Tax Resolution and Financial Freedom:
Using the Financial Planning Process to Deal with Tax Debt

By Scott M. Spann, MA, CFP®, EA

ISBN 978-0-578-01477-7

LifeSpan Financial Planning, LLC
1904 Hubbell Drive
Mount Pleasant, South Carolina 29466

First Edition

Printed in the United States of America

Dedication

To Heather, Caroline, and Andrew

Preface

IRS Tax Debt Resolution: The Financial Planning Approach

Trying to find the best way to resolve tax problems can be a difficult process. Writing about the best practices to help taxpayers is also a unique challenge. When I started this project I had a simple goal of presenting an overview of how to use the tax and financial process to deal with tax problems. I quickly noticed that very few tax and financial planning professionals actually provide comprehensive financial counseling and planning for a group of people that needs help the most. While exploring this specialized area of tax and financial planning, I have learned a great deal about my own approach to the tax resolution process.

My conclusion is quite simple. The ideal solution to tax and financial problems includes a dual focus on tax resolution and financial planning. Rarely are both disciplines combined in an effective manner. Resolving IRS tax liabilities by using fundamental principles of the financial planning process is the most effective way to deal with tax problems. The use of these same principles is also needed to prevent future IRS tax problems.

One thing that I realized during my research and practical application of this approach is that comprehensive financial planning does work for people with federal and state tax liabilities. However, tax resolution planning is a unique process that needs to be structured in a way that increases the likelihood that someone with significant tax issues related to financial management problems will actually succeed in taking control of their situation.

The LifeSpan Process of Tax Resolution and Financial Freedom combines the fundamental principles of tax and financial planning in a holistic manner that focuses on the psychological and behavioral aspects of managing money and taxes. Simply put, most other approaches to tax problems only deal with the elimination of tax debt rather than the elimination of poor financial decision making. In order to achieve freedom from tax debt you must start with a plan that emphasizes smart financial decisions. When the tax resolution process is performed the right way it always places the focus on "big picture" issues.

The Role of Financial Planning

Financial planning is about taking control of your finances and is often defined as the process of meeting life goals through the proper management of your money. The planning process helps people make smart decisions about money and prepare for the demands of the future. More importantly, financial planning is about a better now. Some obvious demands are life's major events: getting an education, buying a home, retiring, providing for your children and even their children. Financial planning also concentrates on day to day concerns such as organizing your finances and preparing for the inevitable surprises that occur in life.

So, how does the financial planning process work when a financial crisis related to a tax problem occurs? Tax resolution is a financial planning challenge that is just as much about replacing ineffective financial behavior patterns of financial decision making with more positive ways of managing money and paying taxes as it is getting rid of the tax problem itself. Therefore, tax resolution planning is a natural fit with the financial planning process.

Financial Life Planning

Is financial planning really all about money? I do not think so. A growing number of financial planning professionals (including myself) have adopted a holistic approach to the planning process. In general, this means looking at the whole person during the life planning process rather than simply focusing on their financial lives. I strongly believe that the "inner game" of money should not be ignored. It is human nature for our belief systems, attitudes, past experiences, goals and values to have an influence on key financial planning and life decisions.

The traditional approach towards financial matters is based on rational decision making. In reality, people do not always behave rationally when personal finances are involved. According to the Certified Financial Planner Board of Standards Inc., more than 40 percent of Americans feel that they are not in control of their finances. This figure was obtained prior to our nation experiencing economic turmoil not seen since the Great Depression. The number of people that lack a sense of confidence related to personal financial management will likely increase as more and more people struggle financially. Financial problems are magnified when people try to move forward without an action plan.

Tax Problems

During both good and bad times many individuals and small business owners can end up owing back taxes. Many also lack a sense of control when it comes to managing their finances. Income tax planning is one of key elements of a comprehensive financial plan. However, most financial plans do not specifically address complicated issues related to tax resolution. This book is designed to help individuals with tax liabilities understand how the financial planning process can work to help them deal with the IRS while working to achieve other short and long-term financial goals. It may also be used as a tool for tax resolution and financial planning professionals to establish tax debt management programs for their clients.

There is no denying the fact that taxes are a problem in this country. Finding the best ways to deal with tax debt is an even greater problem. Many people have tax debt as a result of poor planning, financial ignorance, bad luck, procrastination, etc. Unfortunately, a commonly used planning framework does not exist to alleviate problems related to tax liabilities. Bad financial decisions and overwhelming feelings of desperation and fear can often lead to a cycle of poor decision making (excessive debt, quick fixes, "robbing Peter to pay Paul"). Most of the current tax resolution programs are focused merely on fixing the symptoms (tax liens, wage garnishments) rather than curing the underlying problem (lack of a genuine tax and financial plan). Simply put, tax resolution efforts should focus on the lack of control over money related behaviors.

Seeking Help

If so many Americans have tax problems, where can they turn to for help? Many CPAs, attorneys, and financial planners do not want to invest the time necessary to help with this complex and often time consuming process. Many more professionals lack the desire to work in this difficult and demanding practice area. Tax representation is without a doubt a specialized discipline. The simple fact that many professionals do not want to work in this area is a function of the complexity and frustration that comes with dealing directly with the IRS. In actuality, there is also a frequent sense of frustration felt by the professional working with the tax resolution client. The average person with a tax debt can easily get overwhelmed by the tax resolution process. Procrastination, fear, and avoidance are common traits among many people with tax problems. What is often more frustrating is the fact that they are entering the situation with a major dilemma- the real solution to their tax problems involves developing a financial plan that could have helped them avoid tax and financial problems in the first place.

Unfortunately, too many tax resolution professionals are only focusing on getting their clients out of trouble with the IRS. Not every tax professional is programmed to look beyond the tax issue at hand. It is common practice for both the tax resolution professional and the client to focus solely on the short-term goal of resolving tax problems. Instead, the main goal for every tax resolution engagement should be to achieve dual objectives:

1) To resolve tax issues in the most cost-effective manner based on each person's unique financial situation

2) To create a long-term tax and financial plan that leads to both tax and financial freedom.

My Vision for Tax Resolution Planning

The primary purpose of this book is to provide guidance for individuals dealing with tax problems. It is designed to educate, encourage, and empower delinquent taxpayers with a step by step outline of how to deal with the IRS from a planning perspective. Another purpose is to promote a healthier dialogue between tax planning professionals and financial planners. Tax resolution and financial planning need to be addressed with a specific plan of action that makes sure that the client is focusing on the right thing at the right time. Tax problems are generally a sign of bigger financial problems. A plan of action that promotes positive financial behaviors while preparing for the future will take individuals from a state of being financially stressed to being financially blessed. My vision for the tax resolution planning industry is that an increased number of professionals will eventually combine tax relief efforts with financial planning. I also want to see more people with tax problems recognize the need for a holistic tax and financial plan.

As you assess your need for tax resolution planning you should ask yourself these important questions:

- Do you owe back taxes to the IRS?

- Do you need a comprehensive tax and financial plan to guide your life decisions involving money?

- Do you have a tax lien or wage garnishments?

- Have you failed to file tax returns on time in the past?

- Are you frequently requesting an extension to file your tax returns or make late payments to the IRS or State?

- Do you ever dread dealing with financial matters or avoid them altogether?

- Does the thought of money and taxes make you feel powerless and uncomfortable?

- Are you where you need to be financially speaking?

- Are you ready to get your financial life in order so you can start living free from worry and strife?

- Have you ever thought that a financial plan is something that you need but you never had one or never knew where to start?

- Do you think that planning is only for the wealthy?

If you answered yes to any of these questions then you need to follow the LifeSpan Process of Tax Resolution and Financial Freedom outlined in this book.

It is no secret that money plays an integral role in our lives. Think about the things that you do on a daily basis. Money is right there whether we see it or not. Everyone has their own belief systems related to money. In fact, we all begin creating the framework for how we view money early on in life. It is difficult to see beyond the here and now during any stressful life event. Dealing with tax problems can definitely be classified as a challenging life event that has an impact on all aspects of the life experience.

How people with tax problems choose to respond to this financial challenge will have long-lasting implications. Similarly, the approach that tax and financial planning professionals use when dealing with their clients' tax problems will also go a long way in preparing others for tax and financial freedom.

The goals of tax resolution and financial planning are quite simple. Replace the old way of dealing with money and taxes with a proven system that will help you achieve financial freedom.

S T O P

Engaging in negative financial behaviors
Living paycheck to paycheck
Procrastinating and living in fear
Going deeper and deeper into debt
Worrying about your money
Putting off retirement and other life goals
Being intimidated by the IRS
Allowing interest and penalties on tax debt to grow
Trying to figure out where your $$$ went at the end of the month
Overdrafting your accounts or getting late fees
Arguing with your spouse about money

S T A R T

Planning your future and enjoying life now
Making smart decisions about your money
Taking action and eliminating negative financial behaviors
Paying cash for purchases
Living on less than you earn
Getting out of debt
Investing for retirement and other goals
Dealing with the IRS with confidence
Resolving your tax debt in the most cost-effective manner
Telling your $$$ where to go at the start of the month
Making your money work for you rather than working for it!
Working *with* your spouse

I have worked with hundreds of individuals and families with tax problems. Many delinquent taxpayers have addressed their tax issues and regained control over their finances. These are the success stories and should be the primary reason that tax resolution planners work with people experiencing tax problems. Many taxpayers make a commitment to confront both the IRS and their own financial struggles. They also make an effort to deal with their tax struggles head-on with a plan of action. Most importantly, successful people seeking tax resolution view this seemingly difficult and complex process as an opportunity to create positive change in their lives.

The reality is that some people are able to get out of tax debt for a relatively short period of time. However, after a few years they find their way into tax troubles again and continue to engage in self-destructive behaviors related to how they handle their money and tax obligations. In some cases these people merely transition from one problem to another as their tax debt issues are replaced by another significant financial problem, which is consumer debt.

Unfortunately another group of people choose the paths of denial, resistance, or helplessness. This group tends to avoid their tax problems completely and do not allow themselves to be active participants in the system of change. Instead, they accept defeat and let the system control them. They allow taxes and money to overwhelm them rather than seek a plan for tax and financial freedom.

The Importance of Planning

What differentiates the success stories from the tax and financial failures? In most cases the answer is found in a simple yet highly underutilized concept – PLANNING. An effective financial plan will help overcome the sense of fear, powerlessness, and embarrassment that are often associated with tax problems. The financial planning process is about taking control of your money. If approached with the right perspective, it is also an effective way to regain control over personal problems that money and financial issues help create. The elimination of tax debt and the associated feeling of empowerment will often lead to a greater sense of control. Freedom from tax and financial worries will also open doors of opportunity for people who previously felt tied down emotionally and financially by debt. Planning is the vehicle that will help any individual or family take control and find ways to accomplish important dreams.

The Importance of Taking Action

All of the planning in the world is meaningless if you are unable or unwilling to take action and implement the plan. The LifeSpan Process of Tax Resolution and Financial Planning emphasizes the need to take action and implement a tax and financial plan. Meaningful change takes a great deal of work and hard effort. This step by step process of resolving tax problems is designed to increase the chances of success for those that follow the plan. I encourage all taxpayers undergoing financial stress to realize the importance of both planning and taking action. Tax and financial freedom are closer than you may ever imagine.

How Financial Planning and Tax Resolution Work Together

A strong need exists to bridge the gap between the two disciplines of tax resolution and financial planning. While many tax resolution professionals and financial planners deal with clients facing tax problems with the IRS, there is a limited amount of information available that combines the work of these two disciplines.

As a financial planner specializing in tax resolution planning, I strongly believe that the tax resolution process is a natural fit for the financial planning process. Unfortunately, the majority of tax resolution plans lack critical elements of the financial planning process. The incorporation of a comprehensive financial plan with tax debt management techniques is the most effective way to get out of tax troubles.

Comprehensive tax and financial planning also allows people experiencing a significant life event change (such as dealing with tax debt) to focus on more important life planning goals. This process can open up a world of hope and promise that lies just beyond the immediate and overwhelming situation of debt related problems. An emerging sense of purpose and the need for positive change may also help keep you focused on achieving tax and financial freedom. The pathway to change is much easier to follow if you have a clear set of goals and proper guidance. This is the reason that the LifeSpan Process of Tax Resolution and Financial Freedom is positioned as a proven strategy to help you or someone you know get out of debt with the IRS get on with life.

Introducing the "LifeSpan Process of Tax Resolution and Financial Freedom"

I chose the name LifeSpan Financial Planning, LLC for my financial counseling and tax planning practice for a specific reason. An effective financial plan should do more than simply help individuals and families reach their financial goals. In my opinion, the planning process should include a holistic approach that addresses life planning goals as well as concepts of money management. A "LifeSpan Plan" helps define what is important to each unique individual and addresses underlying dreams and visions across the entire lifespan. It also helps individuals and families find ways to maximize the resources available to accomplish these lifelong ambitions. My main goal as a professional has always been to help my clients achieve important life goals and understand the role that money plays in their lives.

Financial planning is both an art and a science. Life planning is a relatively new approach that is usually seen as the art or human side of financial planning. The process of life planning is used to help people discover their deepest and most profound lifelong goals. This can be accomplished through a process of self-awareness and inquiry. If major obstacles such as significant tax debt or poor financial management exist it is difficult to focus on life and financial planning goals.

Tax problems create a need for tax and financial planning strategies that will solve tax issues the best way possible. On the surface it would appear to be a fairly simple approach. This assumption is based on the belief that most people deal with money in a rational way. The reality is that there are many cognitive-behavioral factors that operate as barriers to change in the lives of people with tax problems. These tax liabilities are significant obstacles that delay or prevent people from accomplishing their innermost dreams in life.

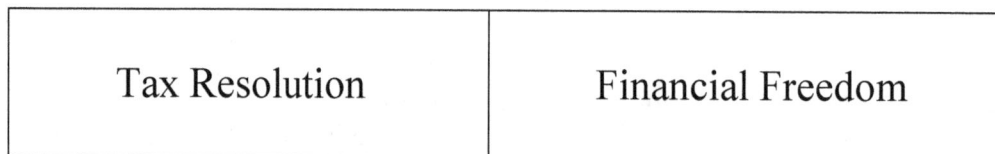

Tax Resolution	Financial Freedom

Tax Resolution and Financial Freedom is a two-stage process that combines two primary areas of focus: tax resolution and financial planning. Tax Resolution and Financial Planning are typically viewed as separate processes. This system simply does not work due to the sometimes conflicting approaches that do not generally work together. You must start the tax resolution process to be able to progress into comprehensive financial planning. The line between the two stages should be viewed as a barrier that stops people from achieving financial freedom. Tax resolution must be achieved prior to working to accomplish most financial planning goals. Otherwise, you will keep running into the brick wall that blocks the path to financial freedom.

As a whole, the "Tax Resolution and Financial Freedom Process" can be overwhelming and confusing. If you break the process into two parts it becomes a more manageable process. A strong need exists to create a new paradigm for dealing with tax problems. Debt is dumb. Tax debt is dumber. Trying to deal with tax and financial problems without a strategic plan is pure stupidity. Good intentions without direction will most likely lead to eventual failure. This step by step plan has been created to provide the direction needed to address tax problems with a plan.

If you currently have a tax problem I encourage you to use this book as a guide to help you accomplish more than just tax resolution. I challenge you to accept this opportunity to achieve total financial freedom. Another goal of this book is to share my vision with other tax and financial planning professionals. If other practitioners embrace the Tax Resolution and Financial Freedom Model they will change how the clients they represent deal with tax problems. The ultimate purpose of Tax Resolution Planning is to help people with a combination of tax and financial problems regain control of their financial lives.

Tax Resolution: Identifying the Need for Change

The tax resolution industry is highly fragmented with the largest tax resolution firm commanding less than 1% of the industry share. Unfortunately, tax resolution firms are unregulated and many of the largest firms do not have stellar track records of service and performance. Recently I surveyed some of the marketing slogans of tax resolution firms advertising on television and the internet. Most of the messages these companies use to reach new clients convey offers of hope and encouragement. However, some companies are marred with extensive customer service complaints and broken promises. Others flat out mislead their clients, misrepresent their services, or market "pennies on the dollar" and "one time only-act now!" settlements. Here are some marketing slogans that I came across recently:

"You could reduce your IRS tax debt to a fraction and be tax debt free"
"Settle for pennies on the dollar- Ex IRS Agents"
"End your IRS Fears"
"Get the IRS off your back"
"Do not be another IRS victim"
"IRS tax problems ruining your life?"

What do all of these statements have in common? They are attempting to reach at the most common emotions shared by a significant number of taxpayers that owe the IRS: FEAR and DESPARATION. The one thing that is missing sometimes is a message that promotes empowerment and accountability while offering the professional expertise that is often needed to help resolve tax problems. It is true that the financial stresses of debt can be overwhelming and debilitating. The IRS and collection agencies can make even the strongest willed person feel powerless and overmatched. Unfortunately, many desperate people make a huge financial mistake when they let fear guide their decision regarding where to seek tax assistance.

Tax representation firms understand the underlying fear and procrastination that is associated with the typical tax resolution client. They also understand that low and middle income people with tax problems do not usually possess a high degree of financial literacy. That is why the typical American with tax problems is at risk of being taken advantage of when dealing with the IRS.

The following are some of the most common mistakes that people make when seeking to resolve tax problems with a tax resolution or tax representation firm:

- Focusing solely on getting rid of tax debt rather than on changing the underlying financial behaviors that helped create the tax problem.
- Financing the cost of tax representation services only to dig deeper in debt.
- Allowing their fears and doubts to increase the chances they will make an emotional decision with respect to choosing a tax representation firm.
- Failing to realize that an Offer in Compromise (resolving tax debt for less than the amount owed) is not for everyone.
- Falling for the lure of a commissioned sales agent providing empty promises they will qualify for an Offer in Compromise when more realistic alternatives exist.
- Hearing what they want to hear ("you can get out of tax debt") rather than what they need to hear ("you can take control of your tax and financial situation").
- Settling for high interest IRS payment plans when other resources are available to pay off the tax debt faster and with lower interest and penalties.
- Getting taken advantage of by not taking the time to do their homework with respect to seeking professional tax resolution guidance.
- Assuming that their tax professional will do all the work and neglecting to send in relevant documents and paperwork needed to proceed with their case.
- Trying to resolve tax problems without a plan.

Rather than simply offering promises of hope and resolution, I prefer to be upfront with my tax resolution clients and let them know that dealing with tax problems is part of a bigger financial process of change. This process may require a great deal of work on their behalf to implement the tax and financial planning recommendations. The end result of the hard work is financial freedom and is definitely worth the effort.

In order to regain control over money and taxes, it is of critical importance to understand that the old way of dealing with money matters has not worked. It is not easy to dispute the need for change when tax liabilities are present. Most people with significant tax problems recognize the need for help with tax and financial planning. This call to action leads to the shared knowledge that the individual client and the tax/financial planning professional are both agents of change. The client is the ultimate beneficiary of the tax resolution process that includes a financial counseling component.

While I would like to believe the bulk of the national and local tax representation firms do indeed operate in their client's best interests, a fundamental change needs to occur within the tax resolution industry. More emphasis needs to be put on treating the root of the tax problem, which is usually a lack of planning and poor decision making on money matters. It is up to tax and financial planning practitioners and their clients to embrace the need for change when dealing with tax problems.

If you or someone you care about has a tax problem the best thing to do is educate yourself, create a plan, and take action. Tax and financial problems do not happen overnight. Likewise, they are not usually corrected overnight either. Patience and persistence are key aspects of tax resolution and financial freedom. Planning is the guiding force that helps drive the tax resolution process. Financial freedom lies ahead at the end of this journey to resolve tax problems.

Dear Taxpayers and Tax Professionals,

The traditional way of dealing with tax debt treats tax problems and money as the primary area of focus. A dramatic shift needs to occur in the tax resolution industry. Rather than focusing only on tax problems and related money matters, more emphasis needs to be placed on the individual with tax debt and their underlying financial management issues. People with tax problems need to carefully examine how they view money and how they view their lives in general. Most importantly, they need a plan to guide them during the tax resolution process and beyond.

If you have tax problems, then tax resolution planning is the answer because it puts you in control of your financial future. The step by step process outlined in this book provides a structured plan that will enable people with tax debt to accomplish two main objectives: tax resolution and financial freedom. This plan works on its own or in conjunction with professional guidance. It takes work to make it work.

Tax resolution is a process. Taking action is a critical point that is emphasized throughout the tax resolution process. The journey in search of tax and financial freedom begins with a simple step. The purpose of this book is to make sure that people with tax problems take that first step in the right direction.

Accomplishing tax resolution and financial freedom is not easy and takes a significant amount of hard work, patience, and persistence to achieve. I realize that the step by step approach used in this book may seem tedious at times. That is expected when you are trying to learn new financial behaviors and change your life in a positive way forever.

If you are reading this book in pursuit of answers to a tax problem I wish you luck on your journey. I sincerely hope that the LifeSpan Process of Tax Resolution and Financial Freedom enables as many people as possible to improve their lives. If you are a tax professional I encourage you to incorporate the basic principles of financial planning into your tax resolution planning practice. Tax resolution does not have to be guided by fear, intimidation, or financial ignorance. I encourage everyone that is seeking to resolve issues related to tax debt to use the planning process to guide future tax and financial planning decisions with hope and confidence.

Best Wishes and Godspeed,

Scott M. Spann

Contents

Part I:
An Introduction to the LifeSpan Process of Tax Resolution and Financial Freedom

An Introduction to the LifeSpan Process of Tax Resolution and Financial Freedom

"America is a land of taxation that was founded to avoid taxation." ~ Laurence J. Peter

"If a person gets his attitude toward money straight, it will help straighten out almost every other area in his life." ~ Billy Graham

Introduction

The effective management of personal finances requires knowledge, organization, and constant vigilance. Tax and financial planning is something that most everyone agrees is important. The reality is that not everyone has a plan in place to help guide their financial decisions. Most of us are simply flying by the seat of our pants when it comes to important money related decisions. It has been well documented that savings rates have been dropping among Americans as a whole. On the flip side, one thing has kept steadily going up in this country- **Debt**.

This alarming trend began in the 1990's when the rate of personal bankruptcy in our country rose by nearly 70 percent, and it continues to rise today, becoming a primary concern for many individuals and families. Just recently the savings rate of our nation hit an all-time low and actually reached negative territory. This is the lowest savings rate since the Great Depression.

Entering the 2009 tax year, millions of people are living paycheck to paycheck, and an increasing number of people are having trouble paying bills and other monthly obligations. Excessive mortgage and consumer debt is overwhelming many families. Record numbers of homeowners are at risk of losing their homes to foreclosure. Others are simply using debt to finance a lifestyle they cannot afford. This leaves people with credit card, vehicle, and other loans that create additional financial stress.

Debt can become an even bigger problem when you owe the Internal Revenue Service. The IRS has aggressive collection measures that usually place this type of debt at the top of the debt hierarchy. If you are concerned about resolving a tax liability and minimizing the impact of taxes, you are not alone. Millions of Americans find themselves with IRS and state tax problems and are seeking solutions to the complex tax code. According to the Internal Revenue Service, delinquent taxpayers account for at least $290 billion a year in unpaid taxes during the 2007 fiscal year. This amounts to roughly 2.6% of the national Gross Domestic Product. If you have IRS tax debt one thing is for certain- **the IRS will never give up and will not go away until your tax liability is resolved.**

The IRS is motivated now more than ever to bring in more tax revenue. Collection activities increased $10 billion over the last 5 years. The IRS collections brought in approximately $43 billion during the 2007 fiscal year. At the end of 2007 the IRS considered $100 billion out of the nearly $300 billion inventory as collectible debt. These numbers were collected with a relatively inefficient system. The IRS still has not perfected the method of identifying which unpaid tax cases are worth pursuing. This is likely to be changed as lawmakers will soon pressure the IRS to improve its collections measures.

The extent to which taxpayers underreport their gross income represents taxes that go unpaid every year. The IRS and the Economic Policy Institute estimate the amount of taxes owed but not paid at $353 billion, equal to about 15% of the total taxes owed. These taxes not paid through our "voluntary and timely" system of taxation are often known as the "tax gap."

Do not expect tax problems to go away anytime soon. In 2009 our nation finds itself in the biggest economic crisis in modern history. Financial institutions are failing in record numbers. A credit crunch continues to loom, and the housing market continues to struggle amid global financial concerns. It is only natural that the tax gap will continue to increase as million of taxpayers face unemployment, reductions in pay, and related cash-flow problems. Do not wait on a federal bailout to get you out of debt. A tax resolution plan should be your own individual bailout plan.

How does the "Tax Gap" affect you?
Unpaid taxes mean that the average law abiding citizen is paying more than his or her fair share. If you are one of the millions that are not current with your taxes the tax gap has a different effect on you. The IRS is seeking to increase its collection efforts. Lawmakers will likely increase their pressure on the IRS to decrease the tax gap. Even with recent improvements the IRS is not moving fast enough in the eyes of many to improve the collection of back taxes. While the IRS recently acknowledged the need to be kinder and gentler in light of the recent financial crisis in our nation, they will not be as willing to deal with delinquent taxpayers that avoid collection efforts and ignore existing tax liabilities.

Congress and others are increasing their questioning of the effectiveness of the IRS collection processes. The IRS is currently implementing measures to improve its collection process. Currently, the IRS primarily focuses their collections efforts on a Three Phase Collection Process. Collection notices, phone calls, and in person visits are the three primary elements of the collection process. In 2007 the IRS sent 16 million collection letters to delinquent taxpayers. They answered 5.4 million incoming phone calls and made 1.9 million outgoing phone calls trying to collect on past due tax debt. In person visits are the final part of the IRS collection process. Over 400,000 contacts were made with delinquent taxpayers at their homes and businesses.

The IRS is constantly working to streamline its collection process. There are a number of reasons why IRS collection activities will continue to grow in the coming years:

- The struggling economy, growing national deficit, war on terrorism, and recent financial bailouts have created a situation where the government needs money badly.
- IRS collection efforts are needed and mandated by Congress to help close the tax gap.
- The IRS continues to hire new employees; the majority of these new hires focus on collections and enforcement activities.
- Budget increases are set to be spent on increased collections and enforcement.
- IRS Commissioner has stated that closing the tax gap is his number one priority.

The pressure on delinquent taxpayers will continue to increase as the federal government recently set in motion plans to increase its tax enforcement efforts in the coming years. In addition, new technology and information sharing among tax agencies make it easier for agencies to pinpoint potential offenders, increasing the number of cases for audit and collection. Financial professionals are challenged with the task of helping clients with tax liabilities resolve their tax problems in the most cost-effective manner. The purpose of this book is to outline various aspects of the Tax and Financial Planning Process and to demonstrate how a comprehensive plan that heavily emphasizes income tax planning can help individuals resolve their tax liabilities and accomplish other financial goals.

The "Taxing" Situation: A Challenging Situation

Dealing with a federal and/or state tax liability can be an extremely daunting and confusing task. Currently, there is no universal framework for using the financial planning process to resolve tax liabilities with the IRS and state taxing authorities. When faced with the task of dealing with the IRS, many people make the mistake of neglecting other financial goals and objectives and do not always make the most cost-effective decisions when attempting to resolve their tax liabilities. More often than not, delinquent taxpayers do not see financial planning as a solution to their tax problems. The reality is that tax problems are often a symptom of a greater financial problem- **the complete lack of a concrete financial plan**.

> "If your tax resolution plan does not include an action plan that focuses on your total financial health then you are significantly increasing the risk for future tax and financial struggles."

Do not feel overwhelmed if you owe back taxes to the Internal Revenue Service or a state taxing authority. The $300 billion plus tax gap is evidence that others are experiencing tax problems. There are a variety of tax resolution options available depending on the individual circumstances surrounding each taxpayer's financial situation. In addition, there is a growing body of financial professionals (CPA's, Enrolled Agents, attorneys, etc.) that specialize in helping their clients overcome federal and state tax liabilities. This has been evidenced by an increasing number of national tax resolution companies and marketing agencies that have chosen to focus on the growing market of delinquent taxpayers. If you have amassed a sizable tax liability, statements such as "get the IRS off your back and get on with your life", "stop IRS wage garnishments", and "settle for less than the amount you owe" most certainly will get your attention if the IRS has not done so already.

Do not be lured into potential traps as you seek help to deal with your tax problems. If your tax resolution plan does not include an action plan that focuses on your total financial health, then you are significantly increasing the risk for future tax and financial struggles. You may be setting yourself up for future failures if you do not approach the tax situation without first addressing your overall financial well-being.

While starting the tax resolution process is an important step to obtaining financial freedom, many tax representation services and tax professionals are not adequately prepared to help provide their clients with comprehensive financial planning. As consumers, it is important that individuals seeking assistance for tax related problems focus on the big picture and engage in a meaningful discussion about their financial plan.

Common Reasons for Tax Problems

It is necessary to determine some of the reasons that people get into tax problems. An understanding of the source of tax problems is very important when developing short and long-term solutions. Sometimes it is easy to pinpoint a tax problem to a single event or financial crisis. More often than not tax resolution planners tend to see a series of poor financial decision making or lack of planning as the root of the tax problem. Still there are many reasons that people end up owing taxes.

Some of the most common causes of tax problems are as follows:

- Self-employment- Not understanding self-employment tax or simply trying to avoid paying tax for self-employment income due to other financial constraints

- Audit- the IRS may not agree with your position on certain items on a return

- Tax protestor (intentional avoidance)

- Failure to pay employment taxes or payroll taxes

- Failure to file (fear of filing can continue year after year and the initial liability is compounded)

- Taxation of retirement distributions

- Capital gains reporting related to the sale of stocks, bonds, mutual funds, etc.

- Changes related to an audit (IRS examination)

- Insufficient taxes withheld from pay

- Loss of job or unstable employment

- Loss or reduction of income

- Cash flow problems (e.g., excessive consumer debt, living off gross income rather than net income)

- Poor financial management

- Reckless spending

- Unable to locate or recover financial records

- Not having enough money set aside for emergencies

- Divorce or other personal problems

- Business failure

- Health problems, medical emergencies; physical and mental problems

As you can see, there are plenty of situations and life events that can lead to tax problems. Regardless of the cause of a tax liability, it is important that individuals overwhelmed by tax debt realize that there are effective solutions available to help manage and overcome it. There are also qualified professionals and effective do-it-yourself techniques available to assist you in this process. Resolving any debt issue can be a difficult process. There is usually no quick fix solution, and debt reduction strategies generally take a significant amount of time and effort. Most importantly, personal goals to reduce tax debt need to be backed by an action plan that specifically addresses the steps that must be taken. Not doing anything is about the worst thing you can do, but what many taxpayers fail to realize is that they need to have a comprehensive tax and financial plan on their side to help guide them.

A Growing Problem

Tax debt is a financial problem that will only create more trouble if not dealt with quickly and appropriately. More and more people are facing tax liabilities that will have a long-lasting effect on the financial well being and quality of life for people choosing to ignore their tax issues. Tax liabilities do more than create financial stress. Tax problems can affect your emotional and physical well-being. Tax debt also tears apart relationships and marriages. Financial differences are frequently cited as the number one reason that couples get divorced.

If you don't deal with your IRS tax problems in a timely manner, any of the following could occur:

- The IRS can levy (seize) your bank account and take your money out of the bank.
- The IRS can file a notice of levy with your employer to levy your wages, salary, and other income. They can take a substantial amount of your paycheck. This also tells your employer that you have a problem with the IRS. The IRS also enforces collection against your 401(k) and other retirement accounts.
- Penalties and interest will continue to accrue.
- The IRS can levy (seize) your assets and sell them at public auction to satisfy your tax liability.
- With court approval, the IRS can levy (seize) your residence and sell it at public auction to satisfy your tax liability.
- The IRS can issue a summons to third parties such as your bank, credit union, employer, and others to determine assets or property owned by you.
- The IRS can issue a summons to you requiring you to appear, testify or produce books, papers, records, or other data.
- The IRS can file a Notice of Federal Tax Lien, which is public notice of a lien in favor of the United States on all property and rights to property belonging to you.
- Tax related stress may also lead to physical and psychological problems

There are other potential consequences for the failure to meet tax obligations. If you do not file your tax returns or pay your taxes on time you may experience a variety of related problems. These problems may include difficulty financing a home or trouble selling property due to tax liens. Tax problems may also make it difficult to obtain business or personal loans without proof of income on tax returns. Not paying taxes also has an impact on Social Security benefits, the ability to apply for college financial aid, and unemployment insurance. The most devastating consequence of tax problems is the loss of control over your financial future.

"I want to deal with my tax problems. I just don't know where to start. What are my options?"

At this point you may be screaming "Help!!!" "Information overload!!!" If you owe taxes, the IRS can provide constant headaches and become one of your biggest nightmares. Just looking at the available options for resolving a tax liability can be just as stressful. Without proper guidance and a strong desire to take control of your financial life, tax problems may continue to grow and compound your financial problems. The good news is the IRS has created a menu of options for delinquent taxpayers to return to good standing with them.

Typical Options When Dealing With an IRS Tax Liability:

- Pay in full using existing resources
- Pay in monthly installments to the IRS
- Reduce the tax liability through an Offer in Compromise
- Have the IRS determine you are temporarily unable to pay and suspend the collection process
- Reduce, eliminate, or pay the debt through bankruptcy
- Wait for the statutes of limitations to expire and subject yourself to liens and other aggressive collection activities

- If the taxes are the result of your former spouse's actions, and you feel that you should not be required to pay the taxes due, you may be eligible for Innocent or Injured Spouse Relief

Finding the Ideal Solution

What is the ideal solution for your tax problems? The answer depends on the "big picture" of your financial situation. There is no one option that is the best choice for each person. A one size fits all approach does not work with tax resolution. The IRS simply wants to ensure that you pay your tax obligation, and they will take various measures to make sure you do so according to their terms. It is up to you, the taxpayer, to make smart financial decisions when choosing among your tax resolution alternatives. Keep in mind that the IRS is essentially the accounts receivables department of the U.S. Government. Their job is to make sure that everyone that should pay taxes does. If a taxpayer is not compliant with IRS procedures they have the authority to collect.

> *"The Internal Revenue Service does not necessarily care that you choose the best tax resolution option available. They simply want to ensure that you pay your tax obligation and they will take various measures to make sure you do so according to their terms. It is up to you, the taxpayer, to make smart financial decisions when choosing among your tax resolution alternatives."*

The bottom line is that avoidance is not an option. Take control of your tax problems, and while you are doing so assume control of something more important- your total financial situation. There are many options available during your quest to deal with resolving a tax liability. However, taking control of your life by establishing a financial plan is NOT an option…it should be viewed as a requirement if you truly want to reduce your financial stress and get on with your life on your terms (not the IRS's). Remember, the IRS is interested in one thing during the collections process and that is collecting taxes that are past due.

If you are faced with the task of dealing with a past due tax liability, you need to understand how to organize your financial life in order to deal with the IRS in the most effective manner. This means putting your goals and objectives first and being proactive. Engaging in the financial planning process is your best option as you begin the journey to tax resolution with the IRS. Tax debt inhibits freedom. It distracts you from other more important goals and objectives.

Debt is Dumb. Tax Debt is even Dumber if not dealt with immediately. Resolving tax debt without a plan is pure stupidity. Tax resolution requires a plan. The tax and financial planning process is the solution to resolve tax problems.

Tax Resolution Planning

How does tax resolution fit into the financial planning process? Tax debt is an extremely complex form of debt that can be resolved during the financial planning process. Unfortunately, the majority of taxpayers do not utilize a formal financial plan when dealing with the IRS. They simply focus on treating the symptoms of the disease rather than treating the nature of the illness itself- failure to plan and poor management of personal finances. Before I outline various tax resolution strategies, it is important to understand how this area of income tax planning fits into the overall financial planning process.

Financial Planning has commonly been defined as the "process of meeting your life goals through the proper management of your finances" (CFP Board of Standards). The financial planning process covers a wide range of financial issues and can touch many parts of your life. A comprehensive financial plan will be able to provide you with advice about general budgeting and debt management, insurance and risk management, investments, employee benefits, income tax, and retirement and estate planning.

According to the Certified Financial Planner Board of Standards, the Financial Planning Process consists of the following six steps:

1. Establishing and defining the client-planner relationship.
2. Gathering client data, including goals.
3. Analyzing and evaluating your financial status.
4. Developing and presenting financial planning recommendations and/or alternatives.
5. Implementing the financial planning recommendations.
6. Monitoring the financial planning recommendations.

What is a Tax Resolution Financial Plan?
Tax debt resolution is a financial planning challenge that fits into the financial planning process. However, tax resolution planning demands more than the typical financial planning engagement. This is primarily due to the complex nature of the tax code. For the delinquent taxpayer, resolving an IRS tax liability is most often the top priority during the financial planning process. Dealing with an IRS tax liability can be daunting task. It may be time consuming and often confusing. Know what kinds of procedures you should follow, what types of information the Internal Revenue Service will need from you, and how the decisions that you make will affect your overall financial situation.

A tax and financial plan is designed to help individuals with tax liabilities achieve goals and objectives related to resolving tax debt while working to accomplish other financial goals (e.g., reducing future taxes, planning for retirement). A comprehensive tax and financial plan follows the same exact steps of the normal financial planning process. The primary difference from the traditional approach to financial planning is the strong emphasis on resolving a federal and/or state tax liability while creating a foundation for achieving other non-tax related goals and objectives.

Tax resolution also requires a significant amount of financial counseling. Currently a limited number of financial planning professionals and financial counselors work with clients with tax resolution needs and concerns. This number is growing as the number of people seeking guidance for tax problems increases.

"Why do I need a comprehensive tax and financial plan? I just want to get the IRS off my back."
This is an understandable objection to undergoing a comprehensive tax and financial planning process to eliminate or reduce tax debt. It can be quite difficult to focus on other short and long-term financial goals when an IRS Notice of Intent to Levy letter arrives in a delinquent taxpayer's mailbox. It is even more unsettling to find out that the IRS has a lien on your home or other properties and will take aggressive collection measures to get you to pay back taxes. However, if you owe the IRS you need to realize that the actions (or lack of action) that you take to resolve your debt are related to many other aspects of your financial life. This relationship emphasizes the importance of using a comprehensive financial plan to deal with the life event of having a tax liability. The ultimate goal is tax resolution and financial freedom.

Throw out the common misconceptions that financial planning is just for the wealthy or only deals with areas related to investing or insurance. When tax debt is present, financial planning is used to eliminate debt and help people assume control over the management of personal finances. Traditional focus areas such as insurance and investments are not a priority during the tax resolution process until the tax debt has been effectively dealt with.

Financial planners have the responsibility to help their clients make smart financial decisions. The challenges of tax resolution are the same, and the primary goal of the tax resolution planner is to help people make smart financial decisions during the process of dealing with tax liabilities. A tax resolution plan uses an intense approach to eliminate tax problems first. This allows people to focus on other financial planning concerns that are not related to tax debt.

Common Financial Planning Focus Areas

- Net Worth & Investment Planning
- Cash Flow Analysis
- Income Tax Planning
- Retirement Planning
- Insurance Planning
- Business Planning
- Education Planning
- Charitable Giving
- Estate Planning

Tax Resolution and Financial Freedom Tips: Best practices when using the financial planning process to deal with tax debt:

1. Set measurable financial goals.
2. Understand the effect of each financial decision.
3. Review and re-evaluate your financial situation on an ongoing basis.
4. Do not delay your tax and financial plan.
5. Set realistic expectations.
6. Take control and realize that you are in charge.
7. Use a tax and financial planning professional for assistance.

There are various unique goals and objectives that fall within the primary focus areas of the financial planning process. Most of these goals cannot be addressed until the tax problem has been resolved. Tax problems are a barrier preventing most financial life planning goals from becoming reality. The only way to become free from the stress of financial problems is to eliminate tax debt. This does not mean that financial planning techniques cannot be used to deal with the tax situation. It requires an approach that focuses on returning to the basic building blocks of the financial planning process. Otherwise, typical financial planning goals will be hard or impossible to reach until tax problems have been resolved.

Typical Financial Planning Areas of Interest or Concern:

- Achieving Financial Independence and Security
- Obtaining homes, cars, boats, and other material things
- Protecting assets and income against loss
- Ensuring a comfortable retirement
- Reducing/minimizing taxes
- Providing money for a child's education
- Taking vacations and travel
- Giving to charitable organizations and private foundations
- Planning for aging parents
- Obtaining health insurance and protecting long-term care needs
- Passing on wealth to the next generation
- Business continuation

Tax Resolution and Financial Planning

Typical financial planning objectives may seem unattainable when faced with having to deal with tax debt. Tax resolution financial planning (or tax resolution planning) focuses on the same major areas of concern in people's financial lives. The only significant difference is that the tax and financial planning process adds an additional area of focus- tax resolution planning. Tax resolution financial planning integrates income tax planning recommendations specifically related to tax liabilities into each of the other areas of focus.

How to Resolve an IRS tax debt using the guidance of Tax Resolution Financial Planning

Is it possible to resolve an IRS tax liability without having a tax and financial plan? Yes, of course! But you may not be using the most cost-effective method available to pay off or pay down your tax liability. More importantly, you are probably just going to end up with bigger problems down the road if you simply focus on a temporary fix to a bigger problem.

Typical Goals of Tax Resolution

- Determine if the amount you owe is correct
- Become compliant with tax requirements
- Stop an IRS wage garnishment
- Remove a tax lien
- Reduce the amount owed to the IRS
- Abate penalties
- Establish an Installment Agreement to pay the IRS over time
- Use existing resources to pay off a tax liability in the most cost-effective manner possible
- Avoid property seizures
- Determine if bankruptcy is a possible solution
- Appeal an auditor's decision

Creating "Big Picture" Tax Resolution Goals

The typical goals of tax resolution remain an important part of the tax resolution process. Last time that I checked, tax problems are the reason that people seek tax resolution in the first place. However, relief from tax debt should not be the only goal for people that owe the IRS.

If you are experiencing tax problems I strongly recommend that you try to do more than just focus on getting out of tax debt. Use the tax resolution process as an opportunity to change your life as it relates to money. If you do this you may actually end up changing your life for the better.

Focus on more than just the typical goals of tax resolution. Take meaningful steps that will also improve your financial well being. A holistic approach to the tax and financial planning process looks at the "big picture". If you start thinking about more than just trying to get rid of tax problems you will develop the freedom to prepare for future tax obligations with confidence. This can be referred to as "tax freedom". As Americans we cannot eliminate taxes from our lives, but we can take control of how we manage our taxes and money from this point going forward!

An amazing thing happens once you achieve tax freedom and resolve your tax problems. Suddenly you realize that you are finally in a position to concentrate on other financial goals. Tax planning becomes life planning. Goals of the past become attainable again. You can finally start taking the steps toward financial independence.

In addition to focusing on the typical goals of tax resolution, you should concentrate on the primary goals of the tax resolution process:

- Eliminate tax problems the best ways possible based on each individual's unique financial situation
- Prevent the occurrence of future tax problems while developing a sense of freedom from past tax problems
- Move beyond the focus on resolving tax problems to achieve financial freedom (however you choose to define financial freedom).

Basic Steps of the LifeSpan Process of Tax Resolution and Financial Freedom

The LifeSpan Process of Tax Resolution and Financial Freedom follows a step by step path to success. Tax resolution is the primary objective. Once tax problems have been resolved and tax freedom has been achieved the focus then shifts to the pursuit of financial freedom. The flowchart at the end of this chapter shows the progression of the tax resolution planning process. The following is a summary of the basic steps that will be outlined throughout the course of this action plan:

Tax Resolution
Taking Control: Making a Commitment to Change
Tax resolution starts with a desire to take control of tax and financial problems. Anyone with tax and financial problems (no matter how big or small) must make a commitment to change. The change process as it relates to taxes and money matters starts with a tax resolution plan. The individual (with the assistance of a tax resolution professional) is the primary agent of change. A tax and financial plan, if implemented correctly, is the best way to resolve tax debt and stay out of future tax troubles.

Establishing Goals and Objectives
Meaningful change requires a holistic or "big picture" financial life plan. This approach helps people concentrate on long-term financial goals and objectives that look beyond the tax issue at hand. Holistic tax resolution planning helps provide meaning to the sometimes difficult task of dealing with tax liabilities. This process starts with establishing realistic goals and objectives and, more importantly, putting those goals on paper as part of a written plan.

Assess Resources
The next step of the tax resolution process is to complete a comprehensive assessment of resources available to deal with the problem. Resources can be internal, external, or financial. The identification of available resources is needed to determine the best tax and financial solution for each individual. This step requires self-awareness and an understanding of common characteristics of successful individuals. It is important to identify models of success if you truly want to become financially successful yourself.

Other resources include an analysis of family and social support systems. This step also incorporates the decision making process of whether or not a tax resolution planner is needed to help provide guidance during the process. Finally, financial resources need to be assessed. Each taxpayer must have an understanding of his or her net worth and cash flow situation prior to attempting to resolve tax debt. You must possess an understanding of where you presently stand financially if you want to reach future life planning goals. An understanding of the current financial status is also needed as you progress into the next steps of the tax resolution process.

Create a Personal Spending Plan
After resources have been determined the focus shifts to creating a personal spending plan or budget. This extremely important step serves as the foundation for all future tax and financial planning steps. The spending plan is an ongoing step that provides guidance for future spending. Personal spending plans allow people to take control over their finances by telling your money where to go before the month begins. Tax resolution, debt reduction, savings, and investing each start with a spending plan.

Tax Resolution Analysis
Once the foundation has been set it is time to actually resolve the tax problem. A tremendous amount of hard work and organization must take place prior to this next step that is referred to as "Tax Resolution Analysis". Many people make the mistake of trying to resolve their tax problems prior to completely understanding where they stand financially. This often leads to prolonged financial stress and tax strategies that do not work or are not the best solution. A comprehensive tax resolution analysis looks at the facts of the tax problem and identifies the most appropriate response based on the financial resources available. The end result of the tax resolution analysis step is to figure out the best possible solution based on the individual facts. An effective tax resolution analysis takes into account unique personal factors while also looking at the tax situation similar to how the IRS will view things.

Implementing the Tax Resolution Plan
The final step towards tax resolution is implementation. Identifying a solution is only part of the tax resolution process. You must also take action and make the tax resolution plan work. Implementation includes resolving the tax liability, staying compliant with future tax obligations, and proactive income tax planning. Tax freedom is the ultimate reward at the end of the tax resolution process. People who choose to take action and participate in the tax resolution process find tax freedom by getting out of debt as quickly as possible, staying out of debt, and making smart tax and financial planning decisions going forward. Subsequently, they are able to progress into the next phase of the tax and financial planning process- the pursuit of financial freedom.

Financial Freedom
Eliminate Consumer Debt
Every single person possesses his or her own unique definition of what the term "financial freedom" means. Life planning goals help determine how to define financial freedom. The Financial Freedom stage of the LifeSpan Process builds on the life planning goals that were established during the Tax Resolution stage. Each step up to this point is geared toward building positive financial behaviors that lead to success during the Financial Freedom phase of the plan. The first step continues to build on the momentum used to eliminate tax debt and concentrates on completely eliminating any high interest consumer debt. This step must take place prior to any savings or investment plans being implemented. The elimination of consumer debt frees up cash flow and sets the stage for building true wealth.

Establish an Emergency Fund
The next step of the financial freedom process is to establish an emergency fund. This important financial behavior of saving for unforeseen events or emergencies provides protection against potential setbacks. Saving for emergencies also develops a saving habit that eventually can be used to aggressively fund an investment plan.

Review Life Planning Goals and Objectives

Tax resolution generally takes time and patience. Life planning goals may change over the course of time. At this point on the journey to financial freedom it is important to take the time to review the goals and objectives that were initially created during the tax resolution phase. Clarify your life planning goals and put your goals in writing. Creating a financial life plan gives meaning to the tax and financial planning process.

Assessing Risk and Protecting the Ones you Love

This step focuses on basic insurance and estate planning needs. Prior to beginning the wealth building process you must first protect yourself, property, and family. Basic insurance and estate planning will help make sure that you are ready for financial freedom. This step addresses the need to insure property such as home and automobiles. It also discusses the need to purchase term life insurance to protect your family or other dependents in the event of death. Basic estate planning such as wills and trusts are also discussed during this step.

Investment Planning

Investing is the best way to reach important life planning goals such as retirement or education funding. The purpose of this step is to focus on setting aside 15% of total household income into tax advantaged investments. A systematic investment plan is needed to achieve financial freedom. Proper asset allocation strategies will help make sure that the investment plan maximizes returns while assuming an appropriate amount of risk.

Eliminate all Forms of Debt

A life without debt allows for more time to actually enjoy life. The debt snowball effect used during the tax resolution process continues with the focus on eliminating consumer debt. The same momentum can be used to eliminate all forms of debt such as mortgages and student loans. A debt-free lifestyle frees up even more money to use toward more important life planning goals.

Identify other Planning Opportunities

Taking control of your tax and financial life opens the door to many opportunities. The weight of tax debt and high interest consumer debt can damage one's spirit and defeat many dreams before they truly get off the ground. Starting a business and charitable giving are examples of other planning opportunities that have the potential to become reality during the financial freedom process.

Financial Freedom

Financial freedom cannot be reached until tax problems have been resolved. Tax resolution stands in the way of most financial planning goals. The LifeSpan Process of Tax Resolution and Financial Freedom emphasizes a step by step process. The process requires a willingness to change financial behaviors and take action. Tax resolution is more than just a life without tax debt. It is a new approach to dealing with tax and financial matters. A tax resolution plan puts you the taxpayer in control of your financial destiny and opens the door to financial freedom.

Tax Resolution and Financial Freedom Tips

Tax Resolution Tips and Financial Freedom Tips are provided throughout the process. I encourage you to use this guidance on your journey for tax resolution and financial freedom. This process will work even if you do not currently have a tax liability. Many people without tax debt have successfully applied the basic principles of The LifeSpan Process of Tax Resolution and Financial Freedom in their lives. A summary of the Tax Resolution and Financial Freedom Tips is located in the appendix.

The LifeSpan Process of Tax Resolution and Financial Freedom relies heavily on the individual. This does not mean you are on your own and professional guidance is not available. Help is available. With or without help, tax resolution planning requires a significant amount of effort and personal involvement. The phrase "Taking Action" is found throughout the tax resolution process. Throughout this book you will notice a text box that looks like this.

Taking Action!!! Resolving tax problems requires planning, patience, and commitment. Most importantly, it requires an ability to take action. The LifeSpan Process of Tax Resolution and Financial Freedom was created to help people take action and seek meaningful change in their lives. When you see a **Taking Action!!!** box you should complete the action steps. Doing so will help keep you on the path to tax and financial freedom.

A few notes regarding seeking tax guidance from a professional:
Every person going through the tax resolution process has different needs. Some people are fully capable of achieving tax and financial freedom on their own, while others simply cannot break through without some degree of professional support. The LifeSpan Process of Tax Resolution and Financial Freedom was developed to work as both a standalone process as well as a collaborative effort with a tax resolution planner. The "Assessing Resources" step will explore your choices in greater detail. Regardless of whether or not you work with a tax resolution professional, the responsibility always rests on your shoulders to make the right financial decisions going forward. Now is the time to take action and start your tax resolution plan. I encourage everyone facing tax and financial problems to seek positive change.

Summary
Tax problems are becoming a growing problem in our country as more and more people struggle financially. There are a variety of causes for tax debt. Regardless of the reason for the tax liability, the IRS is committed to collecting back taxes on behalf of the U.S. Government. The only effective way to address tax problems is through the implementation of a plan.

Choosing a plan of action accomplishes very little until you take action. The LifeSpan Process of Tax Resolution and Financial Freedom is an effective method of addressing tax problems since it emphasizes the need to become an active participant in the tax resolution process. The plan is designed in a step by step manner that develops positive financial behaviors. This process also challenges people to look beyond the tax issue and begin building a foundation for their financial future.

Financial success will be reached if you follow the tax resolution and financial freedom steps one by one. Tax resolution must occur prior to focusing on financial freedom. Tax resolution is a barrier or roadblock on the path to financial freedom. Throughout the book specific tips and guidance are provided for the categories of tax resolution and financial freedom. Follow these steps as you progress through the tax resolution process and you will be ready to live a life of financial independence.

LifeSpan Process of "Tax Resolution and Financial Freedom

First Stage: Tax Resolution

- ➤ Taking Control: Making a Commitment to Change

- ➤ Establishing Goals and Objectives

- ➤ Assessing Resources (internal/external/financial)

- ➤ Creating a Personal Spending Plan

- ➤ Completing a Tax Resolution Analysis

- ➤ Implementing a Tax Resolution Plan

  = TAX RESOLUTION

Tax problems are a barrier on the path to financial freedom. Most financial planning goals and objectives cannot be met until any potential tax problems have been resolved. Once tax freedom has been obtained the focus of the tax and financial planning process shifts to financial freedom and other financial life planning goals.

Final Stage: Financial Freedom

- ➤ Eliminating consumer debt

- ➤ Establishing an emergency fund

- ➤ Reviewing life planning goals and objectives

- ➤ Starting an investment program to fund life planning goals

- ➤ Eliminating all debt (including mortgage and student loans)

- ➤ Identifying other life planning opportunities

  = FINANCIAL FREEDOM

Part II: Tax Resolution Planning

Tax Resolution Step #1:
Taking Control- Making the Commitment to Change

*"It is better to conquer yourself than to win a thousand battles.
Then the victory is yours. It cannot be taken from you." ~ Buddha*

The best time to resolve your tax problems and begin planning for a financial future beyond the tax debt is right now. Tax debt is an emotionally and financially threatening problem that must be dealt with immediately and effectively through a structured plan of action. Before discussing the technical aspects of tax resolution, it is important to explore the human element of dealing with financial matters in general. Many people make the mistake of jumping right into the tax resolution process without a plan or any sense of direction. Deciding to take control of your tax situation and making a commitment to change is a necessary first step on the road to tax freedom.

Rebuilding your financial life takes hard work and discipline. A plan of action will accomplish very little until you take action and actually implement the plan. Resolving tax matters is a combination of mastering tax and financial knowledge and adopting successful behavior patterns to implement the basic steps of "Tax Resolution and Financial Freedom". In essence, the tax and financial planning process is 75% behavioral and 25% knowledge and technique. A simple recipe of 3 parts behavioral action and 1 part knowledge.

Getting Started

The first challenge during the tax resolution process is to accept responsibility for the current debt situation and make a commitment to change. Accountability is imperative. It you cannot accept the fact that you need to change your approach to managing your taxes and personal finances, then you probably will not change much of anything. Own up to your current situation (no matter how you got there) and convince yourself there is a solution. The ultimate goal of the tax resolution process is financial freedom.

Peace of mind awaits those who take action and make the most of their resources. Poor financial decision making has to stop. Destructive financial management behaviors have to be replaced by positive alternatives if you want to achieve peace of mind financially. In essence, the old ways of dealing with taxes and money need to be forgotten and new strategies need to be put in place.

The Internal Revenue Service is not your primary adversary. The number one opponent that you are up against is yourself and the need for comprehensive tax and financial planning. Instead of fighting the IRS, you need to work within the guidelines of their bureaucracy and find ways to resolve your tax debt in the most cost-effective manner. That is, you need to find the best tax resolution method based on your particular situation.

Does this mean you should take their word and always assume the IRS is correct at all times? Absolutely not, but you should understand how they operate and how to deal with them if you have a tax liability. Most importantly, you should view tax debt as a personal challenge and wake up call.

You need to understand more than just how the tax resolution process works. Understanding how to make smart decisions about money is a greatly needed element of the change process. If you do not have a solid foundation of smart financial decision making, now is the time to learn. The ultimate challenge that most people face during the tax resolution process is the inability to overcome problematic money-related behaviors and take control of their financial situation.

Taking Control: Making a Commitment to Change
There are many ways to get into tax trouble with the IRS. Some tax problems are due to honest mistakes by the taxpayer or cash flow problems related to life emergencies. Some are due to fear and procrastination. Others are related to pure negligence and dishonesty. Many more are related to outright protests to the system of taxation in America. One common trait of all delinquent taxpayers who owe the IRS and are actively engaged in resolving their tax liabilities is this one simple fact- **they want the IRS off their back so they can get on with their lives**! That is the reason the first step of the Tax & Financial Planning Process has been labeled "Taking Control: Making a Commitment to Change".

The identification of a tax problem occurs in a variety of ways. A CPA, Enrolled Agent, or tax preparer may bring a tax liability to your attention during the tax preparation process. If you self-prepared your tax returns you may even have identified a tax liability yourself or through the help of tax preparation software. More often than not, the bearer of bad news is the IRS itself. Automated Collection System letters, tax audits, levy notices, and visits from revenue officers are just some of the many ways the IRS can "remind" you of a debt obligation to the United States Department of Treasury.

Once awareness of a tax liability has been established, the decision making process of each taxpayer that owes the IRS begins. The decision is fairly simple and there are two basic options. You can attempt to ignore the IRS and subject yourself to the risk of aggressive collection activities on their part, or you can use this as an opportunity to make a commitment to change in your financial life and take control of your financial future.

The decision to take control sounds more appealing than wage garnishments, bank account levies, and property liens. Surprisingly, many people opt to avoid the IRS altogether and only compound their financial problems by putting them off to the future. For those that are willing to address the IRS tax liability one additional question is present. What is the best way to resolve this tax liability and get on with life?

This is an important area of concern for individuals that owe the IRS. Professional guidance can help determine the most appropriate plan of action to resolve a tax liability. This can help guarantee that you are taking appropriate steps to pay back taxes owed in the most cost-effective manner. Tax professionals can also provide answers to other crucial questions such as:

- Is the amount of the tax liability correct?

- What steps should I take to begin the tax resolution process?
- How does tax resolution planning fit into my overall financial plan?
- How do I remain compliant with IRS procedures and avoid future problems?
- Do I need to use a qualified tax professional or a do-it-yourself approach?
- Do I really have a comprehensive tax and financial plan in place to guide my future decisions?

At this point, most people tend to separate their income tax planning needs from their overall financial planning goals and objectives. From a tax resolution standpoint that is the worst decision to make. Since most debt management issues, especially IRS tax liabilities, can be very emotional and carry such a strong sense of urgency to find an immediate solution, it is easy to think that the tax problem is the only thing that needs to be focused on. Most financial planners would agree that this is an incorrect assessment.

Income tax planning is just one of the areas of focus in a comprehensive financial plan. For a person with tax debt it becomes the most important focus point. Tax resolution needs to be incorporated into the financial planning process to help individuals focus on achieving a variety of short and long term goals rather than just on one goal to deal with the IRS. Fortunately, there is a growing number of professionals (albeit a small group) that focus on this unique need.

Motivation to Change

When I talk to clients about the reasons they are seeking help with tax problems, I get a variety of responses. Some people state they are tired of living in fear of the IRS. Others recognize the need to start planning for the future and assume control of their lives. Many are embarrassed by their failure to meet important financial obligations. These people are intrinsically motivated to seek change. Their primary reason for seeking change is due to a calling from within.

On the other hand, some respond to my inquiry about the reason they are seeking change with brutal honesty. The only reason they are seeking change is because they received a threatening letter or visit from the IRS. Their motivating factor is to avoid a negative financial consequence of their tax debt. Not responding to the IRS's call to action will most likely lead to bank levies, liens, and property seizures. Other external forces can motivate people with tax problems to seek change. Family and friends can often be successful in getting someone they love or care about to take control of their financial problems.

The one thing that matters the most is that you acknowledge the need to assume control of your taxes and money. The most important component of any behavioral modification program is the getting started part. Since we have established that the tax resolution process is 3 parts behavioral and 1 part financial knowledge and expertise, this step should not be taken for granted. If you are not truly committed to change then you will not put forth the effort needed to improve the way you deal with the taxing situation. Ultimately you may never improve your quality of life as it relates to money unless you take a comprehensive look at your financial situation.

Earlier in this book I challenged some of the common advertising within the tax resolution industry. The typical approach to attract tax resolution clients is to offer a desirable solution to the public. This is smart business and makes sense. Offer a service that is needed- tax resolution. Then tell someone who is desperately seeking help that "if you hire us we will help you deal with the IRS and resolve your tax problems".

The part of this I do not agree with is that when you tell someone the only way get out of tax trouble is to hire a professional you can discourage people from accepting ownership of the problem. The one thing that is missing from this approach is the focus on the client's need to take action with how he or she manages personal financial issues. A commitment to resolve a tax problem is not enough. Tax problems help identify a need to take action and completely alter how you view money. Never underestimate the importance of making a genuine commitment to your family and self to follow through on your tax and financial goals. Professional help is available to help provide guidance throughout the tax resolution process. However, the ultimate responsibility is with the individual actually experiencing the tax and financial problems to take control of his or her own situation.

Taking Action!!!

What motivates you? What motivated you to seek tax and financial freedom? Make a list of the reasons you are motivated to change your financial future.

Write down some motivating statements to keep you focused along the journey toward tax and financial freedom

---

Psychology of Debt

Debt affects everyone in different ways and can have a devastating impact on one's psychological well-being. Many psychological factors exist that can potentially lead to debt problems. It is important to deal with the issues that led to the tax debt prior to implementing any debt reduction strategies. Otherwise, similar tax problems may pop up again creating a vicious cycle. That is why this section is part of Tax Resolution Step #1: Taking Action: Making a Commitment to Change.

Rising debt levels in our society are becoming excessively burdensome to many individuals and families. Debt can be both emotionally and financially damaging. If not dealt with proactively, debt can threaten the accomplishment of short and long-term financial goals. Most people know they have trouble managing their personal finances. What the majority of people in financial crisis fail to understand is the psychological nature of debt.

Everyone has a unique view of money. The early lessons that are provided by parents, teachers, friends, and society help shape our belief system. Money lessons shape our views about personal finance and affect our views about how to manage money. Gaining a basic understanding of the psychological basis for financial behaviors is important during the tax resolution process. Self-awareness and inquiry is an essential part of trying to find effective solutions to any tax or financial problem.

Psychology is the study of human behavior. One area that needs to be explored more within the field of financial psychology is what psychological, demographic/economic, or attitudinal factors are predictors of debt problems. So far it appears that there are many potential predictors of why people travel down the path of a debt filled existence. Psychologists typically have focused on variables such as the following:

Demographic and economic factors- Some studies indicate that poor people are more likely to be in debt. Having a low income in relation to social class is also related to debt problems. Additional research indicates that associating with people in debt themselves may increase the risk of debt.

What demographic or economic factors shaped your early beliefs about money and debt?

Did you grow up with the haves, the have nots, or the have not paid for what they haves?

Psychological Factors- There is a belief that people with an external locus of control may have a greater chance of experiencing debt problems. Locus of control refers to individual beliefs about what causes negative or positive events in one's life. An external locus of control refers to the belief that other people, a higher power, or the environment controls life decisions. Internal locus of control means that the individual believes he or she has control over their life (tax resolution planning requires this belief). Low self-esteem and low self-efficacy beliefs may also be related to debt problems.

Do you believe that you have the ability to take control of your financial situation?

Have you ever had self-esteem problems related to money?

How confident are you in your ability to achieve tax and financial freedom?

Attitudinal Factors- One of the most reliable predictors of debt may actually be related to attitudes people possess toward debt. Research displays that people with more debt-tolerant attitudes are more likely to be living in debt.

If you have tax debt, how do you feel about the fact you owe taxes to the IRS?

What early money lessons were you taught by your parents or others?

What are your general thoughts about debt?

The presence of debt problems affects more than just the individual in debt. Tax debt can create additional strains on relationships with a spouse or other family members. Similar to most problems that go unaddressed over long periods of time, financial problems related to debt will compound if not eventually dealt with. This is undoubtedly the case with past due tax liabilities and related penalties and interest.

Biopsychosocial Impact of Debt (a.k.a. The Triple Whammy)
The presence of debt affects more than just the wallet. Debt problems can also create an increased risk of health, psychological, and social pressures. Following a debt reduction plan will do more than improve your finances. The following problems are associated with debt.

- **Health Problems-** Being in debt is associated with an increased risk of digestive track issues, migraines, and even heart attack. Other related problems are high blood pressure, insomnia, lower back pain or tension, and concentration problems.
- **Psychological Problems-** Anxiety, depression, stress
- **Social Problems-** Marital tension and debt stress have a negative impact on relationships in general. Trouble focusing on work can also result in poor productivity and increased problems at your job.

This information is not rocket science and should come as no surprise. Stress related to tax debt can cause serious health and psychological problems in addition to financial problems.

As you progress through the steps of the tax resolution process, focus on the past lessons you were taught about money. Also, think about the impact that debt has had on your life. Self-awareness related to the psychology of debt is important because it helps overcome future barriers to change. It also helps identify the most appropriate solutions for the problem.

While learning from the past is important, I also encourage people to move beyond past money lessons and look forward to a new way of life as far as money is concerned. Do not let the past hold you back or tie you down. Focus on the positive rewards that lie ahead when you reach the ultimate goal of financial freedom. The negative problems associated with tax debt are presented as a reminder of the important crossroads that every person with a tax liability finds himself or herself.

In one direction is the seemingly comfortable way of dealing with financial matters. This is the old way of doing things and is without a doubt the status quo. The old way gets people into tax and financial problems in the first place. Either look back and continue with the status quo or seek change by heading forward into the direction of hope, the decision is yours.

Financial freedom is in the other direction. At times the journey will not be easy. You will be challenged to change how you view money and you will be forced to replace negative financial behaviors with positive alternatives. You will also have to stick with a plan and stay on track while everyone else calls you crazy for not being satisfied with the old ways of doing things. Just remember that the old ways of doing things led you into debt in the first place.

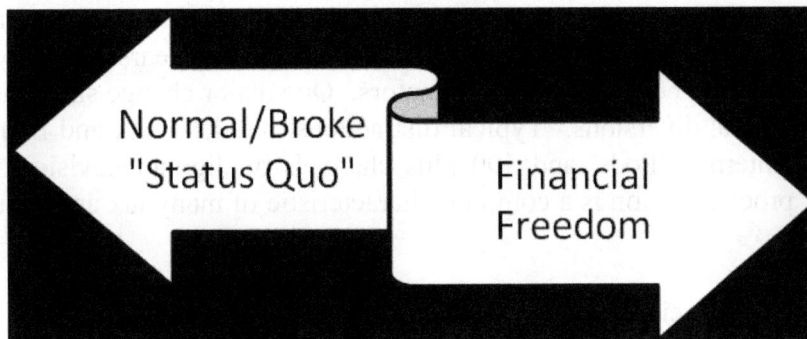

In which direction are you headed?

If you are dealing with tax and consumer debt problems you are in a key transitional period of your life. The choice is quite simple. You can continue to make the same mistakes over and over again and expect things to change or you can change your financial behaviors and adopt a positive system of change that will lead you to tax and financial freedom.

Remember that the definition of insanity is doing the same thing over and over again and expecting different results. You can take comfort in knowing that most people around you will choose this option. The average person in this country is broke. Whether or not they have tax debt, the average person is faced with major debt problems.

Many of us live in a constant state of ignorance or denial when it comes to financial matters in general. If you fall into this category do not hide behind a lack of knowledge related to tax or financial matters. Most Americans understand the importance of financial planning, yet lack the education and expertise to follow through with the creation and implementation of a financial plan. Annual tasks such as preparing an income tax return are often viewed as an adverse situation similar to going to the dentist or doctor. The subject of taxes can evoke a wide range of emotions. Denial, anxiety, fear, anger, hopelessness and depression are just some of the words that are commonly associated with tax debt management.

Procrastination

Tax Procrastination is a common trait shared by many people with past due tax payments. Many people delay filing and subsequently delay paying taxes for a variety of reasons. The IRS estimated that 10.2 million people out of 135.3 million filers would apply for a 6-month extension in the 2006 tax year. In order to resolve tax problems and achieve financial freedom you have to address procrastination issues early on during the tax and financial planning process. Never allow fear or financial ignorance the opportunity to take control of your life as it relates to money.

You have probably heard the saying, "Why do today what you can put off tomorrow?". It seems that a significant number of people with tax problems experience a tendency to put off or get overwhelmed by tax and financial obligations. Procrastination is defined as putting off things that you should be doing now. Most people procrastinate at some point in their lifetimes. Approximately 20% of people in this country are classified as "chronic procrastinators". Thirty years ago only about 5% of Americans considered themselves to be chronic procrastinators. One major change since the 1970's is the increased number of technological diversions. Typical distractions that delay tax and financial planning include email, cell phones, internet, iPods, and 400 plus channels of digital television with video on demand. Not surprisingly, procrastination is a common characteristic of many tax and financial planning clients.

We live in a society that reinforces the need for instant gratification. There are countless temptations in the world to distract people. You may have the best intentions to start planning and stay on task until procrastination rears its ugly head.

Motivation is another factor related to procrastination. The more motivated people are, the more likely they will avoid procrastinating behaviors and vice versa. Other predictors of procrastination include lack of self-confidence, aversion of money matters, impulsiveness, and distractibility. Many individuals with tax problems report a lower expectancy that they are actually capable of succeeding with tax and financial planning tasks.

If you have a problem with procrastination something has to be done about it if you want to improve your financial life and get other important life tasks accomplished. This means sooner rather than later! Procrastination can damage both your overall health and your total wealth.

Some common causes of procrastination in people with tax problems include the following:

- Lack of clearly defined goals
- Confusing or difficult to understand tasks
- Fear of failure
- Fear of success
- Underestimating the difficulty of tasks
- Poor decision making skills

Whether you believe you can or believe you can't, you're probably right
People generally procrastinate because they do not know what to do or how to do it. The LifeSpan Process of Tax Resolution and Financial Freedom clearly explains the steps needed to resolve a tax debt and move on with your life. The costs of not taking action now are significant when you have an existing tax liability. The IRS will take aggressive collection measures if you do not respond to your tax

obligations in a timely manner. The longer it takes for you to pay off past due taxes, the more interest and penalties you will end up paying over time. Procrastination also leads to opportunity costs when the money you eventually pay to resolve your taxes could have been used to invest in other goals.

Combating Procrastination: Strategies for Change

"To do" lists provide good reminders of what needs to be done. However, a "to do" list is also a good way to delay things actually getting done in a timely manner. Have you ever had good intentions in the past in relation to financial planning tasks? Some common tax and financial intentions are listed in the statements below:

- "I need to file my taxes on time this year."
- "I really need to set up a savings fund just in case an emergency occurs."
- "We should pay off our credit cards."
- "Let's get our paperwork to our accountant."
- "I need to get my financial planning forms to my planner."

Unfortunately, the good intentions listed above lack direction. A better alternative as you follow the steps of the tax resolution process is to develop what I refer to as "implementation intentions" or "planning intentions". In the tax resolution world, planning intentions decide how, when, and where you are going to accomplish the steps of the tax and financial process. They increase the likelihood you will follow through on the important steps needed to improve your financial well-being.

Many of the action plan recommendations throughout the Tax Resolution and Financial Freedom process include tips to help you move from a goal intention to action. In reference to the stages of behavior change, planning intentions help move from contemplation and preparation to action and maintenance.

Taking Action!!!

In order to ensure that you follow the steps of the Tax Resolution and Financial Freedom process, you need to make planning intentions. Good intentions lead to procrastination. Planning intentions define how, when, and where you will perform each step of the process. During the tax resolution process be sure to define the specifics (how, when, where, etc.) of your planning behaviors. Put your planning actions in writing and hold yourself accountable. Never miss a deadline.

The need to change financial behaviors is significant when tax liabilities are present. This step has explored the need to understand the reasons for the tax debt in order to be in position to avoid creating the same mistakes again. If you want to take control of your financial future you need to become a better planner and remove the word "Procrastination" from your vocabulary. Planning is a proactive response that leads to positive change. Responding to pressures from the IRS to resolve tax debt without a comprehensive plan is simply being "reactive". You can deal with the past mistakes related to your income tax planning by being proactive. The best alternative is to take control of your life and secure your financial future with a comprehensive tax and financial plan.

"Whether you think that you can or you can't, you're usually right." - Henry Ford

The Role of Self-Efficacy

- Do you believe in your own ability to attack tax debt head on?
- How confident are you in your own ability to take control of your financial future?

These are questions that each person experiencing tax problems must answer. Your internal belief system plays a key role during the tax resolution process. Albert Bandura, Ph.D. is regarded as one of the most influential social psychologists of our time. One of his greatest accomplishments as a psychologist has been related to an extensive body of research conducted on the topic of self-efficacy.

Self-efficacy is essentially your belief in your ability to be effective as a person. This effectiveness is generally defined in terms of managing your own life. More specifically, self-efficacy refers to the belief that you can competently deal with individual tasks. Bandura's research has demonstrated that self-efficacy has a significant impact of individual thoughts, feelings, behaviors, and accomplishments.

The concept of self-efficacy can be applied to the tax resolution process. Learning new financial behaviors and taking control of one's financial life can be a seemingly difficult and overwhelming process. The perception of the tax resolution process is directly related to your likelihood of success as you begin the journey in search of financial peace. If you perceive that your tax problems are something that you can handle then you are more likely to perceive the situation as a challenge. If you believe that the tax situation is beyond your abilities, then you are likely to experience personal distress.

According to Bandura's social cognitive theory, people with a strong sense of their capabilities 1) view difficult tasks as challenges to be mastered; 2) develop a deep interest in their activities; 3) set challenging goals and maintain a strong commitment to them; and 4) recover quickly from setbacks and disappointments. This describes the ideal belief system that you must have when approaching the tax and financial planning process.

In contrast, people with a weak sense of self-efficacy 1) view difficult tasks such as tax resolution planning as threats to be avoided; 2) lose confidence very easily and dwell on personal deficiencies and other obstacles to achieving desired results; 3) have low dreams and aspirations and weak commitment to goals; and 4) are slow to recover from minor setbacks and disappointments in life. These examples of low self-efficacy represent everything that you need to avoid during the tax resolution and financial planning process.

Self-efficacy beliefs provide the foundation for human motivation, well-being, and personal accomplishment. In order to resolve your tax problems and take control of your financial life, you need to be motivated and remove any self-doubt about your ability to succeed. Keep in mind that you are not expected to be a financial genius to proceed through the steps of tax resolution and financial freedom. You do not need to know everything about taxes and money to succeed. You simply need to know just enough to be dangerous! Do not allow fear and doubt to stand in your way of learning new ways to manage your finances.

Taking Action!!! You may not know everything about tax and financial planning at this point. That is okay! You are just getting started with the tax resolution process. Before you continue with the tax resolution steps you should ask yourself these simple questions to measure your own self-efficacy.

1. Do you believe that you will successfully get out of debt?
2. Are you capable of achieving financial freedom?

If you answered yes to both of those questions then you are ready to continue. It is that simple. If you do not believe you are capable of resolving your tax problems and achieving financial freedom with or without professional guidance, then you probably need to evaluate your belief system before you continue. If you have a low sense of self-efficacy and self-doubt it is strongly recommended that you seek professional guidance and support in order to proceed through the tax resolution steps.

Are you ready to change financial behaviors?
Once you have a firm belief that you are capable of taking control of your financial situation you need to act on this belief. If you have ever made a New Year's resolution you probably understand the difficulty of changing any behavior. Perhaps you were not ready for change. Maybe you did not know how to implement change the best way. Frequently these resolutions are abandoned due to frustration and discouragement. Lasting change is rarely a simple process. If you have ever tried to lose weight, stop smoking, exercise more, etc. you probably realized that a simple solution does not exist for everything. Behavior change can be difficult to maintain over the course of time. Tax and financial planning undoubtedly involves a substantial commitment of time, effort, and emotions and is a form of behavior change. Fortunately, there is a technique that has proven to be the most effective method of achieving tax and financial freedom- Tax Resolution Planning.

Problem behaviors can include procrastination, fear, avoidance, ignorance, addiction, and blame (to name a few). Some other examples of problematic financial behaviors include reckless spending, deception, and lack of teamwork. Understanding the elements of the change process can help you stay on track while dealing with the IRS. Behavioral psychologists tend to focus on three important aspects of behavioral change: antecedents, behaviors, and consequences. It is important to understand these elements when you start developing new financial strategies and use the planning process to change your financial behaviors.

Examples of Positive and Negative Financial Behaviors

Positive Financial Behaviors	Negative Financial Behaviors
Set goals and review progress regularly	Failure to file tax returns on time
Save or invest on a regular basis	Owe taxes to the IRS or state
Develop and follow a spending plan	Compulsive spending- Buy on impulse
Plan ahead for large purchases or expenses	Operating without a budget or spending plan
Pay cash for planned major purchases	Minimum monthly payments on credit cards
Maintain 3-6 months income for emergencies	Borrowing money to pay basic living expenses
Pay off credit card bills in full each month	Bank overdraft charges and late fees
Check your credit report at least once a year	Late payments on bills
Communicate about money with spouse	Argue with spouse over money matters
Use a written plan of action to guide decisions	Put off planning

> **Taking Action!!!**   Make a list of some areas of your financial life that have been a problem for you in the past. Choose the top three negative financial behaviors that you would like to improve. Go ahead and make a list of positive financial behaviors that you would like to work on during the tax and financial planning process.

As you begin the tax and financial planning process, keep in mind that you are trying to replace negative financial behaviors with positive ones. The tax resolution process fails when the proper preparation and actions are not taken. You must follow each step of the Tax Resolution and Financial Freedom Process. By approaching tax resolution goals with an understanding of how to best prepare, act, and maintain new financial behaviors, you will be more likely to succeed.

The ABC's of Behavior Change

Most people find it difficult to give up or change things that are familiar. For many people seeking tax resolution, negative financial behaviors occur on a regular basis. Since negative financial behaviors are usually present for long periods of time it often helps to understand the characteristics of the behavior itself.

A very simple yet effective method of assessing financial behaviors is called the "ABC" approach. Behavioral psychologists typically use this method to make observations on the **A**ntecedents, **B**ehaviors, and **C**onsequences of the behavior that needs to be changed. In other words, "What comes directly before the behavior?", "What does the behavior look like?", and "What comes directly after the behavior?"

This approach is relevant to the tax resolution discussion because poor financial behaviors need to be replaced by positive alternatives. For example, fear of filing a tax return (antecedent) could lead to the behavior of procrastination. The resulting consequence is a failure to file penalty with the IRS and potentially additional tax debt if the taxes were not paid. To change this cycle you need to alter the behavior. Once you recognize fear or avoidance related to filing a tax return you need to stay focused on the short and long term benefits of financial freedom. The resulting consequence could be a small reward such as dining out or a trip to the movies. Of course, the ultimate consequence is tax and financial freedom which allows people to use money to help accomplish life planning goals.

Consider the example of a self-employed individual trying to manage personal and business finances without a plan or vision (antecedent = no financial plan, no budget, no emergency fund). Living off of gross income rather than net income ends up being the resulting behavior. Of course an associated behavior is the failure to make estimated quarterly tax payments to the IRS. The consequence as you can imagine is an IRS tax debt (and related penalties). If he replaced the behavior of living beyond his means with the creation of a personal spending plan he could end up identifying a way to pay off his estimated taxes.

The ABC process is very basic, but with tax resolution planning you sometimes need to take the baby steps before you run the race to financial freedom. Take a few moments to analyze your problem financial behaviors. Try to identify any patterns. If there are consistent antecedents and/or consequences, then your tax resolution plan should target them in order to increase or decrease the target behavior.

ABC's of Tax Resolution Planning

Antecedent (What comes first?)	Behavior (What do you do?)	Consequence (What is the result?)
Example: Fear of dealing with tax issues	Procrastinating behaviors	Tax debt continues to grow, IRS begins collection process
Spending money without a plan (no budget in place)	Expenses exceed income	Credit card debt, unable to pay income taxes

As you embark on this tax resolution and financial planning mission you should embrace the idea of change. Dealing with tax problems can be a significant challenge. Tax resolution planning requires you to take a different approach to managing taxes and personal finances. The tax resolution process may be difficult and frustrating at times and you should always prepare for and expect minor setbacks. If you take the steps one at a time and prepare to take control of your life as it relates to money you will be able to obtain meaningful change.

Taking Action: Elements of Change

1. **Readiness to change**
2. **Barriers to change**
3. **Expect setbacks**

The concept of tax resolution planning involves taking action. If you want to change your financial life and get out of tax debt you have to take action. You have to want to change and be ready to accept it with courage and a positive attitude. Improving your financial well being requires a constant pursuit of meaningful change in all aspects of your life.

Many barriers to change exist along life's journey no matter what the challenge. In the tax and financial planning world these barriers could be procrastination and fear. Other obstacles such as lack of support or marital discord may also stand in the way of change. Whatever your personal barriers are you need to go ahead and accept the fact that there will be obstacles. You should expect to incur setbacks and prepare for them. This does not mean that you should accept failure. You simply need to prepare for the minor setbacks and never allow them to stop you on the journey to financial freedom.

Assessing the Change Process

Behavior change is an ongoing process and in theory progresses through a series of stages. These theoretical stages were introduced by James Prochaska, Ph.D. and are generally referred to as the Transtheoretical Model of Change (Stages of Change Theory). I know that is a big word. Do not focus on it as much as the importance of assessing where you are in the change process while seeking ways to resolve tax problems. As you progress through the Tax Resolution Steps (and then focus on the Steps to Financial Freedom) always keep in mind as to which stage you are in.

1. **Pre-contemplation-** person does not intend to take action in the next six months
    Example: IRS letters are completely ignored, unwilling to discuss the need to file past due tax returns, continue to spend more than you earn, no personal spending plan, may not even realize a tax problem exists

2. **Contemplation-** person intends to take action in the next six months
    Example: Realizes the need to deal with tax issue, understands the need for a tax and financial plan, lack of awareness where to turn to for help and guidance, do not understand the financial mess they are in, tried to create a budget in the past but failed, defensive (pulled into action before they were ready)

3. **Preparation-** person intends to take action in the next 30 days
    Example: Researching available tax resolution options, deciding whether or not to seek professional help, beginning stages of organization, gathering tax and financial documents

4. **Action-** person has taken action, but for less than six months, hardest most demanding step, make a commitment to place the tax resolution and financial planning process as the top priority for the next six months,
    Example: Seeking help with tax resolution issues, creating a personal spending plan, determining the best particular tax resolution alternative, working the steps of tax resolution and financial freedom

5. **Maintenance-** person has take action for more than six months, stress is the top reason people regress at this stage, there is a need to create positive choices or alternatives to deal with stress (social support/talking, exercise, relaxation)
    Example: Staying current with IRS payments, filing future tax returns on time, reviewing personal spending plan on an ongoing basis, communicating regularly with spouse about money

6. **Termination-** person will not revert to self-defeating, self-destructive financial behaviors; learning new behaviors and making them a part of who you are, similar to the challenge that people are faced with addiction
    Example: Tax freedom is achieved by paying off the tax liabilities. Future tax and financial problems are avoided by consistently using positive financial behaviors. Developed the ability to take control of money and focus on other parts of life.

    The LifeSpan Process of Tax Resolution and Financial Freedom promotes the termination of problematic financial behaviors. The best way to do this is to learn better alternatives such as planning, eliminating debt, avoiding debt, saving and investing.

Change: Are you ready?

Let's take a moment to look at how the steps of the change process can be applied to dealing with tax liabilities. In order to achieve tax freedom you must develop new patterns of financial behaviors. When looking at the ABC's of your tax problems (antecedent- behavior- consequences) you may be able to identify some patterns. The primary goal of tax resolution planning is to stop the cycle and create a new, more effectives patterns that promote debt reduction and wealth building

Take a few moments to think about these questions. You may want to take a notepad and write down your responses.

- Are you ready to take control of your life as it relates to money?
- How have you dealt with money matters in the past?
- Do you have difficulty getting your finances organized?
- Are you clueless about the best savings and investment options?
- Have you ever avoided opening an IRS letter or bill from a debt collector?
- How would you describe your spending habits?
- Do you accept responsibility for your tax problems, or is there someone else to blame?
- What are some of the problem behaviors that you need to change in order to focus on dealing with a tax problem in the most cost-effective manner?

Seven R's of Behavior Motivation and Change

The LifeSpan Process of Tax Resolution and Financial Freedom was designed to help people resolve tax problems and focus on building wealth and a life of financial independence. The process emphasizes changing financial behaviors and developing a new approach to tax and financial planning.

Recently the National Endowment for Financial Education sponsored a think tank of professionals on the topic of financial psychology. The topic of the Seven R's of Behavior Motivation and Change were discussed in the context of financial change. The concept of the Seven R's that were discussed during the forum can be applied to the tax resolution process.

As you progress through the steps of the tax resolution process keep these "R's" in mind and explore the following questions:

Readiness- Are you ready to take control of your financial future?

Resources- Will you need professional guidance during the tax resolution process? Are your spouse, family, and friends on board with your mission to get out of debt? Are you prepared to assess your financial resources?

Relevant- Do you feel that the tax and financial planning process is a relevant and useful way to resolve your tax debt? Do you understand the connection between your views about money and how you have handled financial decisions in the past?

Respect- How does your tax debt and financial situation affect how you feel about yourself?

Responsibility- Do you understand that you are the primary agent of change? Will you share responsibility with another person or take the journey alone?

Reward- What is your definition of financial freedom? Why are you pursuing tax resolution goals? What will be the final reward for your hard work?

Replication- How committed are you to the process of improving your financial life? Will you be able to stay focused and stay on track financially? Are you prepared to make tax and financial planning a habit that you repeat over and over again in pursuit of financial independence?

The Seven Rs for Behavior Motivation and Change are explained in greater detail in the appendix. Tax resolution and financial planning will work to eliminate tax problems and improve your financial standing if you follow the process of changing financial behaviors. When changing your approach to taxes and money you must create good habits and repeat them over and over again. Positive financial behaviors such as spending with a plan, paying off debt aggressively, and saving on a regular basis must be replicated over time if you want to resolve tax and financial problems. It is your responsibility to yourself and your family to take control of your financial future. The reward is financial freedom. You get to decide what financial freedom means to you. The basic concept of the Seven Rs of behavior change will follow you throughout the LifeSpan Process of tax and financial change.

Message for Couples

As you make a commitment to change and take action you need to keep in mind that tax and financial planning is a joint effort that you both need to work on together to accomplish. Managing personal finances can be a difficult task when a tax liability exists. Financial planning is even more difficult, if not impossible, if a couple is not working together as one.

One common problem in marriages is a disagreement on how to manage money. Unfortunately, comments such as "you spent how much on that?" are more common than the ultimate question- "how much should we be spending?" It is not surprising that financial disagreements are often cited as the number one reason couples end up getting divorced. Many couples struggle with the task of openly discussing their finances. The tax resolution process requires couples to work together to achieve a common goal of freedom from tax debt. This means that both parties need to take action and make the commitment to change financial behaviors.

Money and taxes should not be viewed as an issue of mine and yours. As a couple you should view everything as an "ours" issue. Talking about money with anyone can be very difficult because money is such a taboo subject in American culture. When that special someone is your spouse the talk can be even more complicated.

Why does money have such a powerful impact on our relationships? This is a difficult question that I encourage couples to explore. Money represents different things to each partner. One partner may view money as a symbol of power and success. The other may see money as a symbol of comfort and security. If the topic of dealing with tax debt and taking control of personal finances makes one or both parties emotionally uncomfortable or defensive, you should seek the help of a financial planner or financial counselor. Professional counseling is also available for couples experiencing problems communicating about money.

Make a commitment to one another to handle your tax problems as a couple. This is important even if the tax debt was assumed prior to the marriage or a non-liable spouse is involved. Simply determining that your partner's tax debt is not your problem is not going to work. Blaming will also do nothing to help the situation. Other unhealthy habits include sabotaging personal spending plans by secret spending or hiding financial decisions from the other spouse.

Each spouse should be accountable to the other. Aim to create a tax resolution and financial plan that works for both of you. Make sure that the commitment to work toward financial freedom is a vision that you both share. If only one person is doing the work then you have a major problem brewing.

Communicating About Money
How we communicate with each another can be just as important as the message you are trying to get across to the other person. If you have a recent history of tax or financial problems it is easy to let emotions and the past take over the discussion. When talking to a spouse or significant other about

money it is also easy for things to get lost in translation. Always be aware of how you are actually communicating with a spouse or loved one about money matters. Never forget that how you say things is just as important as what you actually say. Talking about money is not something that comes easily for most people. Try following these basic communication tips when talking about taxes and money matters.

1. **Set a date**
   Schedule a convenient time to talk about money. Try to pick a time during the week when you are both available to have a calm discussion free from any distractions (e.g., no children, no television).

2. **Establish open lines of communication**
   Remember that what you say is sometimes not as important as how you say it. Use "I" messages to improve communication.

3. **Talk about your life experience with money**
   What lessons did you learn early in life about money?

4. **Give and Take**
   If you are going to ask your spouse to sacrifice something you need to be willing to do the same.

5. **Set boundaries on what can and cannot be discussed**
   Stay focused. Do not bring up off-limit topics.

6. **Avoid secret-spending**
   Be open and honest with your spouse.

7. **Agree on a personal spending plan**
   A budget or personal spending plan will not work unless you both work the plan together.

8. **Discuss your financial matters on a regular basis**
   This is a key element to staying focused and on track.

9. **Seek professional assistance if necessary**
   Know when to seek assistance. If you cannot talk to your spouse or significant other about money then you may need help. Marital counselors and financial planners can both be helpful.

Using "I…" Messages

1. "I feel…"
   Make a clear statement of how you feel.

2. "When you…"
   Name the specific behavior that caused you to feel that way.

3. "Because…"
   Say why the behavior or event is upsetting.

Summary

Tax problems need to be dealt with through the use of a coordinated action plan. Taking control and making a commitment to change requires hard work and discipline. This first step of the LifeSpan Process of Tax Resolution and Financial Freedom sets the stage for the entire journey to tax and financial freedom.

Tax and financial planning has a significant psychological component, and is highly behavioral by nature. If you practice the positive financial behaviors related to tax planning you will succeed. It is important to understand which stage of behavior change you are in. If you are not ready for change or ready to overcome the potential setbacks along the road to tax resolution then you are setting yourself up for failure. However, if you unleash the motivation to change your financial behaviors related to taxes and money management you are bound to succeed. It should not be too difficult to find an excuse to motivate yourself to change as long as the IRS is trying to collect back taxes.

Do not make the mistake of only focusing on resolving tax liabilities. Taxes are one part of a comprehensive financial plan. Look at the big picture and focus on changing your total approach toward money matters. This holistic tax resolution approach requires taking a brand new outlook on the topic of debt. Tax resolution also requires a basic understanding of the psychology of debt. Tax debt is caused by a variety of factors. Each individual has their own personal story and unique views about money. It is relevant to explore some of the psychological factors of debt in order to stay on track with a debt elimination plan.

However, it is not necessary to get caught up in the past. Everyone has their own reasons for getting into debt. Learn from past mistakes and then move on. The tax resolution process uses knowledge about the past to create an action plan for the future. The tax and financial planning process is forward thinking and is most concerned about taking control and committing one's self to new financial behaviors. Avoid the tendency to procrastinate by proactively taking action by using new financial behaviors related to tax resolution planning. Procrastination and fear leads to more tax problems and creates a financial mess. Combat procrastination by identifying positive financial behaviors and understanding the need to take consistent action.

If you understand the basic concepts of ABC's and the Seven R's of Behavior Motivation and Change you will be on the fast track to success. Always set clear goals and "planning intentions" to help you determine how, when, and where you will implement the steps of the Tax Resolution and Financial Freedom process. Explore your own financial behaviors and focus on replicating your new planning behaviors as outlined throughout the tax resolution process. The end result will be the creation of a new habit that will become a way of life. Everything starts with the initial step of taking control and making a commitment to change.

Finally, if you are married or in a committed relationship you will both need to be actively involved in the change process. Make an effort to communicate openly with your spouse about the tax problem. Seek help as needed. Always make an effort to work on the tax and financial planning goals together. Financial discussions can become very difficult (especially if they have not occurred on a regular basis in the past).

The journey to tax and financial freedom starts with a single step. The underlying causes of debt differ from person to person and can be difficult to fully understand. The willingness to take action and assume control of your financial future is the answer to issues related to tax debt. Taking action also means that you are making an important commitment to the change process itself. If you attack this challenge with enthusiasm and desire you are just beginning to create the positive momentum that is needed to become financially free.

Tax Resolution Step #2:
Establishing Goals and Objectives

"It's a dream until you write it down, and then it's a goal." ~ Anonymous

"Which one of you, when he wants to build a tower, does not first sit down and calculate the cost to see if he has enough to complete it?" ~Luke 14:28

"You control your future, your destiny. What you think about comes about. By recording your dreams and goals on paper, you set in motion the process of becoming the person you most want to be. Put your future in good hands - your own." ~ Mark Victor Hansen

Once you have made a commitment to get rid of tax debt and take control of your finances you need to get organized. This means organizing and prioritizing your goals and objectives. In order to determine the most effective way to resolve a tax liability and achieve other financial goals you need to first define your personal and financial goals.

Establishing goals defines the expectations of the tax resolution process. Goal setting also establishes an expected time frame for achievement and defines the level of importance. An outline of specific goals and objectives should address your personal values, abilities, and needs. Tax resolution planning is not a one size fits all approach. When setting goals be sure that your goals are measurable and realistic. Since goals are the central focus of tax resolution planning you should be as detailed as possible when creating them.

Most people have a variety of life planning goals that they would like to accomplish during the tax and financial planning process. Unfortunately, stressful life events such as dealing with IRS tax problems can create distractions from long range planning. If you look beyond the primary goal of resolving tax debt you will see that most people have more important life ambitions they would prefer to focus on. Some examples of life goals include retiring, sending a child to college, purchasing a dream house, taking a special vacation, or funding a new business.

When it comes to the subject of establishing goals it is important to think big. Do not allow the presence of a tax problem to force you to lose sight of your goals and objectives. Debt may present a barrier on the path to financial freedom but it does not have to be a permanent obstacle. Start the process of turning dreams and visions into reality by putting pen to paper and turning your dreams into realistic goals.

Financial Life Planning
The discussion of goals and objectives goes far beyond tax matters during the LifeSpan Process of Tax Resolution. It can easily be assumed that everyone pursuing the goal of tax resolution wants similar results. Common goals are to stop IRS collection letters, file past due tax returns, eliminate tax problems, respond to a recent examination, and to get out of tax debt and regain tax compliance. Financial life planning takes goal setting to a new level. Previously, we discussed the need for meaningful change. The life planning approach adds meaning to the tax and financial planning process.

If you truly want to resolve tax problems and get on with your life you need specific goals and objectives to guide your pursuit of change. Many people with tax problems go through the tax resolution process with one goal and mind and that is to fix the tax problem. That is a worthy goal but it has its limitations. If the underlying problem that led to tax debt is not effectively resolved future tax and financial problems will likely occur.

Life planning goals focus on the "big picture" and provide a deeper meaning to the tax and financial planning process. Focusing on improving your life as it relates to money is the real challenge that you should be called to achieve. This means finding ways to understand how smart money related decisions will have an impact on your life plan.

Financial life planning requires a focus on what matters to you the most in life. It starts the thinking process about what is important to you about money. When establishing tax and financial goals you should consider the role that money plays in your life. How does having a tax debt interfere with your lifelong dreams and ambitions?

Tax Resolution Planning: Financial Life Planning Goals and Objectives
Tax resolution goals are fairly straightforward and do not differ significantly from one person to another. The primary goal is quite simple. Get rid of tax debt. Stay out of tax trouble in the future. Here are the most common tax resolution goals.

- Resolve tax debt with IRS

- Resolve tax problems with a state taxing authority

- Prepare past due tax returns

- File your past due tax returns

- Stay current with estimated tax payments (if applicable)

- Obtain IRS files

- Determine actual amount owed

- Determine the most cost-effective tax resolution alternatives

- Implement tax resolution plan

Establishing your Life Planning Goals and Objectives
Whether you are working with a professional or creating your own financial plan, a comprehensive list of goals and objectives is an important starting point in the establishment of a tax and financial plan. Even if you are not working with a planner you should start the planning process with specific goals and objectives. First, start by making a list of your financial goals and objectives. Then rank these goals and objectives from the most important to the least important. Establishing personal goals and objectives is

your opportunity to identify what is most important to you. There are no right or wrong answers! This may seem like an easy step. However, this step should not be neglected. Goal setting will help define what you look to accomplish during the tax resolution financial planning process.

Take Action!!!
Rank the following tax and financial planning goals from 1 to 12. Tax resolution should automatically be your top priority during the tax resolution and financial freedom process.

The following are some of the most common tax and financial planning goals that people generally set. I encourage people to be honest with themselves when ranking goals and objectives. Do not feel constrained by this list by any means. Add your own goals if this list does not include an important area of concern in your life.

Rank from 1 (most important) to 12 (least important).

Level of Importance	Tax and/or Financial Planning Goal
	Resolve a tax problem with the IRS or a state tax authority
	Increase Net Worth through, savings, investments
	Establish a debt reduction plan to manage consumer debt
	Manage income and expenses to maintain good cash flow
	Minimize current income taxes
	Ensure a comfortable retirement with income to maintain desired lifestyle
	Provide education funds for children or grandchildren
	Maximize the benefits of owning a business, provide for business continuation
	Provide cash and income for survivors in the event of death
	Protect assets and income against loss in the event of disability
	Protect property from loss by natural or legal disaster
	Pass money and property on to the next generation, minimize potential death taxes
	Achieve Other Goals (Be Specific). Examples include: change jobs, career change, self-employment, learn a new skill or hobby, lose weight, improve physical fitness. Other goals: _____

After you have ranked your goals and their level of importance take the top three and write them down. Make sure that your goals are SMART and follow the guidelines below.

How SMART are your goals?

S = Specific (Be clear and precise)

M = Measurable (Identify how will you measure progress and success)

A = Attainable (Set goals that you are capable of accomplishing)

R = Realistic (Know your limitations but never underestimate your own abilities)

T = Timely (Set a time frame regarding when you would like to accomplish your goals)

The Three Most Important Goals in My Life

1.

2.

3.

(Provide an estimated time frame for accomplishing these goals in parentheses.)

Life Planning: What is your life vision?

Financial life planning is about more than just money. A financial life planning approach can provide a deeper meaning to the management of personal finances. Every person going through the tax resolution process needs a vision, purpose, and a plan if they want to succeed. George Kinder is a well respected financial planner and a leading proponent of the life planning movement within the financial planning industry. His financial counseling process includes three questions that are popular for their ability to help clients focus on what really matters to them about money. I have adapted a version of these questions for the tax resolution client.

The main purpose of this exercise is to begin thinking about what you want your money to do for you. The first question is designed to initiate the process of thinking about all of life's possibilities; the second and third questions are created to help people with tax troubles focus in on their priorities in life.

Since the accumulation of excessive tax and consumer debt has such an immediate and overwhelming impact on household finances it is easy to lose sight of long-term goals and dreams. Looking beyond the current state of financial stress is an important way to help prioritize goals during the tax resolution process. It also helps to have something to work to achieve while reinforcing the need to attack your tax problems with passion and enthusiasm.

The life planning questions below should be used to help you identify what you want to get out of life. Since money plays such an integral role in our lives it is important that you are able to understand your values that lie beneath the surface of your financial world.

Take Action!!! Ask yourself the following questions.

1. Imagine that you have paid off all of your tax and consumer debt. You owe absolutely nothing and have enough money to take care of your needs, now and in the future. How would you live your life? Would you change anything?

2. Imagine that you visit the doctor and he or she says you have only five to ten years to live. You will not feel any pain or sickness, but you will never know when death will actually come. What will you do? Will you change your life? How?

3. Finally, now try to imagine that your doctor says you have only one day left to live. Ask yourself: What did I miss? What did I not get to be or do? Do I have any regrets?

Life Transitions:

The three questions exercise is designed to tap into your heart's core. What are your values? What is your vision? Now is the time to start thinking about a life without any debt. Setting a goal to resolve a tax liability is usually the #1 priority during the tax resolution process as it should be. It can be difficult to look beyond the stress of the here and now when it comes to tax and financial matters. Establishing life planning goals add more meaning to the tax resolution process.

Some other life planning goals could be as simple as a special trip, development of a new hobby, career change, or unique personal challenges. At this point many people may wonder why I would even suggest bringing up the life planning discussion. Long-term goals such as retirement sound great but you may ask "what does this have to do with my tax problem". My answer to this question is "everything". If you do not have an idea of where you are going you probably will never get there.

As expected, tax resolution is generally the number one priority during the tax resolution planning process. It is easy to become near sighted and only focus on the immediate goal of reducing tax debt. However, I frequently remind people undergoing this difficult but liberating process that hope and financial freedom lies ahead on their journey. If you are not living a well-rounded life your journey to tax and financial freedom will likely be unfulfilling.

If you do not plan for a life beyond debt there may not be a life of financial freedom to enjoy when and if you ever reach a debt-free place in life. Psychological research (and common sense) indicates that goal setting is an important part of any behavior modification program. In theory, tax resolution and financial planning is 75% behavior modification and attitude and 25% actual tax and financial knowledge. That is the reason that the previous step called "Taking Action" is such an important part of the tax resolution process. In order to take action you need proper direction. Goal setting is an integral part of the tax resolution action plan.

Goals start with a vision of what life could be in the future. Think big. Your vision can include anything and is only limited by your imagination and potential. For many people overwhelmed by tax and financial problems the vision starts with a life without tax debt and financial stress. It can be difficult to look beyond the current crisis. I firmly believe that comprehensive goal setting across all aspects of the life planning spectrum will help provide meaning and direction during the tax resolution process. When setting goals you should not limit your vision to the areas of tax and financial planning.

Life planning goals generally fall into seven different categories.

- Family
- Career
- Social
- Physical
- Spiritual
- Financial
- Intellectual

While this book concentrates on the financial visions and goals you should strive to set goals in the other six areas of your life. Dealing with tax and financial matters can be a life changing event if approached properly. Do not neglect other parts of your life during the tax resolution process.

As you work to resolve tax problems you should address your overall work-life balance. Start thinking about your life goals. Ask yourself these questions:

Do I have well defined life planning goals?
What are my current areas of strength?
What are my biggest areas of weaknesses?
How will the development of my goals help me during the tax resolution process?

> **Taking Action!!!** Go ahead and establish your life planning goals across the seven categories. Break them down into categories of short and long-term goals. Make sure that you set SMART goals that are specific, measurable, attainable, realistic, and have an estimated time frame.

Summary

Establishing well-defined goals and objectives is a critical element of the change process. Goals are necessary during tax resolution. They should be SMART goals that are specific, measurable, realistic, and have an estimated time frame for completion. Life planning goals provide meaning to the entire tax resolution process. Well defined goals give the entire process of getting out of debt relevance. Goals should also be the inspiration for the hard work and effort that goes into the planning activities.

Tax resolution involves so much more than just relieving tax problems and resolving debt issues. The tax resolution process is a commitment to a new approach to both taxes and money. A new way of life requires direction and guidance. Goals and objectives provide direction for people seeking tax resolution. The pursuit of financial freedom is often associated with these goals.

The specific steps on how to accomplish important tax and financial planning goals lie ahead in the LifeSpan Process of Tax Resolution and Financial Freedom. Goal setting comes first in order to define why you are engaging in tax resolution planning to begin with. Think long and hard about the values, visions, and purpose in your life. Next, focus on how your personal finances may play a role in turning these dreams into reality. A carefully designed set of goals and objectives provides the outline for the tax and financial planning process. Of course, you may always modify certain goals over the course of time. In general though, the goals at the heart's core generally tend to stay consistent over time.

Tax Resolution Step # 3:
Assessing Resources

"Contentment is natural wealth, luxury is artificial poverty." ~ Socrates

"Self-assessment is universal truth." ~ Anonymous

The previous tax resolution steps stressed the importance of taking action and establishing goals and objectives. The next step is to assess the "resources" you have available to accomplish these goals. For individuals with tax problems these "resources" ultimately determine the recommended tax resolution option that best fits each person's unique financial position. Available resources are critical elements of the change process in relation to tax debt. Every available tool will be needed to attack tax and financial problems.

Resources can be both internal and external. They come in the form of personal strengths and abilities. Social support and professional guidance are available resources during the tax and financial planning process. The willingness to change and the courage to make sacrifices are other examples of skills required when seeking financial change. Resources also include tax and financial knowledge. Everyone going through the tax and financial planning process has a different amount of resources that affects their ability to implement tax resolution recommendations.

This step is designed to help evaluate where you stand in terms of resources that will help you accomplish tax and financial freedom. Information is everywhere. Not everyone has the ability to take the available knowledge and follow through with it. An assessment of resources helps determine whether or not professionals should be used during the tax resolution process. The self-evaluation of resources also helps identify existing strengths and weaknesses related to money. Finally, this step also addresses the financial resources available and prepares for tax resolution.

Throughout the course of this resource assessment step you should be able to answer the following questions:

➤ Are you ready to take action?

➤ Which characteristics of financially successful individuals do you possess?

➤ What areas do you need to improve on?

- What is your financial mission statement?
- Do you have the support system in place to proceed through the financial life planning process?
- Should you seek professional guidance and use the help of a tax resolution planner?
- Where do you stand financially speaking (net worth and cash flow)?

Assessing Resources: Internal Self- Assessment

During the initial step of the tax resolution process we explored the importance of taking action and making a commitment to change. This step touched on the topic of self-awareness as it relates to the psychology of debt. Many characteristics common among individuals with tax liabilities were identified. They are not meant to point fingers or ridicule. This information compiled based on years research and practical work with tax problem clients.

Procrastination and poor financial management behaviors were discussed as frequent problems for many people with tax debt. If you possess these traits and problematic behaviors you need to assess ways to prevent them from sabotaging the tax and financial plan. Rather than focus on negative behaviors such as procrastination or poor communication we should turn our energy to positive traits that should be emulated. These positive traits should be used as a guide for everyone going through the tax resolution and financial freedom process.

> **Taking Action!!!** As you continue through the steps of the tax resolution process, take a moment to assess your own strengths and weaknesses.
> What are some of your biggest strengths as a person?
> What are a few areas you need to improve on in your daily life?

Internal self-assessment requires an analysis of both strengths and weaknesses. The next focus during the self-assessment process is to identify some of the top qualities or traits to strive for during the quest for financial independence. Consider the traits that we are going to review as predictors of success. If you do not possess all of these qualities it does not mean that you will not succeed during the tax resolution process. However, the lack of a significant number of these qualities may prevent you from achieving total financial freedom in the long run unless you make an effort to improve in your areas of weakness.

Models of Success

Now that we have taken some time to examine some of the characteristics of people with tax and consumer debt, let's take a moment to look at the common traits of the wealthy and successful in our country. After focusing on some negative and self-defeating behavior patterns in need of change, it is important to identify the positive behavior patterns that you can adopt during the tax resolution planning process. This will enable you to model your personal behavior after successful individuals that simply "get it" when it comes to managing their money.

It is essential that you always remember that the tax resolution process is part of a bigger challenge- TAKING CONTROL OF YOUR FINANCIAL FUTURE. I encourage you to start thinking not only about how you got into this mess, but how you can change your behavioral patterns involving money and adopt new, more productive behaviors.

Tax resolution is about using the understanding of past financial behaviors to figure out what needs to be changed. Development of positive financial behaviors will allow change to happen. This new approach to life and financial planning means there is a need to have models of success. It is generally not good to only place the focus on negative financial behaviors. That is the old way of approaching tax and financial matters. Instead let us shift our focus to positive models of success. Based on the work of Thomas Stanley's *The Millionaire Mind*, I have selected a set of positive behavior patterns of wealthy and successful individuals.

The Common Traits of Millionaires and Financial Secure Individuals

An analysis of the personality traits of millionaires and financially successful individuals is more than relevant during the tax resolution process. It is required. In order to achieve tax resolution and financial freedom you need to be able to identify some of the most common characteristics of people who have already accomplished success. You also need to strive to possess these qualities.

As you read these traits ask yourself if you possess these qualities. Be honest with yourself as you assess your internal resources. If there are a few areas that are in need of improvement write them down and make a list of ways that you would like to improve. Keep in mind that you are not expected to currently possess all of these traits. However, the closer that you can get to 100% of these traits the easier your journey may be.

1. Integrity

"**Integrity** is doing the right thing, even if nobody is watching." - Author Unknown
Successful people never sacrifice their integrity and are always honest with themselves and others. If you behave with a high degree of personal integrity you have a greater likelihood of financial success. Most importantly, you will live a life of strong resolve and consistency. There are many wealthy individuals in this country who have amassed large sums of wealth through corruption and deception. The acquisition of wealth without integrity is not a sign of success. True financial success requires high standards of integrity through good and bad times.

2. Courage

"Promise me you'll always remember: You're braver than you believe, and stronger than you seem, and smarter than you think." - A.A. Milne
"**Courage** is resistance to fear, mastery of fear - not absence of fear" - Mark Twain

Change requires personal sacrifice. To live like nobody else with a sense of financial freedom requires the courage to take risks and live like nobody else until you reach your goals. Often successful people are risk-takers, but more importantly they are courageous. They tap into the courage that lives deep inside them and use it to break ground, try new things and put themselves out in front. When making a commitment to learn new strategies and techniques you are taking risks.

It takes courage to admit failure and pick oneself off the ground and try again at anything in life. Courage is also needed to change one's approach to taxes and finances. Some of the most successful people in this world have failed time and time again only to get up again and display the courage needed to accept the next challenge in life.

3. Willingness to Act

"Faith means belief in something concerning which doubt is still theoretically possible; and as the test of belief is **willingness** to act, one may say that faith is the readiness to act in a cause the prosperous issue of which is not certified to us in advance." - William James

Knowing and doing are two separate things. The key ingredients of tax and financial freedom include three parts behavioral change and one part knowledge and expertise. Knowing what to do during the tax resolution process is important. Having the willingness to act on this knowledge is more important.

Successful people are willing to dig in, do the work and learn new things. They are simply willing to do whatever it takes to create the life they want. TAKING ACTION is a core theme throughout the Tax Resolution and Financial Freedom Process. Be willing to take the steps needed to improve your financial life.

4. Commitment

"There is a difference between interest and **commitment**. When you are interested in doing something, you do it only when circumstance permits. When you are committed to something, you accept no excuses, only results." Author Unknown

"The best way out is always through." - Robert Frost

Commitment provides the necessary energy and dedication to keep moving forward. Committed people do more than just have the willingness to take action. They keep taking action over and over again.

Creating a plan alone will not automatically fix your tax and financial problems. Tax resolution generally takes a great deal of commitment. As the old saying goes, anything worth having in life does not come easily. Financial freedom is worth the hard work and effort. Freedom to live a financially secure life awaits those who are committed to doing everything it takes to succeed.

5. Purpose

"The **purpose** of life is a life of **purpose**." - Robert Byrne

"Many people have a wrong idea of what constitutes true happiness. It is not attained through self-gratification, but through fidelity to a worthy **purpose**." - Helen Keller

Living a meaningful life starts with a sense of purpose. Successful and happy people have usually spent time considering their unique purpose in life and have taken steps to fulfill that purpose. Successful people know exactly where they are going and why they want to get there. They have a clear personal vision to guide them in their personal lives, their family lives, and their careers. Purpose provides the energy and focus to help us achieve life planning goals.

6. Creativity

"The **creative** is the place where no one else has ever been. You have to leave the city of your comfort and go into the wilderness of your intuition. What you'll discover will be wonderful. What you'll discover is yourself." - Alan Alda

"The world is but a canvas to the imagination." - Henry David Thoreau

We all have an innate sense to create in our lives. Successful people have learned to tap into their creative spark and do so in a way that enriches their lives and the world around them. They are constantly questioning the crowd and traditional expectations. They create their own unique definitions of success and rarely subject themselves to a herd mentality. For many this could include doing things differently from a financial perspective. Saving for emergencies rather than spending to keep up with others takes some imagination. Creative budgeting and finding ways to entertain on a limited budget are other examples of financial creativity.

Other creative endeavors help successful people charge their cognitive batteries and inspire goal driven accomplishments. Creativity requires independent thinking. It also helps us tap into our ability to understand the difference between needs and desires through independent thinking and self-awareness. A creative mind helps prevent us from getting stuck in life. It helps us move forward and find new meaning and importance in our daily struggles.

7. Balance

"The best and safest thing is to keep a balance in your life, acknowledge the great powers around us and in us. If you can do that, and live that way, you are really a wise man." - Euripides

The happiest and most successful people usually lead well-balanced lives. They take time for their families and fun times and celebrate the whole of their lives, not just parts of it. A holistic approach to tax and financial planning works because, without balance life can seem empty and unrewarding. The most successful people in this world are well rounded people that find happiness and joy in various aspects of their life experiences.

It is no small coincidence that the seventh trait of successful people is balance. This fits perfectly with the Seven Goal Areas of Life Planning. The elimination of debt and creation of wealth is a meaningless endeavor if you lack balance in your life. Strive for balance in your life as you continue on the path to financial freedom. Focus on other goal areas such as family, physical health, spiritual, career, social, and intellectual pursuits.

8. Persistence

"Most of the important things in the world have been accomplished by people who have kept on trying when there seemed to be no hope at all." - Dale Carnegie

"When you come to the end of your rope, tie a knot and hang on." - Franklin D. Roosevelt

Be persistent in the right areas. Financial planning behaviors must occur on a regular basis for them to become habits. Perseverance leads to prosperity. Never give up on your quest for tax resolution and financial freedom. Most people with significant tax debt succumb to the urge to give up before they really even start the tax resolution process. Make a commitment to yourself and your family to be persistent with your financial life plan and always stay focused on your long-term goals no matter how hard the journey may be.

9. Spirituality

"We need to find God, and he cannot be found in noise and restlessness. God is the friend of silence. See how nature - trees, flowers, grass- grows in silence; see the stars, the moon and the sun, how they move in silence... We need silence to be able to touch souls." - Mother Teresa

"Faith is the force of life." Leo Nikolaevich Tolstoy

Successful people have a strong amount of spirituality in their lives. A strong relationship with their God helps guide them through good and bad times. Spirituality also provides an understanding that our actions and behaviors have a greater meaning and purpose in the grand scheme of things. Faith also provides encouragement and strength during difficult times such as experiencing tax and financial problems.

The Bible teaches us many valuable lessons about money. Some people mistakenly believe that money is the root of all evil. The scripture tells us that the love of money is the real problem. A life of faith helps people accept the role as an agent of change.

10. Love of Learning

"Man's mind, once stretched by a new idea, never regains its original dimensions." - Oliver Wendell Holmes

"**Learning** is like rowing upstream: not to advance is to drop back." - Chinese Proverb

Successful people never lose the desire to learn. Whether through reading, attending classes, learning new hobbies or exposure to new life experiences, knowledge is a key to success. The love of learning inspires successful people to be open minded and willing to advance their minds. Every person that you meet and every life event provides an opportunity to learn something.

11. Adaptable/Flexible Thinkers

"If you are truly **flexible** and go until... there is really very little you can't accomplish in your lifetime." - Anthony Robbins

"It is not the strongest of the species that survives, nor the most intelligent that survives. It is the one that is the most **adaptable** to change." - Charles Darwin

Adaptability and flexible thinking is a vital trait of successful people. Success demands thinking outside the box. Adaptable and flexible thinkers see both positive and negatives in every situation. They also possess the ability to adapt their style of thinking in different situation. Open-mindedness and curiosity are excellent traits to possess when faced with difficult problems.

12. Patience

"**Patience** is waiting. Not passively waiting. That is laziness. But to keep going when the going is hard and slow - that is **patience**." – Unknown

"He that can have **patience**, can have what he will." - Benjamin Franklin

Success takes time to build. You cannot begin building meaningful wealth until you are completely out debt. In this day and age of instant gratification very few people have the patience needed to succeed financially.

Dealing with tax problems and getting out of debt takes time and a great deal of patience. Tax and financial problems do not usually occur overnight. Therefore, they probably cannot be dealt with in a short amount of time. You probably have heard the old saying that anything worth having in this world takes time to get. Patience does not mean sitting around and waiting. As the quote above indicates, you need to keep going and take action even when the going is hard and slow.

Incorporate these characteristics and personality traits into your life. The only constant in life is change. If you are going to change your financial life then you need to adopt the behaviors associated with these characteristics of success.

> **Taking Action!!!** Self-assessment time again. Do you possess the 12 traits of successful people? Assess your own personality traits and the characteristics that you possess. Rate your current level from 1-5 (lowest to highest). Circle the 3 characteristics that you would like to focus on improving the most. Make a list of specific ways that you can improve in these areas.

Mission Statement

Mission statements are key elements of any strategic planning process. Businesses use them all the time to provide a sense of unity and understanding for employees embarking on a common mission. Individuals should also have a clear sense of vision. Personal mission statements should be used to help define your purpose and values as you work to achieve tax and financial freedom. Mission statements are used to define what you want to focus on and the goals you want to accomplish in particular areas of your life.

Take a few moments to create your own financial mission statement. It does not have to be long and complex. Try to capture your vision of how you can use the tax resolution and financial planning process to improve your financial life and overall sense of well being.

As an example I will provide you with my company's mission statement.

"We value each and every client and his or her desire to achieve tax and financial freedom. We will help our clients reach their financial and life planning goals by providing unmatched levels of integrity, empathy, and professionalism. The success of our company should be directly related to the financial success of our clients. We will honor God through our actions and commitment to help others."

> **Taking Action!!!** Create your own financial mission statement. This pledge should be your motto to guide you throughout the tax resolution process.

I pledge that I will …

_____

_____

_____

_____

_____

_____

Once you have identified the model behaviors of the wealthy and successful you are ready to continue with the tax resolution process. Although we have not specifically addressed the specific tax resolution alternatives that will resolve your tax debt, we are moving in that direction. Every step has a purpose and every activity you complete gets you one step closer to resolving tax debt. If you do not recognize a need to change your money related behaviors by this point you probably should stop right here. The tax resolution planning process is not a get rich quick scheme; this is not a debt consolidation plan, and there is no magic wand or quick fix to resolve every tax problem. However, if you follow the "Basic Steps to Tax and Financial Freedom", you will regain a sense of control over how you deal with money issues. An effective tax resolution plan is the solution that will lead you to the financial promise land.

Assessing Resources: Getting External Resources Organized

Evaluating your Support System

Support can come in many different ways. Tax and financial professionals are available to provide support (CPA, EA, CFP®, attorneys, financial counselors, marital counselors, pastoral counseling, etc.). Family and friends can also provide valuable support. It is important to have a support system in place to assist you during the tax and financial planning process. Planning requires action if you expect to see any positive results. A support system can help provide you with the guidance and accountability needed to stay on track. Family, friends, and support groups can be very helpful and understanding if you effectively communicate your needs. On the other hand, if you are married and trying to achieve financial freedom, you are simply fighting a battle that cannot be won until both parties work together. If you are in a situation where your spouse is not willing to play an active role in the tax resolution and financial planning progress then you need to change your approach.

Assessing Social Support: If married, are you and your spouse working together to resolve your tax problems? If you are single, do you have friends or other social support available to listen and guide you along the way?

Should I use a tax professional to help me deal with the IRS?

There are two agents of change that are necessary to change financial behaviors.

Individuals: If you have a tax problem and need financial guidance, then the ultimate agent is staring right at you every time you look into the mirror. You have the ability to make wise choices regarding your money and taxes.

Professionals: Tax professionals such as CPAs, EAs, tax attorneys, financial planners, and counselors are all available to help others change financial behaviors. The tax professional has specialized training and experience that helps guide clients through difficult tax and financial situations. The ideal situation occurs when individuals and professionals work together for the common goal of tax resolution.

Create Order Out Of Chaos (Choosing your Team)

It is possible to successfully take on the IRS by yourself. However, if you feel overwhelmed or need some professional reassurance that you are making the best decisions, consider using a qualified tax professional. Enrolled agents, tax attorneys, and CPA's can assist you with an audit, collection, or appeals problem with a taxing authority.

Deciding to Use a Tax Professional

Pros	Cons
Professional Guidance	Cost
Expertise in dealing with the IRS	You can represent yourself in front of the IRS
Evaluate all tax resolution options	Most tax representation professionals do not provide financial planning
Negotiate on your behalf	No guarantees- IRS has the final word.

Whether or not you decide to use a tax professional to assist you in dealing with a tax problem, you should not neglect your financial planning needs. It is possible to successfully create and implement a financial plan by yourself. However, it is not a practice that is recommended if you already have tax planning issues. In fact, financial planners themselves should use the guidance of other professionals in their own financial lives. Why? Making smart decisions about money and personal finances can be emotional, and as human beings we are all subject to irrational thinking and bad decisions.

Tax Resolution and Financial Independence are not worth taking a gamble on with a do-it-yourself approach. Objective, independent advisors are out there that will align themselves and work in your best interests…not the interest of the IRS, investment firms, insurance companies, etc. As a fee-only financial planner, I admit that I am biased toward the advice and guidance that tax resolution planners provide their clients. This is because I have seen what happens to people that do not have quality help from a tax resolution professional. It is very easy to get lost in the resolution process when flying solo. The choice is a personal decision. Always do your homework and research your alternatives wisely.

The "Do It Yourself" Approach
Some people insist on taking a do it yourself to tax and financial planning. The tools and techniques as well as knowledge and self-help resources are all available to help the do it yourselfers. As a financial planner I am admittedly biased against the idea of tackling the tax resolution process without some professional guidance. Even the best financial planners, CPAs, attorneys, physicians, etc. have a network of colleagues that they rely on for professional guidance.

Set measurable goals and a specific time frame for completing tax resolution and financial planning objectives. If you are unable to resolve tax problems on your own, hit a roadblock, or simply decide you need professional guidance, then seek help immediately. Be sure to know in advance what questions to ask a tax resolution specialist or financial planner.

Choosing a Tax Resolution Specialist

Enrolled Agents, CPAs, and attorneys are the only professionals allowed to practice before the IRS. Simply having the ability to represent clients before the IRS does not guarantee that a professional has the knowledge and experience to help their clients resolve tax problems. Remember that the goal is more than seeking tax freedom. The ultimate goal is to achieve financial freedom. This means gaining control over your finances and obtaining a true understanding of the role that money plays in your life. Therefore, you should seek a professional who will do more than help you resolve your tax problems.

You want a qualified professional that will work with you to develop new strategies to help you stay out of tax trouble and design a tax plan to reduce your future taxes as much as the tax laws will allow. Some tax resolution planners will also provide financial counseling and planning services to help you create new more effective ways of dealing with your money. If your tax resolution specialist does not provide financial counseling or financial planning you should hire someone who is willing to work with other professionals that will help you take the next step toward financial freedom.

Note: The questions located on the next page can be used to help you choose the tax resolution specialist that is right for you. In addition, refer to the "Choosing a Tax Resolution Planner" guide that is located on page 51 and in the appendix.

Tax Resolution Tip: Never let fear guide your decision in selecting a tax resolution specialist. Always complete your homework, ask lots of questions, and never feel pressured into making any immediate decisions.

How do I choose a financial planner that understands the tax resolution process?

There are many professionals that consider themselves financial planners. Do not confuse the term financial planning with investments or insurance. This is a common misconception. Many financial planners also provide tax preparation services. A small number of financial planning practitioners are also Enrolled Agents, CPAs, or tax attorneys that provide tax representation services. An even smaller (but growing) number of financial planners are capable of providing tax resolution services.

Even if a financial planner does not provide tax preparation or tax resolution services, they can coordinate the implementation of these solutions with other professionals. Good financial planners should not be expected to understand all of the ins and outs of dealing with the IRS. However, they should be expected to take the time to understand that tax resolution concerns create financial planning and counseling opportunities. For individuals with tax debt, long-range income tax planning is an area in which a Certified Financial Planner™ professional can be most helpful.

As you progress through the stages of the LifeSpan Process of Tax Resolution and Financial Freedom, it is essential that you choose a financial planning professional that understands income tax planning and how tax resolution fits into the process of developing and implementing a financial plan. Financial planning recommendations need to be coordinated with tax resolution strategies.

Financial Planning is a professional field with a broad scope of practice. Essentially anyone with some business savvy and the ability to pass an investment adviser exam can call themselves a financial planner and provide financial advice for a fee. It is imperative that the consumer be aware of the level of expertise of a potential tax and financial planner. Not every financial planner has extensive income tax planning training. Also, keep in mind that due to the specialized nature of financial planning for individuals with tax liabilities, it may be difficult to find a professional in your area that is proficient in understanding how tax resolution planning fits into the financial planning process.

The best alternative is to work with a tax resolution, financial planning or financial counseling professional (preferably a CFP®, CPA, EA, or AFC) that understands tax resolution is your #1 priority. Seek out fee-only advisers who clearly define the services offered and how they are compensated. In general, you should not purchase any investment or insurance products as you focus on resolving tax problems and other debt issues. A solution to the tax problem must be identified prior to making any other financial planning decisions.

Questions You Should Ask Your Tax Resolution Planner:

- When choosing a financial planning professional it is important to do your homework and ask specific questions that are geared to answer the following types of questions:
- How can you help me achieve my financial goals?
- What is your philosophy or approach to the financial planning process?
- Do you provide both income tax planning services and tax representation?
- Are you able to represent me in front of the IRS? (EAs, CPAs, tax attorney)
- If not, do you work with a team of professionals that specialize in tax representation?
- How will you be compensated?
- What are the fees and how are they determined (hourly, flat rate)?
- Does the financial planner or a member of his team prepare tax returns?
- How long have you been in business?

- What are your professional qualifications and educational background?
- Ask yourself: Does your financial planner appear to have the heart of a counselor and the patience of a teacher?

Financial Freedom Tip: Seek the assistance of a tax professional, financial counselor or financial planner that will take the time to understand your tax resolution needs. Choose a professional that is empathic and will take the time to educate you about the tax resolution process. You are seeking someone with the heart of a counselor and the patience of a teacher.

It is also important to understand the professional designations and educational backgrounds of tax resolution and financial planning professionals.

CFP®- Certified Financial Planner- CERTIFIED FINANCIAL PLANNER™ certificants are individuals who have met CFP Board's education, examination and experience requirements, have agreed to adhere to high standards of ethical conduct and who complete CFP Board's biennial certification requirements, including continuing education. They use the certification marks CFP®, CERTIFIED FINANCIAL PLANNER™. A CFP® practitioner is a financial professional authorized to use the CFP® certification marks who has identified himself or herself to the CFP Board as being actively engaged in providing financial planning services. All CFP® certificants have voluntarily submitted to the regulatory authority of CFP Board.

EA- Enrolled Agent- An Enrolled Agent (EA) is a federally-authorized tax practitioner who has technical expertise in the field of taxation and who is empowered by the U.S. Department of the Treasury to represent taxpayers before all administrative levels of the Internal Revenue Service for audits, collections, and appeals.

CPA- Certified Public Accountant- The CPA designation is awarded by the American Institute of Certified Public Accountants (AICPA) to accountants who pass the AICPA's Uniform CPA Examination and satisfy the work experience and statutory and licensing requirements of the state(s) in which they practice.

AFC- Accredited Financial Counselor- This designation is awarded by the Association for Financial Counseling and Planning Education (AFCPE) to individuals who pass AFCPE courses, meet experience and ethics requirements and submit three letters of reference. An AFC is a financial counselor who has certified skills to assist individuals and families in the process of financial decision making. Accredited Financial Counselors must maintain up-to-date knowledge in the fields of personal finance and financial counseling.

ChFC- Chartered Financial Consultant- The title Chartered Financial Consultant (ChFC) is used by financial professionals-including accountants, attorneys, bankers, insurance agents and brokers, and securities representatives-who have earned the ChFC designation by completing The American College's eight-course education program, met experience requirements and agreed to uphold a code of ethics.

RIA- Registered Investment Adviser- Any individual or firm providing securities advice for compensation as part of a regular business of giving investment advice must register with the Securities and Exchange Commission (SEC) or appropriate state securities agencies as an investment adviser, unless specifically exempted from registration. Financial firms and individuals managing $25 million or more of assets have to register with the SEC, while individual advisers and firms managing less than $25 million have to register with the state securities agency in the state(s) in which they practice. Individual advisers with less than $25 million under management, but who have clients in more than 30 states, also may register with the SEC. Investment advisers may recommend stocks, bonds, mutual funds, partnerships or other SEC-registered investments for clients.

Tax Attorneys- A relatively small percentage of attorneys provide financial planning services, usually specializing in estate and tax planning. In the context of financial planning, a planner may ask an attorney to provide specific legal advice for a client, particularly in the areas of taxation or estate planning. An attorney may also be called upon to prepare the legal documents necessary to implement recommendations in areas such as wills, trust documents or business ownership planning.

"Choosing a Tax Resolution Planner"

During the tax resolution process there are some important things you should look for when choosing a tax and financial planning professional to help you resolve your tax issues. Remember that you are interviewing professionals to provide a service on your behalf. Work is required on your part to make sure that you resolve your tax debt and take control of your financial future.

1. Seek a CPA, Enrolled Agent, or tax attorney that specializes in helping people with tax problems. Avoid working with sales consultants that are not the actual professionals who will be dealing with the IRS or state taxing authority.

2. Ask about the tax professional's general approach to the tax resolution process. Do they simply focus on the tax debt, or do they provide income tax planning and financial counseling?

3. Do not sign any post-dated checks or high-interest finance agreements. Get the terms of the tax resolution engagement in writing and do not feel pressured to sign anything until you have reviewed the client-practitioner contract or engagement agreement.

4. Find out if individuals other than the person you are speaking with will be working on your case. If so, ask about their qualifications and preferred methods of communication. Do not be alarmed if your tax professional uses a team based approach. Simply be sure that each team player's role is clearly defined.

5. Determine what your responsibilities will be during the course of the tax resolution process.

6. Do not set unrealistic expectations for your tax professional or for the tax resolution process in general. Dealing with tax problems can take time and involves a considerable amount of effort on the part of both taxpayer and tax professional. Take ownership of your tax issues and play an active role while working with your tax resolution professional.

7. Trust your instincts. If the promises of a tax resolution planner sound too good to be true then they usually are. Remember that not everyone will qualify for an Offer in Compromise. The Internal Revenue Service determines whether or not taxpayers qualify for various tax resolution options. This means that tax professionals cannot guarantee a particular outcome for your dealings with the IRS.

8. Inquire about the cost of services. Make sure that the fees for service are based on the estimated amount of time that will be needed to deal with the tax problem rather than the amount of taxes owed.

Financial Resources

Many people make the mistake of jumping right into the tax resolution process head first without a general idea of their actual financial situation. If an excessive amount of debt exists it is not that hard to figure out a problem may exist. When monthly expenses exceed monthly income people generally understand they may be living beyond their means. Tax resolution planning requires more than just a basic idea of financial resources that are available to resolve the tax debt and accomplish other goals.

You need to know exactly where you are before you can figure out where you are going. This means that you need to know where you are financially speaking in order to determine the tax solution that is right for your situation. The assessment of financial resources starts with an analysis of your net worth and cash flow. Personal financial statements are the roadmap that will guide you from where you are today to where you want to be in the future. They also provide important points of reference that can help you measure your progress over time. There are two basic personal financial statements that everyone should prepare during the financial planning process. They are the cash flow statement and the net worth statement (balance sheet). This process is a critical part of both tax resolution and financial planning.

Net Worth Analysis

How much are you worth?

Do you have a clear understanding of where you stand financially? Most people do not know their net worth, but it provides revealing details about how years of either good or bad spending habits affect your overall financial well-being. In order to take control of your financial situation and resolve your tax liability, you need to know exactly where you stand today.

Tracking your financial position and progress gives you a great sense of control - you know where you are going financially. It helps you to make wise decisions about financial matters. From a tax resolution standpoint, your personal financial statements are the keys to determining the most appropriate methods to reduce or eliminate your tax liability.

A net worth statement is essentially a roadmap for securing and building your financial future. It is also commonly referred to as a balance sheet. The net worth statement provides a snapshot of your current financial situation. Figuring out your net worth is a fairly easy calculation. Your net worth is simply defined as the difference between all the things of value that you own, and all the debts you owe. In financial terms, your net worth is your assets minus your liabilities.

Financial Planning Tip: Complete a net worth analysis. Keep in mind that the net worth statement has absolutely no bearing on your worth as a person. Regardless of where your net worth falls, be sure to understand that personal wealth has many different meanings to each individual. For some it is a measure of accomplishment and success. For others wealth serves as a tool for accomplishing life goals.

When you review your net worth, be sure to ask yourself these questions:

What is important to me about money?

How do I define wealth?

Wealth is…
1. _____
2. _____
3. _____

This brief assessment will help you confirm your goals and objectives and will also help you prioritize your issues and concerns during the tax resolution and financial planning process. Your feelings about money and wealth have a strong impact on your ability to implement tax and financial planning recommendations.

Total Assets: A list of current estimated value of your assets might include the following: home, personal assets, collectibles, jewelry, cash in banks and money market accounts, cash surrender value of life insurance policies, IRA & Keogh accounts, pension and 401(k) accounts, stocks bonds, mutual funds, annuities, real estate, and personal property. Add them up and you'll have a figure that represents your Total Assets at the moment.

Total Liabilities: Next, make a list of your liabilities, which might include the following: mortgage, bank loans, car loans, charge accounts, property taxes, IRS debt, college loans, etc. Add these up and you'll have a list of your total liabilities. Hopefully, it's less than your assets!

Your Net Worth: Your personal net worth is the difference between your total assets and your total liabilities.

$$\text{Total Assets - Total Liabilities = Your Net Worth}$$

A net worth statement is a snapshot of your financial situation. The worksheet on page 58 will help you add up all of your outstanding liabilities and subtract them from your assets. This is an important step in assessing how you are doing financially. No matter what you think the outcome may be, DO NOT neglect this important assessment of financial resources. Identifying your current financial position is necessary to help you overcome the obstacles related to the tax liability that stands before you. There are three potential outcomes for your net worth analysis.

- Assets Equal your Liabilities
- Assets are Greater than your Liabilities
- Assets are Less than your Liabilities

Once you have completed a net worth analysis, you are in a position to review how specific assets and liabilities relate to a Tax Resolution Financial Plan. Before actually completing your net worth analysis it is important to take a look at some assets and liabilities in greater detail.

Assets
Liquid Assets
Liquid assets are assets that you can readily convert into cash. They provide a source of funds for emergencies and for investment opportunities. Some examples of liquid assets include the following:
- Cash
- Money Market Accounts
- Savings
- Cash Value Life Insurance

- U.S. Government Series EE Bonds
- Certificates of Deposit

A note about emergency funds: It is generally recommended that you maintain sufficient funds for emergencies following the resolution of your tax liability. A reserve of 3-6 months' living expenses is recommended for an emergency fund. Three months is generally sufficient for an emergency savings fund if you are married and both you and your spouse are working. For single individuals or married couples with one spouse working full-time, six months living expenses is recommended.

Financial Planning Tip: The tax resolution process may require you to tap into an emergency fund if you already have a savings fund. If this occurs be sure to establish a plan to rebuild your emergency fund prior to beginning any other savings or investment plans. Keep in mind that you will need a source to make payments to the IRS if you set up an Installment Agreement to pay your tax debt over time or if you qualify for an Offer in Compromise. Maintain a "Starter Emergency Fund" of at least $500-$1,000 in the event of emergencies as you progress through the tax resolution action steps.

Personal Residence

Home ownership is a key part of the American dream for most people. In recent years more and more Americans have been able to accomplish this dream. If you own your home or any other real estate, it is important that you understand the estimated value of your property. In real estate, fair market value is the price a buyer will pay and a seller will accept for a property under reasonable and ordinary conditions. Real estate values are constantly fluctuating and your home may be currently valued significantly higher than the amount you paid for it.

Why is it important to have an estimate of my property value?

Real estate is often the biggest asset held my most individuals. The IRS takes a look at all assets when determining the resources that you have available to pay your debt obligation. Special quick sale values are used based on the percentage of your home's fair market value. If you are a homeowner they will most certainly look at this asset and use it as leverage to get you to pay your tax liability as soon as possible. Therefore, it is important to use a reasonable value when presenting your estimate of real property value in documents sent to the IRS.

Avoid overestimating the value of your property. Likewise, do not underestimate your property value. This could be viewed negatively by the IRS as an attempt to misrepresent your financial information. The IRS will generally allow individuals to have up to 20% equity in their home before they consider it to be an asset in the resolution of your tax liability. Conversely, if you have more than 20% equity in your primary residence, the IRS will consider it in the resolution of your tax liability.

If you bought a home or refinanced within the past 5 years you may not be surprised to find out that you may owe more on your mortgage than the house is actually worth. The recent housing crisis has resulted in a significant decrease in real estate values. As of October 2008, at least one in six households had negative equity (e.g., owe more than the house is worth).

There are many resources available to help you estimate the value of your home through the analysis of recent sales information for homes in your area. Zillow.com is a website that provides a free estimate of home values based on public records.

Personal Use Assets

Personal assets are those you purchase primarily for personal long-term use and enjoyment. These include furniture, vehicles, jewelry, art, antiques, collectibles, and other personal property. Be realistic when estimating the value of your personal property. If necessary, consider having a professional appraisal of these items. This will allow you to estimate the value of your personal use assets and may also be used to ensure that your items are adequately insured. Some home use assets include furniture, home furnishings, household goods, appliances, and sporting goods or hobby related equipment. Collectibles (art/antiques) include items that have a potential investment value in addition to a personal interest value.

Investment Assets

Investment assets are those you purchase for the long term in order to satisfy future goals such as retirement, educational financing, and other goals. Stocks, bonds, CDs, mutual funds, real estate investment trusts (REITs), rental property, and retirement accounts are just some of the examples of investment assets that are commonly used to accomplish financial goals. When including investment assets on your net worth statement, be sure to include their most recent values. Examples of equity assets include stocks, stock mutual funds or other investments based on stock market investments. Fixed-income assets include bonds, bond mutual funds, CDs, preferred stock or other bond type investments.

Tax Resolution Tip: If you are currently investing money in stocks, bonds, mutual funds, annuities, or other investment vehicles (including retirement plans) you should STOP your investment plan contributions until your tax liability has been resolved. If you participate in a 401(k) or other retirement savings plan and your employer matches contributions you should still contribute up to the maximum amount your employer will match (if possible from a cash flow standpoint).

Business Assets

Business assets consist of the ownership value of any business you may have an interest in such as a partnership, corporation, or sole proprietorship. Many business owners have no clue what their businesses are worth. Business owners also tend to overestimate the value of their business due to their emotional involvement. If you are a business owner engaged in the tax resolution process, it is essential that you understand the difference between the liquidation and fair market values of your business. The appraised value of a business has a direct impact on the tax resolution process. Be sure that you use a realistic fair market value of any business interests on your net worth statement.

For purposes of resolving your tax liability the IRS will use the "liquidation value" of your business assets, which is the amount you could realize from a forced sale of the assets. This amount is often far less than the fair market value of the assets. While it is important to realize that the IRS can seize business assets, it is unlikely that they will if you are actively working with them to resolve your tax debt.

It is important to note that assets that are available to you are also available to the IRS for lien, levy, or seizure to pay your tax liability. These assets include savings, checking, money market accounts, stocks, bonds, IRAs, any accessible funds in other retirement savings plans, real estate, cash value life insurance, certain business assets and any other accessible assets with equity.

Liabilities

Short-term Liabilities

Short-term liabilities are those obligations that you generally plan to repay within 6 to 12 months. Some examples include short-term loans, credit cards, personal loans, installment loans, federal and state tax liabilities.

Long-term Liabilities

Long-term liabilities are those that you plan to repay in more than one year's time. Typically, you incur them for one of two purposes: to finance long-term investments or the purchase of major personal assets. Student loans, mortgages, and long-term loans are the most common types of long-term debt found on the personal balance sheet.

The Good Debt vs. Bad Debt Debate

The elimination of tax debt is the main goal of the tax resolution process. Tax debt is one of the most problematic types of debt to have. When you stop to think about debt, is there really any good form of debt?

It is nearly impossible for the majority of people to live debt-free. There is no shortage of lenders in this country who are willing to provide loans for houses, cars, RVs, boats, and all of the other so-called necessities and toys that get us into trouble financially. Credit card companies are just as eager to issue credit so consumers can purchase the American dream and rack up some huge finance charges in the process. Discussions about debt are becoming more common as an increasing number of people are aware of the potential debt crisis that faces our nation's consumers.

Debt is a tool that can be used to purchase homes, cars, businesses, and many other planned major purchases. If used wisely, debt can help you accomplish important financial goals. Debt also reduces net worth and creates additional expenses that can become a difficult burden to overcome. Many people find themselves with serious debt problems due to these common reasons:

- They experience financial stress caused by unemployment, medical bills or divorce.
- They display an inability to control spending
- They do not have plan for the future and do not save money on a regular basis.
- Many people lack the knowledge of financial and credit matters and do not seek professional guidance to help with these difficult decisions.

It is important to understand more than just the total amount of debt that you have. You also need to understand the different categories of debt. Debt is commonly divided into two different categories: tax-deductible and non-deductible. It is important to realize that tax deductibility does not necessarily mean that this debt is a "good" form of debt. A comprehensive tax and financial plan can help you understand the role of debt in your financial life. The LifeSpan Process will help you eliminate all forms of debt (including tax liabilities) and help you focus on increasing your net worth.

Net Worth Analysis

Taking Action!!! Use the following instructions to complete a net worth analysis using the worksheet on the next page. Be sure to list all assets (everything you own) and liabilities (everything you owe to others). Make copies of the form or use a similar personal balance sheet/net worth statement. The form on the next page will give you an estimate of your actual net worth. List the value of any assets in the 1st column. Liabilities (debt) such as tax debt, credit card, and loans should be entered in the 2nd column.

Be as accurate as possible. Do not worry if you do not have the exact value of certain assets or liabilities. Use a best guess estimate if needed. Fair market value is the price at which property would change hands between a willing buyer and a willing seller, neither having to buy or sell, and both having reasonable knowledge of all the relevant facts. Various commercial firms and trade organizations publish guides, commonly called "blue books," containing complete dealer sale prices or dealer average prices for recent model years. For your vehicle's estimated fair market value you could use a Kelley Blue Book estimate. Visit their website at www.kbb.com to estimate your vehicle's value. Real estate appraisals may be obtained from a variety of sources. Web sites such as www.zillow.com are frequently used to obtain a quick estimate if you do not have a general idea of your home's value. Do not include any leased assets on your net worth analysis. If you do not own it or are responsible for paying the liability, then do not include it.

After you have entered each of the columns you should start adding the value of assets. Then subtract the total debt. The resulting amount is your Net Worth. Complete a net worth analysis each month so you can track your progress. If you have been living with significant debt the net worth analysis can be frustrating initially when you notice what your net worth is. However, a net worth analysis can also be a great motivational tool as you watch your debt decrease and your net worth increase on a monthly basis by following the tax resolution plan.

Net Worth Worksheet

Date:

ITEM	ASSETS	(minus) LIABILITIES	(equals) NET WORTH
Real Estate (Home)	$	$	$
Other Real Estate – Rental or 2nd Home	$	$	$
Car 1	$	$	$
Car 2	$	$	$
Car 3	$	$	$
Cash on Hand	$	$	$
Checking Account 1	$	$	$
Checking Account 2	$	$	$
Savings Account 1	$	$	$
Savings Account 2	$	$	$
Money Market Fund	$	$	$
Mutual Fund Account 1	$	$	$
Mutual Fund Account 2	$	$	$
Mutual Fund Account 3	$	$	$
Mutual Fund Account 4	$	$	$
Retirement Plan 1	$	$	$
Retirement Plan 2	$	$	$
Retirement Plan 3	$	$	$
Retirement Plan 4	$	$	$
Stocks (not part of retirement)	$	$	$
Bonds (not part of retirement)	$	$	$
Cash Value (Insurance)	$	$	$
Household Items	$	$	$
Jewelry	$	$	$
Antiques	$	$	$
Boat	$	$	$
Credit Card Debt	$	$	$
Other Debt (excluding house)	$	$	$
IRS Estimated Tax Debt	$	$	$
State Tax Debt	$	$	$
Other	$	$	$
Other	$	$	$
TOTAL NET WORTH	$	$	$

Cash Flow Analysis

The final component of the "Assessing Financial Resources" includes a detailed cash flow analysis. Understanding your monthly cash provides valuable insight as to where you are now financially. Your cash flow situation has a direct impact on your tax resolution alternatives.

If you owe taxes to the IRS and you are seeking a payment plan or proposing a settlement, you need to have an idea of your cash flow situation. The IRS is about to take a detailed look into your financial life. Most of the clients that I deal with do not have a good grasp on where their money is going on a monthly basis. In order to pay off or pay down your tax liability, you need to first understand where your money is coming from and where you are spending it. Analyzing your cash flow is the next step during the process of evaluating your financial position. After you have prepared a personal net worth statement, you need to examine your income sources and expenses. This process is referred to as a Cash Flow Analysis.

Determining your cash flow is an essential part of Tax Resolution and Financial Planning. A thorough assessment of your income and expenses will help do the following:

- Indicate your ability to pay the IRS

- Identify your ability to save and invest

- Determine if you are living within your means

- Help target problem spending areas

- Allow you to prepare for emergencies and unforeseen events

- Point out differences in basic and discretionary expenses

- Create a "Personal Spending Plan"

Tax Resolution Tip: The creation of a "Personal Spending Plan" is an essential part of the tax resolution process. The initial spending plan that you create during the tax resolution process begins with a detailed Cash Flow Analysis. Review your current income and expenses using the cash flow worksheet on the next page. Compare your monthly spending to national averages.

National Spending Patterns:

How does your spending compare to these broad national spending patterns?

Category	National Spending	Budgeted Amount	%
Food	14.8%		
Clothing	5.3%		
Housing	25.0%		
Personal	8.7%		
Medical	20.4%		
Transportation	12.0%		
Other	13.8%		
Totals	**100%**		100%

Source: Statistical Abstract of the United States: 2008. Table No. 655 Personal Consumption Expenditures in Current and Real (2000) Dollars, By Type: 1990 to 2005

Keep in mind that these are national spending averages. The average American is in debt and will most likely stay in debt. Tax Resolution and Financial Freedom is about taking control of your money and getting out of debt. Do not assume you need to be in line with all of these averages. This is a helpful method of identifying potential problem areas where your spending is significantly higher than it should be.

Analyzing the Numbers

Once you have completed the cash flow analysis you should have a better understanding of where your money is being spent. Take a moment to review your spending habits and break down your spending into the categories of basic and discretionary expenses.

Your basic lifestyle expenditures are those expenditures that are difficult to reduce without changing your basic standard of living. The "Big Four" - housing, food, clothing, and transportation - account for the largest part of basic lifestyle costs. Discretionary expenses are those recurring annual expenditures over which you can exercise a good deal of control, both in the amount and timing of the expenditure.

Ask yourself the following questions regarding the cash flow analysis:

Does your income currently exceed your expenses? If not, how big a concern is this for you? Where does the bulk of your money go on a monthly basis? Are you allocating more than 10% of your income to discretionary spending items?

Assessing your financial resources and completing the cash flow analysis steps should prepare you to create a personal spending plan. In order to achieve financial success you need to transition from trying to figure out where your money went during the previous month and plan where you want it to go in the future. An effective spending plan begins with a thorough cash flow analysis.

Cash Flow Worksheet

Monthly Income (after taxes)		AMOUNT
Income/Salary (from all sources)		$
Investment Income		$
Other Income		$
TOTAL INCOME		**$**

Monthly Expenses

Housing		Food	
Mortgage/Rent	$	Groceries	$
Home Repairs/Maint. Fees	$	Eating out	$
Homeowners Assoc. Fees	$	Other	$
Other	$	**Total Food**	$
		Total Housing	$

UTILITIES		Auto/Transportation	
Electricity	$	Car loan	$
Water	$	Auto Insurance	$
Gas	$	Gas	$
Home Phone	$	Maintenance	$
Mobile Phones	$	Parking	$
Trash	$	Lease	$
Cable/Satellite/Internet	$	Other	$
Other	$	**Total Auto/Trans**	$
		Total Utilities	$

Insurance		Loans/Lines of Credit	
Homeowners/Renters	$	Credit Cards	$
Health/Medical	$	Home Equity Loan/Line	$
Disability	$	Personal Loans	$
Life	$	Student Loans	$
Dental	$	Other	$
Other	$	**Loans/Lines of Credit**	$
		Insurance	$

Personal		Entertainment	
Care products/Health Club		Movies/Vacation/Tickets	$
Other		**Entertainment**	$
		Personal	$

Clothing		Miscellaneous	
New Clothes		Gifts/Dues/Subscriptions	$
Dry Cleaning/Other		**Total Misc.**	$
		Total Clothing	$

		TOTAL EXPENSES	$

Total Monthly Income: _____ (Minus) Total Expenses: _____ (Equals) Net Cash Flow _____

Summary

The assessment of resources during the tax and financial planning process is necessary to gather information that will be used to resolve the tax problem. The resources that require the most emphasis can be broken down into the categories of internal resources, external resources, and financial resources. Internal resources include individual characteristics and personality traits. Basically, an internal resource refers to what makes a person tick. Everyone undergoing the tax resolution process must complete a self-assessment of strengths and weaknesses. An honest analysis of your own ability to make financial change a reality will help make sure that you are prepared for the planning process.

Self-assessment also includes a review of common traits and characteristics of millionaires and successful individuals. The best way to learn new behaviors and habits is to create "models of success". Learn from other successful people how they approach the world and accept challenges in their lives. Reviewing the qualities of financially successful people usually provides good insight into one's own set of unique skills and traits.

Some of the best predictors of success include the following traits and characteristics of people that have already achieved tax and financial freedom: integrity, courage, willingness to act, commitment, purpose, creativity, balance, persistence, spirituality, love of learning, flexibility, and patience.

The assessment of internal resources culminates with the creation of a mission statement to guide you throughout the tax and financial planning process. A well thought out mission statement takes your own strengths and puts these internal resources into action.

The next type of resource assessment involves external resources. In order to solve any problem in life a support system is helpful. Change is difficult. Financial change can be exceptionally challenging due to the emotional and behavioral elements of the change process. Attempting to experience the change required during the tax and financial planning process can be quite difficult without the support of a spouse, friends, or other family members. In order to assess external resources you need to identify your support system and begin to put together a team that will help you throughout the journey toward tax and financial freedom.

An important part of this assessment process includes determining whether or not professional tax guidance is necessary. Every tax situation is different, and the decision should be based on each individual situation. The fact remains that tax resolution planners exist and are available to help people resolve tax problems and focus on other financial life planning goals. It is also important to recognize that no matter what level of external resources are employed to help your tax situation, the successful outcome depends on your own willingness to take action and seek meaningful change.

The final resource that needs to be assessed is the most important resource as far as tax resolution is concerned. Financial resources determine your ability to resolve any tax or financial problem. The assessment of financial resources includes a review of your net worth situation. Finally, a brief review of the cash flow situation must occur. The assessment of financial resources has proven to be the guiding force during the tax resolution process. A snapshot of your personal financial statements also sets the stage for the next step of the LifeSpan Process of Tax Resolution and Financial Freedom- "Creating a Personal Spending Plan". While the cash flow analysis is not an actual budget, it makes the process of establishing a budget much easier because you now will already have a good idea of where your money is currently going each month.

If the word budgeting conjures up dreaded images and bad memories you are not the only person to feel discomfort. In my professional practice I try to avoid using the word "budget" because it is often associated with negative emotions, marital stress, and feelings of constraint. I prefer the term "personal spending plan" since a spending plan allows you to take control of your money and tell it where to go each month. The typical person gets to the end of the month and tries to figure out where all the money went. As you are probably aware by now, the typical family in this country is broke and will stay that way until they change their attitudes and behaviors as they relate to money.

As you prepare to take the next step of the tax resolution process (Creating a Personal Spending Plan), think of this stage with an "out with the old and in with the new" mindset. The old way of approaching cash flow management is usually passive. The activity that you just completed was also passive. Most people get to the end of the month and try to figure out where their money actually went. The new way is proactive and involves the creation of a personal spending plan. This process of spending with a plan puts you in control.

Old way ("Traditional Budgeting") = Passive
New Way ("Personal Spending Plan") = Proactive

If you are afraid of feeling tied down by a "budget" you should feel comfort in knowing that a "personal spending plan" will help set you free financially. The cash flow analysis is designed as an important building block for the next step of actually creating a personal spending plan.

Tax Resolution Step #4:
Creating a Personal Spending Plan

"I have learned that success is to be measured not so much by the position that one has reached in life as by the obstacles which he has overcome while trying to succeed." ~ Booker T. Washington

Creating a Personal Spending Plan

The definition of insanity may be doing the same things over and over again and expecting different results. I think the key defining element of seeking financial change (and eliminating insane amounts of debt) is doing the right things over and over again and actually getting positive results. Spending with a plan is the right thing to do, and it must be done over and over again.

The creation of a personal spending plan is one of the most important steps of the tax resolution process. A personal spending plan is also the foundation for achieving financial freedom. On the surface a spending plan or budget is extremely basic. Most people do not even have a simple budget much less a spending plan to guide their financial decisions. The purpose of this tax resolution step is to create a personal spending plan that will help you make sure that your money is working for you the best ways possible. Spending plans are also needed to resolve your tax debt and reach your other life planning goals.

A budget is generally defined as: a) an itemized summary of estimated or intended expenditures for a given period along with proposals for financing them, b) a systematic plan for the expenditure of a usually fixed resource, such as money or time, during a given period, and c) the total sum of money allocated for a particular purpose or period of time.

When used as a verb the word budget means to plan in advance the expenditure of something. These definitions each focus on the action of planning. Budgeting is defined as estimated projection of the amount of certain expenses. During the tax resolution process you should use the word budget as a verb and take action. Tell your money where you want it to go rather than trying to figure out where it all went or worse, spending more than you have available and relying on credit cards and debt to get you through the month.

Unfortunately, most people approach the budgeting process the wrong way and do things backwards. They use a legal pad, spreadsheet or budgeting software and track where spending occurred across various categories (food, utilities, credit card bills, etc.). This is a great way to see where your money went during the previous month. But it is a horrible way to plan where your money will go in the future. During the previous step we analyzed where your money has been going in the past. Going forward, you should use the information gathered during the cash flow analysis to create a spending plan or budget.

The budgeting process is often misunderstood because it is typically viewed in a negative manner by the people who need one the most. We have discussed at length how many individuals in debt display problematic financial behaviors. One of the biggest problem behaviors is trying to manage personal finances without a plan. The lack of a personal spending plan or budget is common in the majority of people with tax problems. Many people are resistant to change when it comes to budgeting. Some tax resolution clients view a budget as a form of constraint that inhibits freedom. This is ironic because a personal spending plan will actually lead to financial freedom if used consistently.

Every single household spending plan is unique and each person will be presented with his or own set of challenges. Do not expect your personal spending plan to work perfectly the first time around. It may take a few months to figure this process out. This is normal. Whatever happens on a month to month basis, DO NOT QUIT and NEVER allow frustration to get in your way. Remember that the LifeSpan Process of Tax Resolution and Financial Freedom requires you to take action to replace negative financial behaviors with positive alternatives. The old way of doing things got you into this mess. Replace the old way with a new and improved way of handling your personal finances.

Spending with a Purpose

A personal spending plan is an essential tax resolution strategy for saving and spending money. It is designed to help you guide the money you have coming in the most appropriate places. This means making sure that you are able to meet your fixed expenses, prepare for occasional expenses, reduce debt and eventually reach your savings goals more easily. Spending plans will allow you to:

1. **Resolve your tax debt as quickly as possible**
   If your primary goal is to eliminate tax debt you must have a spending plan in place to make sure that you can aggressively pay off as much as possible on a monthly basis.
2. **Prepare for expenses**
   Some expenses are fixed such as vehicle payments, mortgages, and insurance. Others are variable such as groceries, utilities, and gas. Likewise, there are some expenses that occur on a regular basis and others that only occur once or twice a year. If you have a spending plan that prepares for these expenses ahead of time you will avoid financial roadblocks on the path to financial freedom.
3. **Be ready for the unexpected**
   Emergencies are bound to happen. Unforeseen events and emergencies such as medical bills, car problems, and home repairs can create financial stress. We cannot predict the future, but we can prepare for the unexpected. Establishing a plan to prepare for the unexpected will allow you to proactively deal with potential setbacks.
4. **Make sure that you have the funds available to pay your tax liability**
   If your mission is to eliminate tax and consumer debt you need to know exactly where your money is going to come from each month to pay the IRS and/or a state taxing authority. If you have a payment plan and miss one payment then you will subject yourself to aggressive collection measures.
5. **Take control of how you spend your money**
   Creating a personal spending plan is a critical part of the tax resolution planning process. In order to take control of your financial situation you must first take control of how you spend your money. As you begin to pay more attention to your personal spending, you may soon realize that

you are spending a significant amount of money on certain items without realizing it. This realization can be very important as you determine how to spend your money in order to reach your tax and financial planning goals.

Tax Resolution Tip: Always stay focused and do not get discouraged with the process of creating a personal spending plan. This is the key to your financial future. The path to financial freedom starts with a personal spending plan that puts you in control of your money.

How does a Personal Spending Plan work?

A personal spending plan is a written plan to guide your spending habits and provide you with important direction for your money. Operating without a budget or personal spending plan can put you on the fast track to tax problems and debt while giving you a strong sense of feeling completely out of control financially. Following through with the budgeting process and sticking with a personal spending plan will help you assume control of your finances and will empower you to make smart financial decisions.

You cannot eliminate your tax and financial problems without a spending plan. You will not achieve financial freedom with a savings and investment plan. A personal spending plan will help you resolve your tax problems. Subsequently it will allow you to reach financial freedom by maximizing your ability to pay off your tax debt as quickly as possible and then save or invest as much as possible for your life planning goals.

Be prepared for everyone around you to think you are going insane when they see you are implementing a spending plan. Friends and family may act confused or completely freaked out by the fact that you have seen the light and are now operating on a budget. Most people just do not get it. They are probably spending without a clue themselves. That is why most Americans are in debt. It is important to realize this in advance because you should be prepared to explain to your friends and family why you are choosing to manage your money in a more effective manner. There is no need to be embarrassed or ashamed by the fact that you actually have the courage to say enough is enough- I am taking control of my life!

Most budgets fail because they lack purpose. During the tax resolution and financial freedom process your purpose is clear. Eliminate the tax problem, get out of debt, and focus on more important financial and life planning issues. When you create and stick with a personal spending plan never lose sight of the main purpose of following a budget in the first place- ***tax and financial freedom***.

Taking Action!!!

You should have already started taking the basic steps of creating a personal spending plan during the cash flow analysis exercise (Assessing Resources: External). Go ahead and use your cash flow worksheet to guide you during the creation of your personal spending plan. Set up a personal spending plan prior to beginning the tax resolution analysis. Be sure to set aside enough money to pay any estimated taxes or installment payments to the IRS or state.

Ask yourself these basic questions prior to establishing your spending plan:

- When you reviewed your current spending in the previous section did you notice any particular areas of concern?
- How did your budgeted spending compare to national averages?

- What percentage of your overall spending consists of discretionary expenses?
- Are there any particular categories in which you should focus on reducing your spending?

Instructions

Creating a personal spending plan does not have to be difficult. Use the Personal Spending Plan Worksheet to guide you along the process. Feel free to personalize your spending plan as needed. This is your plan and you need to adapt it to your specific needs. Get started by taking these basic steps:

1. **Figure out your net income from all sources**

   Start by determining your net income, or take home pay. Be as accurate as possible. Do not forget that your objective is to tell every single dollar where to go and what to do before the month begins. If you are self-employed or have variable income use a best guess estimate to predict your expected income. I recommend that you err on the side of caution and use a conservative income amount. Any income in excess of your amount should immediately be applied to saving, giving, or paying off debt.

2. **Determine an amount to be saved for goals and emergencies**

   Saving and giving should always come first in the personal savings plan. Saving and investing should not occur until you are out of debt. Prior to the resolution of your tax debt, all of the monthly savings should be used to pay off tax debt. Charitable giving is another area of focus during this step. Giving is a personal issue that should be incorporated into the personal spending plan. Since this is an often spiritual and religious area I will leave it up to each individual to decide the appropriate level of giving based on your unique situation.

   A Few thoughts about charitable giving: You will notice that giving is listed at the top of the Personal Spending Plan Worksheet. Charitable giving of time, money, and talents is a very personal and spiritual topic that I encourage you to explore during the tax and financial planning process. Each person is unique and has his or her own belief system related to the topic of giving. However, the personal spending plan that is incorporated into the LifeSpan Plan for Tax Resolution and Financial Freedom focuses on putting giving and saving at the beginning of the spending plan. They come first for a reason. I encourage you to explore the reason of whether or not you choose to put them first in your spending plan.

   A few thoughts about saving: Despite the fact that savings is not a top priority until you resolve your tax problems you should not neglect savings altogether. If you have an existing emergency fund in place you will likely need to use some if not all of your savings to get out of debt. Make sure you leave at least enough for a "starter emergency fund". A single person should keep at least $500-$750 in emergency savings. Married couples should strive to begin setting aside enough funds to reach a $1,000-$1,500 starter fund goal. If you have never had an emergency savings fund or have simply relied on credit cards or loans, then now is your chance to start changing your financial behaviors. While you may not be able to initially set up a fully funded emergency fund, you should still get into the habit of saving and have money available in the case of an emergency.

3. **Estimate all of your expenses (monthly, quarterly, or annually). Include everything and estimate realistically for the unknown or variable expenses.**

   It is essential that you understand the difference between basic and discretionary expenses. Basic expense categories include food, clothing, housing, medical, personal, and transportation. Food, clothing, and shelter are the most important expenses that you need to survive. Most everything else is negotiable. A key element of the personal spending plan is identifying the difference between needs and desires.

During the tax resolution process you should focus on reducing basic expenses as much as possible. It is also generally recommended that you work to keep your discretionary spending at 10% or less of your income. Discretionary dollars are the funds remaining after basic expenses and other essential commitments that will allow you to achieve your long-term financial goals.

4. **Set aside money each month for the items that do not occur monthly (insurance, property taxes, homeowners association, vacations, gifts, etc.)**
    Some bills do not occur on a monthly basis. Unless you have a plan in place to set aside funds for those expenses you will continue the debt cycle. If you have expenses that occur once or twice a year you still need to incorporate them into your spending plan. Take the total amount that you plan on spending for the expense during the year and divide that amount by 12 to determine your monthly amount to set aside. For example, if your real estate tax bill comes every December and is $1,200 you need to set aside $100 per month from January through December. When December arrives you will have the funds available and do not have to resort to negative financial behaviors such as borrowing money or worse, not paying your tax bill.

    This is a fairly simple concept, yet very few people have a spending plan that prepares for expenses that do not occur on a monthly basis. If you do not prepare for these infrequent expenses your spending plan will not work and your budget will fail. Therefore, you absolutely have to plan for these expenses. Use the personal spending plan worksheet to identify your irregular expenses and make sure that you have a plan in place to budget for them.

5. **Be sure to include the "Potential Budget Busters"**
    Little expenses add up in a hurry. Some examples of potential budget busters include the following small ticket items that can have a big impact on your spending plan:
    *   Trips to the vending machine at work or school
    *   Coffee breaks at places like Starbucks, Dunkin Donuts, or the neighborhood newsstand
    *   Miscellaneous school related expenses (supplies, field trips, projects, etc.)
    *   Fast food and drive thru windows
    *   Other miscellaneous expenses

    Other budget busters are less subtle but still represent potentially problematic financial behaviors that need to be addressed with a personal spending plan:

    *   ATM withdrawals
    *   Debit and credit card purchases
    *   Wal-Mart, Lowes, Home Depot, Target, and other big box stores
    *   Vehicle repairs and maintenance
    *   Entertainment
    *   Family celebrations
    *   Vacations

6. **Use the envelope system**
    One of the most effective ways to help control spending is the "envelope method". Establish a monthly dollar amount for expenses that generally cause problems for you. Everyone has different

problem areas. The most common problem areas are generally groceries, clothing, restaurants and entertainment. Once you determine the categories for which you will be using the envelope system, such as groceries or eating out, go ahead and put that amount in an envelope that is designated for that category each month. Once the envelope for that category is empty you cannot spend any more money on that category for the month. Establish envelopes for other discretionary expenses as well, such as the potential "budget busters" (gifts, entertainment, and miscellaneous expenses).

The modified envelope system is an alternative that works for people that do not feel comfortable carrying cash. If you do not like keeping cash around the house or on your person you should consider this alternative. Keep an envelope or notebook card in your wallet or purse with the total amount you plan on spending for each envelope system category. Keep receipts in the envelope and immediately subtract the amount spent form the allowable amount. This will provide you with a running total, and you will actually see the amount available.

Another budgeting technique that works for some people is to establish periodic monthly holidays from discretionary spending. For example, you could choose once each quarter (i.e., every third month) to eliminate all discretionary spending (restaurants, entertainment, etc.) for the month, while in other months you do the best you can to stay within your budget (which might permit some limited discretionary spending in those months). Another option would be to eliminate any discretionary spending for one or two weeks out of the month. The budgeted amount could be used to accelerate your debt payments toward your taxes.

7. **Balance your Budget**
The goal for your spending plan is for the total income minus expenses to always equal ZERO. You will have a plan for every dollar. Know where it should be spent before the month begins. During the cash flow analysis you tracked where your money is generally spent during a typical month. If you have a tax debt you are in the process of learning new financial behaviors. The personal spending plan is a critical part of the tax resolution process.

8. **Review your spending plan regularly**
The best way to experience success with a personal spending plan is to track your income and expenses regularly. I recommend that you review your spending plan on a monthly basis (at a minimum). During the first few months you should review your spending every two weeks. Stay focused and do not lose sight of the ultimate purpose of your personal spending plan- *Tax and Financial Freedom.*

In 3-4 months you should be able to accurately predict your monthly spending. Most importantly, you will begin to experience a renewed sense of control over your money. After 6 months of working with a personal spending plan you will have created a habit that you should not stop. The more you practice your new financial behavior the more you will actually enjoy seeing your money start to work for you. This is much more enjoyable than constantly feeling like you are working for your money and debt obligations.

Taking Action!!!
Set aside at least half an hour a day for two consecutive days to complete your "Personal Spending Plan". Do not allow yourself to make excuses. This is a TOP PRIORITY during the tax resolution process.

---

15 Proven methods of increasing cash flow

1. Create a Personal Spending Plan and review it on a regular basis.

2. Consider a part-time job or find ways to increase your income from your current job.

3. Sell any non-essential assets that you can live without. Do you have any personal assets that you could sell? If so, try to sell these items on Ebay, Craig's List, classifieds, garage sales, etc.

4. Focus on basic expenses (food, clothing, shelter).

5. Reduce discretionary expenses as much as possible (restaurants, entertainment, tickets to movies, games or concerts, etc.)

6. Get rid of "life of luxury and a world of debt loans" or toys that eat away at your cash flow (timeshares, boats, cars with high monthly payments).

7. No big vacations or major purchases (unless necessary) until you are out of debt. If you have to replace a car, pay cash for a reliable used automobiles. Avoid leasing. If a loan is unavoidable, pay it off as soon as possible and always buy USED.

8. Trade in a vehicle for a lower cost but reliable alternative.

9. Use the envelope method to control spending. Consider taking a "vacation" from discretionary spending for a few weeks or as long as a month. This extreme "no" discretionary spending plan does not have to eliminate fun from your life. It actually challenges you to find creative sources of free entertainment and "staycations" (vacations at home or near your home town).

10. Eliminate cable, satellite television, or other subscription costs. Get rid of gym memberships

11. Stop using credit cards; avoid installment and personal loans unless they are used to pay off tax debt. Stop the cycle of debt.

12. Communicate with your spouse or significant other. Establish a support system and create a sense of accountability for your financial decisions.

13. Temporarily cut or reduce your charitable contributions.

14. Tell your money where to go BEFORE the month begins rather than trying to figure out where it went AFTER the month is over.

15. Seek help if you have a behavior problem or addiction such as gambling, alcohol, drugs, or compulsive spending. These psychological problems have severe financial and personal consequences but can be dealt with through self help, group support, or professional guidance.

Personal Spending Plan:
Monthly Income Sources

SOURCE	NET MONTHLY AMOUNT	NOTES
Salary 1	$	**Provide Take Home Pay Amount**
Salary 2	$	**Provide Take Home Pay Amount**
Salary 3	$	**Provide Take Home Pay Amount**
Commissions 1	$	
Commissions 2	$	
Bonus	$	
Self-Employment Income (if applicable)	$	
Alimony Income	$	
Annuity Income	$	
Cash Gifts	$	
Child Support Income	$	
Disability Income	$	
Dividend Income	$	
Interest Income	$	
Pension Income	$	
Rental Property Income	$	
Royalty Income	$	
Social Security Income	$	
Trust Fund	$	
Unemployment Income	$	
Other 1	$	
Other 2	$	
Other 3	$	
TOTAL INCOME	$	

Instructions: Make copies of this form so you can create multiple spending plan worksheets throughout the tax resolution process. Be sure to list the net monthly amount (take home pay after taxes). This Personal Spending Plan activity is not interested in your gross income. Gross numbers do not serve our planning purposes because you need to work with how much you actually have to spend after taxes each month.

Do not forget to list all of your income sources on this worksheet. The total income should equal ALL the money coming in each month.

This sheet will let you know how much cash you have available to spend. Insert your total monthly income amount on page 86.

LifeSpan Process Personal Spending Plan Worksheet:
Monthly Expenses

ITEM	MONTHLY TOTAL	ACTUAL SPEND	COMMENTS
CHARITABLE GIVING	$	$	
SAVING AND INVESTING	$	$	
HOUSING			
First Mortgage	$	$	
Second Mortgage or Home Equity Line	$	$	
Home Repairs/Maint. Fees	$	$	TRANSFER TO SAVINGS
HOA/Neighborhood Regime Fees	$	$	1/12th of the annual amount
Prop. Taxes/Insurance	$	$	1/12th of the annual amount
Other	$	$	
UTILITIES			
Electricity	$	$	
Water	$	$	
Gas	$	$	
Home Phone	$	$	
Mobile Phones	$	$	
Trash	$	$	
Cable/Satellite	$	$	
Internet	$	$	
Other	$	$	
TRANSPORTATION			
Car Payment 1	$	$	
Car Insurance 1	$	$	TRANSFER TO SAVINGS
Car Payment 2	$	$	
Car Insurance 2	$	$	TRANSFER TO SAVINGS
Gas - Total For All Cars	$	$	
Repairs/Oil/Tires/Tags	$	$	Set aside money here
Car Replacement Fund	$	$	START SAVING FOR THIS
Car Taxes	$	$	
Other	$	$	
PERSONAL			
Personal Care/Hair	$	$	
Cleaners/Laundry Service	$	$	
Baby Sitter	$	$	
Disability Insurance	$	$	
Health Insurance	$	$	
Doctor/Dentist	$	$	TRANSFER TO SAVINGS
Personal Medications/Drugs	$	$	TRANSFER TO SAVINGS
Life Insurance	$	$	TRANSFER TO SAVINGS
Other	$	$	

Monthly Expenses (Continued)	Monthly Total	Actual Spend	Comments
HOUSEHOLD			
Food/Groceries	$	$	USE ENVELOPE SYSTEM
Eating Out	$	$	USE ENVELOPE SYSTEM
Entertainment	$	$	USE ENVELOPE SYSTEM
Clothing	$	$	TRANSFER TO SAVINGS
Miscellaneous Budget Busters - Husband	$	$	Use the ones that apply
Miscellaneous Budget Busters - Wife	$	$	Use the ones that apply
Budget Buster Money/Misc.- Child One	$	$	Use the ones that apply
Budget Buster Money/Misc - Child Two	$	$	Use the ones that apply
Budget Buster Money/Misc - Child Three	$	$	Use the ones that apply
Wal-Mart/Lowes/Home Depot/Target etc.	$	$	
Gifts	$	$	TRANSFER TO SAVINGS
Other	$	$	
OTHER EXPENSES			
Vacation Fund	$	$	TRANSFER TO SAVINGS
Christmas/Birthday Gift Fund	$	$	TRANSFER TO SAVINGS
School Tuition	$	$	TRANSFER TO SAVINGS
School Supplies	$	$	TRANSFER TO SAVINGS
Child Support	$	$	
Organization Dues/Club Dues/Gym/Sports	$	$	TRANSFER TO SAVINGS
Credit Cards (add up all minimums)	$	$	
Student Loan #1	$	$	
Student Loan #2	$	$	
Miscellaneous Loans	$	$	
Personal Loans	$	$	
IRS Tax Debt Payments	$	$	Include IA/OIC Payments
State Tax Debt Payments	$	$	Include IA/OIC Payments
Other Miscellaneous Expenses	$	$	
Other Miscellaneous Expenses	$	$	
Other Miscellaneous Expenses	$	$	
Other Miscellaneous Expenses	$	$	
Other Miscellaneous Expenses	$	$	
TOTAL MONTHLY EXPENSES	$	$	
TOTAL MONTHLY INCOME	$	$	

MONTHLY ENVELOPE TOTAL:	$	Add all envelope system items at start of month
MONTHLY SAVINGS TOTAL:	$	Add all Transfer to Savings items

Personal Spending Plan Tips: The LifeSpan Process Spending Plan Worksheet is designed to help give you a good idea of where you money is being spent. An effective spending plan tells your money where to go before the month begins. Use the best estimates as possible. Do not worry if you do not know the exact amounts. You should be as realistic as possible in planning your spending. This is a "Zero Based Budget". Spend (and save) every dollar on paper before the month begins. Income - (minus) Expenses = ZERO

In order for the personal spending plan to work you should transfer money to savings for each expense amount that does not occur monthly. Also, be sure to obtain cash at the beginning of the month for your envelope plan categories.

Financial Roadblocks

There is no doubt that financial roadblocks will stand in the way of your pursuit for tax resolution. Some of the typical obstacles that will impede your success may include lack of teamwork, ending the cycle of compulsive spending, procrastination, fear, denial, and basic everyday life stressors. Whatever financial roadblocks are standing in your way now (or may appear in the future), you will need to confront these obstacles by taking action.

A personal spending plan, if implemented appropriately, is one of the best methods of assuming control of your financial future. If you stay committed to this step by step process and continue to follow through with the tax resolution plan you will succeed. Be prepared to deal with setbacks and stick with your spending plan. A financial life plan starts with goals, an assessment of resources, and a spending plan. These initial steps build the foundation for your plan to live a life without debt.

Do not get frustrated if you have trouble sticking with your personal spending plan. Sometimes it takes a few months to get things right. Expect for this process to feel a little uncomfortable or painful at times. Remember that your initial discomfort will be well worth the effort when you achieve total tax and financial freedom.

Summary

The LifeSpan Process of Tax Resolution and Financial Freedom differs from other tax relief plans because it requires you to create a personal spending plan prior to implementing your tax resolution plan. The traditional approach to tax resolution generally looks at the collection potential of the IRS first. This approach is important because the IRS only uses certain allowable expenses to determine your ability to pay an outstanding tax debt. Unfortunately, looking at the situation from the IRS's perspective is the wrong way to approach tax resolution planning because it does not place the emphasis on the client's actual cash flow situation. A tax resolution analysis only takes into account the information that the IRS will be looking at. It does not always look at real world spending issues.

Every single person with a tax problem needs to honestly assess their own ability to pay the IRS through a tax resolution analysis. Before you begin the tax resolution analysis step you first need to establish a spending plan. It is essential to create a personal spending plan prior to analyzing the IRS's ability to collect on your tax debt. Spending plans provide the foundation for financial freedom. A tax resolution analysis only provides clues about the tax issue. Think big picture and focus on more than just resolving tax debt. Focus on the ultimate pursuit of meaningful financial life planning goals.

Spending plans are constantly changing with our lives. You may have to revise your personal spending plan again once your tax resolution alternatives have been determined. That is okay. This is the purpose of a personal spending plan. Personal spending plans are always subject to change and should become a monthly process. Review your personal spending plan at least once a month for at least the next year. Make it a habit. Creating a personal spending plan or budget will likely prove to be the most important financial behavior that you will need to repeat over and over as you proceed through the next steps of the tax resolution process.

Tax Resolution Step #5:
Tax Resolution Analysis

"Creditors have better memories than debtors." ~ Benjamin Franklin

"The hardest thing in the world to understand is the income tax." ~ Albert Einstein

The Tax Resolution and Financial Freedom process includes a step by step approach to getting out of tax debt and getting on with your life free of debt. The end result is ultimately a sense of freedom that places you in complete control of your financial behaviors. Now that you understand your current financial situation you are in a position to start implementing your goals. You have decided to take action to improve your finances starting with the elimination of tax debt.

Let us review where we are at this point in the tax resolution process. So far you have taken action and made a genuine commitment to do more than just deal with the tax problem. You should be totally committed to completely getting out of debt. Determining your actual net worth and completing a cash flow analysis provides you an understanding of exactly where you stand financially. This is because you need to have a solid grasp of your own financial situation before the IRS takes a look at your ability to pay a tax liability. By taking the previous steps you put yourself in control of your financial destiny and help make sure that you do not waste your time and money on tax resolution alternatives that are not in your best interest. That is the reason that the assessment of your internal and external resources has to occur prior to beginning the tax resolution process.

The previous steps also should have provided a solid foundation for the tax resolution analysis. Most tax resolution alternatives require that you take a comprehensive look at both your spending and the equity that you may have in any assets that you own. Your financial information should already be right at your fingertips and readily available to apply as we take this next step to determining the ideal tax resolution alternative for your situation. Additionally, you already have a personal spending plan in place that can easily be updated and revised once you put a plan in motion to take care of your tax debt.

Overview of the Tax Resolution Process

How much are you worth to the IRS?

The total equity in your assets and your income and expenses play a critical role in determining the options available during the tax resolution process. Now that you have completed a balance sheet and cash flow analysis, let's see how the IRS views your financial situation. Getting organized and mobilized may have been hard work and will continue to be a tough process. Fortunately the steps of the Tax Resolution and Financial Freedom process have already provided the necessary structure to simplify dealing with the IRS.

Tax Resolution Financial Planning:

Key Components of Analyzing and Evaluating Financial Status

> **Net Worth Analysis**
> **Cash Flow Analysis**
> **Tax Resolution Analysis**

One of the primary purposes of the Tax Resolution Analysis is to assess if your financial resources are sufficient to pay your tax debt in full. If so, you need to make smart decisions when choosing among your available menu of choices. If you do not have existing resources you need to figure out if you are a potential candidate for the OIC program. Some tax resolution firms and so-called "offer mills" lure potential clients with the promise of dealing with tax debt by paying less than the original amount owed through an offer. I prefer an approach that emphasizes the promise of financial freedom. The only way to reach financial freedom if you have a tax debt is to resolve your tax liabilities the best way possible according to your unique financial situation.

If you are not an OIC candidate, the tax resolution process will help identify your potential alternatives to pay down tax liability. It does not benefit you to submit an OIC if you have little or no chance to qualify. This is where most people act impulsively and make the wrong tax resolution decisions that can eventually cost hundreds and thousands of dollars. Undergoing a pre-screening process that is objective will save you time and money.

The following steps of the tax resolution analysis will be discussed in detail throughout this chapter:

Steps of the Tax Resolution Analysis Process

1. Understand the Tax Liability
2. Identify Reasons for the Tax Liability
3. Obtain an Estimate of the Actual Tax Liability
4. Determine Total Equity in Assets: Net Worth (Available Equity)
5. Determine Monthly Disposable Income: Cash Flow (IRS Allowable Expenses)
6. Determine Estimated Minimum Settlement Amount (Future Income Potential + Total Equity)
7. Identify Tax Resolution Alternatives

Tax Resolution Analysis Step #1:

Understanding the Tax Liability

It is nearly impossible to solve a problem if you do not know what the problem actually is. This is definitely the case with a tax liability. It is necessary to gather as much information about the details of the tax liability in question. First determine if a tax debt actually exists. If so you should verify whether or not you are actually the responsible party. In the event that you are not current with filing your tax returns you will need to get current and compliant with IRS filing requirements.

Once you have completed the previous steps and have established a personal spending plan, begin gathering all necessary documents that relate to your tax liability. This includes items such as correspondence from the IRS, copies of the IRS Master File, tax returns and any additional information that relates to a tax liability. Be prepared to answer the following types of questions:

- Are you current in filing tax returns for each of the past ten years?

- What is your best guess estimate of your federal and/or state tax liability (including penalties and interest)?

- How have you filed your income tax returns in previous tax years (single, married filing jointly, married filing separately, head of household)?

- Have you used a different filing status during the past ten years?

- How many total exemptions will you claim when you file your tax return (including yourself and spouse)?

- If you own a business, how does your business report income (Sole Proprietor, Partnership, S Corporation, C Corporation)?

- Which tax years are involved?

- What type of back taxes do you owe (employment or income)?

- Do the original returns need to be amended?

- Who is responsible for paying the tax debt?

Filing past due tax returns

If you have unfiled tax returns you are not alone. It is not uncommon for some taxpayers to go one or more years without filing a tax return. Many times I have seen that a taxpayer fails to file a tax return in a year when financial and life circumstances changed. For reasons related to procrastination, fear, lack of funds, or any other combination of factors a tax return was not filed. An amazing thing happens at first when a tax return is not filed within the system of voluntary compliance- Nothing! Sometimes weeks, months, and years may pass before the IRS requests a tax return or issues a tax assessment for a previous tax year.

Whatever the reason for not filing, tax problems only get worse if a non-compliant taxpayer starts worrying about his or her financial situation but does nothing to change the problem. Everyone has reasons and a life story that explains why a tax return was not filed. It is important to understand and address your individual reasons to avoid future filing problems. The tax resolution process is focused on the future and moving forward. Try to not dwell on your past mistakes or reasons for not filing a tax return. Focus on taking action and following the tax resolution steps.

Common Reasons for an Unfiled Tax Return

- Poor recordkeeping or loss of records due to disaster
- Disability or illness
- Divorce
- Job loss or extended unemployment
- Missing W-2 or 1099 information
- Unable to find the records needed to file a return
- Inability to pay the tax on a return
- Fear that filing a tax return would call attention to an individual's tax and financial situation
- Inability to find the forms needed to prepare a return for a previous tax year

---

The importance of filing a tax return

Are you current with the filing of your federal and state tax returns through the most recent tax year? For various reasons, you may not have filed your federal income tax return for this year or previous years. Possibly you may not have known whether you were required to file. You may not have filed because you owe additional tax that you cannot afford to pay in full, or you may not have filed because you expect a refund and just have not taken the time to complete the return.

Regardless of your reason for not filing, you should file your past due tax returns as soon as possible. Contact a qualified tax professional if you need assistance preparing a tax return. Filing a tax return is an important issue of compliance for each American required to file a return based on existing tax laws. Tax return information is used for more than just determining the amount of taxes owed to the federal government. They can be required to obtain financing for a home or other loans.

Tax returns may be used to apply of college financial aid. They are also used to calculate Social Security benefits and to calculate compensation in the event you have to file for unemployment insurance. Unfiled tax returns can result in losing the right to receive refunds (must be claimed within 3 years of the filing due date). The biggest consequence of not filing a tax return is the lack of control that creates a barrier between you and financial freedom. Filing past due tax returns puts you in control of your life again and allows you to move closer to accomplishing your life dreams and ambitions.

Failure to file your return on or before the due date may result in penalties and interest. However, if you filed on time but did not pay in full, you will be subject only to the failure to pay penalty. Interest is charged on taxes not paid by the due date, even if you have an extension of time to file. Interest is also charged on penalties.

Substitute for Return

If you do not file voluntarily the IRS is allowed to take enforcement steps for people that do not comply with their filing obligations. The IRS may file what is known as a Substitute for Return (SFR). This means that the IRS can prepare a return that does not include credit for most deductions and exemptions that you would ordinarily have been entitled to receive. If you are married with children and have itemized deductions for the past 15 years the IRS will still file a return in their favor and only use a standard deduction. Substitute for Returns most often favor the IRS and can be replaced by filing an actual tax return. They are simply placeholders to start the tax assessment using whatever information the IRS has available to them (1099's, W-2, etc.). You should always check to see if filing an actual return would reduce the tax assessed by the IRS through a Substitute for Return. This could substantially reduce the actual amount of taxes owed.

How far back do past due tax returns need to be filed?

IRS policy currently indicates that you need to be current with filing a tax return for the last six years. The IRS may require you to file a tax return for more than just the past six years if you are filing for an Offer in Compromise or own certain types of business such as a corporation or partnership. Of course you should file more than the last six years if you need to replace an IRS Substitute for Return.

Obtain information needed to prepare a tax return

If you need to file a past due tax return you should make arrangements to do so immediately. It is very difficult to file an accurate tax return for up to six years without the assistance of a tax professional. Make sure that you put together IRS records for the years in question. Some examples of the documents that may be needed to file a past due tax return include the following:

- W-2 forms- displays the wages for tax year
- Proof of income
- Social Security statements (1099-SSA)
- 1099 forms- information from banks and other financial institutions showing dividends and interest (1099-Int and 1099-Div)
- Retirement distributions (1099-R)
- Brokerage statements (1099-B), along with statements showing when investments were bought and sold
- K-1 statements reporting profits from partnerships, trusts, and small businesses,
- Record of income and expenses for any rental property
- Record of income and expenses for your self-employment
- Supporting information to document expenses claimed on the return- itemized deductions, dependent care expenses, business expenses, etc.
- Copies of the last two tax returns that were filed
- Social Security numbers for dependents

If you do not have the information available to prepare a past due tax return you may need to contact the IRS to obtain income information. Call the IRS at (866) 681-4271 and request a copy of your record. You may also use IRS Form 4506 to request a copy or transcript of the following tax forms:

1) Copies of filed individual tax returns (1040)

2) Tax return transcript

3) W-2 forms and 1099 information

Taking Action!!! If you have past due tax returns that need to be filed you should make arrangements to prepare your tax returns immediately. If you decide to pay someone to prepare your tax return, you need to choose that preparer wisely. Taxpayers are legally responsible for what is on their own tax returns even if they are prepared by someone else. Therefore, it is important to choose carefully when hiring an individual or firm to prepare personal returns.

Tax Resolution Analysis Step 2:

Identify Reasons for the Tax Liability

The identification of the reason for the tax liability must not be neglected during the tax resolution process. During the introduction to the tax resolution process several causes of tax problems were identified. It is important to understand the reasons for the tax problems and their underlying causes. Do not forget the ultimate goals that you have for the Tax Resolution and Financial Freedom process. You should be trying to deal with your tax problems and replacing the problematic financial behaviors with positive ones. This process requires accountability, so be honest with yourself. Now is not the time to dwell on past mistakes. You need to use the knowledge of past mistakes or uncontrollable circumstances as a motivator to guide you along the process of change.

Here is a review of some of the most common events or circumstances that may lead to tax trouble:

- Self-employment- Not understanding the self employment tax or simply neglecting to pay estimated taxes for self-employment income
- Tax protestor
- Failure to pay employment taxes or payroll taxes
- Taxation of Retirement Distributions
- Capital gains reporting related to the sale of stocks, bonds, mutual funds, etc.
- Changes related to an audit
- Insufficient taxes withheld from pay (W-4)
- Loss of job or income reduction
- Cash flow problems related to living beyond your means
- Poor financial management
- Not having enough money set aside for emergencies
- Divorce or other personal problems
- Business failure
- Health problems, medical emergencies; physical and mental problems

What is the actual reason for your tax liability?

_____

_____

_____

_____

In the next section we will focus on income tax planning strategies that can be used to avoid future tax problems and enable you take control of your personal finances.

Tax Resolution Analysis Step 3:

Obtain an Estimate of the Actual Tax Liability

Do you owe the IRS?
Once you are current with filing all required tax returns you need to determine if the amount owed is actually correct. You will need to use copies of tax returns and IRS correspondence letters to determine how much you actually owe. If you do not know how much you owe or have not received a tax bill from the IRS you can request information from them to obtain an estimate of your tax debt including penalties and interest.

> **Taking Action!!!** Did you know it has been estimated that approximately 50% of all IRS letters go unopened by taxpayers due to fear and procrastination? Begin gathering all IRS letters and tax return information available for the tax years in question. Do not be afraid to open letters from the IRS! They contain valuable information regarding the tax resolution process.

IRS Correspondence:

If you have received a letter from the IRS, some anxiety and discomfort may accompany the contents of the IRS notice. **Do not panic if you receive an IRS notice.** After a tax return showing a tax liability is filed, the IRS immediately begins their collections process. During this collection process the IRS sends a series of letters notifying taxpayers that they are attempting to collect debt owed to the IRS. The most common reasons for an IRS notice are as follows:

1) To collect information about a taxpayer's account;
2) To notify a taxpayer of a change to their account; or
3) To attempt to collect a balance due.

IRS collection notices become increasingly more urgent. The more time that passes without a response, the more likely "forced" or "involuntary" collection actions will occur. If you receive an IRS collection notice, you should be aware of the typical time frames related to IRS correspondence.

IRS Collection Notice Time Frames

Notice	Time Frame (Calendar Days)	Explanation of Notice
Tax Return Filed/ Tax Assessed	IRS date of acceptance	
1st IRS Notice Sent to Taxpayer	Within 60 days	This is the first notice of the IRS collection process. This notice provides the taxpayer with information regarding their tax debt and rights to appeal
CP 501	30 Days	**YOU OWE TAXES**…Please pay your taxes within 10 business days.
CP 503	30 Days	**IMPORTANT NOTICE**…Immediate action is required or the IRS will begin to collect.
CP 504	30 Days	**URGENT!** The IRS intends to levy certain assets. RESPOND NOW. The IRS may also levy state tax refunds and file a Federal Tax Lien.
Letter 1058	30-45 Days	Notice usually sent by a Revenue Officer and will levy at his/her discretion.
CP 523: Installment Agreement Defaulted	45 Days	Taxpayer has defaulted on an Installment Agreement and the IRS will levy assets.

Do you agree with the amount the IRS claims you owe? The most important step in resolving IRS debt is to first determine if you actually owe the IRS money. If you believe that an IRS bill or notice is wrong you need to contact them or a tax professional immediately. Call the phone number on the bill, send a written response to the IRS office that issued the tax notice. Visit a local IRS office, or call 1-800-829-1040.

Freedom of Information Act

If you just want to know what type of information is in your IRS file, you can access your information without fear of drawing attention to your particular situation. Congress passed legislation called the Freedom of Information Act that requires government agencies, including the IRS, to disclose such information when requested.

- Freedom of Information documents can also be used to explain why, how, when and where the tax problems started.
- Having this information is helpful as it discloses the IRS information used to assess taxes, penalties and interest against the taxpayer.
- If you are having any difficulty figuring out how much you owe the IRS you should consider using the Freedom of Information Act to obtain your IRS Master File.
- Often the information you receive can help you better understand all of the important details of your tax liabilities.

IRS Master File
If you do not know the amount of your tax liability you can always obtain a copy of your IRS records. The IRS Master Files will show when tax returns were filed, how much tax, penalties, and interest were assessed and when these assessments were made. An assessment is a formal addition and recording of tax debt on IRS accounts. The assessment date is the start of the formal 10-year statutory period of collection. It will show the amounts and dates of any payments or credits that were posted to the account. It will also show any adjustments made to the account, the current status of the account, and information to determine when the collection statute expires. Any other actions taken by IRS will also be shown. The IRS will furnish a transcript of the information on the Master Files if a request is made from the taxpayer or his/her representative with a valid Power of Attorney.

Business Master File
Small business owners can request a Business Master File from the IRS. All tax data and related information pertaining to individual business income taxpayers are posted to the Business Master File so that the file reflects a continuously updated and current record of each taxpayer's account. All settlements with taxpayers are effected through computer processing of the BMF account and the data therein is used for accounting records, for issuance of refund checks, bills or notices, answering inquiries, classifying returns for audit, preparing reports and other matters concerned with the processing and enforcement activities of the Internal Revenue Service.

IRS Collection Activities
The tax resolution process is designed to empower individuals with tax problems to take control of their tax and financial problems. Developing new financial behaviors to replace years of poor financial decision making requires determination and persistence. I prefer to use a positive approach when dealing with people undergoing such a life changing event. That is why the end result of the tax and financial planning process is financial freedom. This means freedom to accomplish your life goals and make your visions become reality.

IRS collection activities are negative events and represent anything but freedom, and therefore should be avoided. You must be proactive and take action to avoid IRS collection measures such as wage garnishments, bank account levies, property seizures, and liens placed on your property. It is important to know what the IRS is capable of doing. Most people find this knowledge a helpful motivator to stay on track with the tax resolution process. If the collection process has already started you should still proceed through the tax resolution process quickly and accurately to start resolving your tax problems on your terms rather than simply accepting defeat and allowing the IRS to control your financial life.

What does the IRS typically attempt to levy?
The IRS may intent to levy any federal payments due, retirement benefits, Social Security benefits, wages, or employee travel advances or reimbursements. The IRS can also levy property such as real

estate, automobiles, business assets, bank accounts, wages, commissions, and other income. A levy is a seizure of property. The IRS will try to levy assets unless you TAKE ACTION. Why allow the IRS or any creditor to take control of your assets on their terms. If you owe taxes you need to pay them. However, you need to have a plan to pay them on your terms and not the terms of the IRS.

The IRS may involuntary collect the tax debt owed to them through different types of levies. A levy is served after the IRS has exhausted <u>all</u> other collection efforts to encourage taxpayer compliance. Levies commonly attach a taxpayer's bank account, salary and wages, and/or business accounts receivable.

The IRS is required to release levies in several circumstances, including:

- The levy is creating an economic hardship.
- The taxpayer agrees to make an Installment Agreement.
- The liability is no longer owed.
- The 10-year statutory collection period has expired.
- The levy was wrongfully served.
- An Offer in Compromise is accepted for review.

The two circumstances most often utilized to request a levy release are when the levy is creating an economic hardship or when the taxpayer agrees to make an Installment Agreement. In both of these situations, the taxpayer must provide a Collection Information Statement for Individuals and Self-Employed Individuals (Form 433-A) and/or Collection Information Statement for Businesses (Form 433-B). To obtain a levy release, the taxpayer must also file all required tax returns and be current in estimated payments or Federal Tax Deposits, if required.

The IRS usually will not release a levy until the taxpayer has proposed a solution to the delinquent tax problem and demonstrated that they will remain in compliance with future obligations. In certain circumstances, the IRS may release a levy if the taxpayer promises missing tax returns or financial information by a fixed date, but this cannot be counted on. It is always best if the taxpayer can get all of the needed documentation before contacting the IRS for a release of levy.

Will the IRS file a lien against my property?
A tax lien is a lien imposed on property by law to secure payment of taxes. Tax liens may be imposed for delinquent taxes owed as a result of failure to pay income taxes or other taxes. The IRS will file a lien under most circumstances to guarantee payment of your tax liability. Liens give the IRS a legal claim to your property as security for payment of your tax debt. Liens arise when the IRS assesses a liability, sends a Notice and Demand for Payment, and you do not fully pay the tax debt within 10 days after notification. Unpaid tax liens can remain on your credit record for 15 years while paid tax liens remain for 7 years. Act quickly to avoid aggressive collection measures and negative credit reporting. A lien may harm your credit record and affect your ability to get a loan for a home or car.

Estimated Amount of your Tax Liability
How much do you owe the IRS (including penalties and interest)? Enter the estimated amount of the tax debt below:
Amount Owed: $_____

If you agree with the amount owed and do not have any doubt as to the amount the IRS states that you owe go ahead to Step #4: Determining your Ability to Pay: Tax Resolution Analysis.

What if I do not agree with the amount the IRS says that I owe?

A variety of options are available should you disagree with the amount of taxes the IRS claims that you owe. The IRS does make mistakes from time to time. It is up to the taxpayer to take the initiative to correct any IRS mistakes. Consider these available options should you disagree with the assessed amount of your tax liability: file an amended return, appeal an IRS audit, request innocent spouse relief, or file an Offer in Compromise- doubt as to liability.

File an amended tax return

Preparing a tax return is not always a simple and straightforward task. Mistakes and errors are bound to happen with our nation's complicated tax code. If you need to revise your tax return you should file an amended tax return. The most common reasons to amend a tax return include the following:

- Changing your filing status
- Reporting additional W-2 or 1099 income
- Claiming additional dependents
- Removing previously claimed dependents
- Correcting personal exemption amounts
- Making changes involving tax credits
- Adjusting above the line deductions, standard deductions, or itemized deductions
- Correcting business income and expenses reported on a Schedule C

In order to amend a return you will first need to complete a new Form 1040. Next, report the differences between the original return and your new return on Form 1040X. There is a time limit involved so be sure that you file an amended return before it is too late to do so. IRS rules state that you have 3 years from the date your original return was filed or 2 years from the date you paid the tax, whichever is later, to amend a tax return.

Appeal an IRS audit

An IRS audit can be a very stressful and confusing situation to deal with. The IRS uses the audit or examination process to verify that the tax reported on a tax return is correct. The changes on a return as a result of an audit can either work in your favor or against you depending on the situation. Most audits take place in the form of letters from the IRS requesting an explanation of various items on a tax return. The IRS may also simply request supporting documentation. According to the IRS' 2007 Data Book, only 22.49 percent of all tax return audits were actually conducted in person during the 2007 fiscal year. The majority of all tax audits are correspondence audits.

The likelihood of an audit is fairly low. Only about one percent of all individual tax returns filed actually received an IRS audit in 2007. If you are audited you need to know your rights and respond immediately by appealing to the IRS for a second look if you disagree with their initial assessment. You may be able to represent yourself in an IRS audit. However, in most cases it is advantageous to seek professional guidance with the audit process. The most important thing to realize is that you have rights and a successful audit appeal could potentially lower or eliminate your tax liability.

The following are some basic tips for appealing an IRS Audit:

1. Refer to the IRS audit letter for instructions on how to file an appeal, request an informal review, or appeal your case in Tax Court.
2. The IRS generally allows you to appeal its decisions to the IRS Appeals Office. The Appeals Office is independent from the audit department. Their goal is to settle your appeal without having to take your case to Tax Court.
3. Respond to the initial notice letter in a timely manner. Start the appeal by writing a protest letter. Send the letter to your local IRS district director. You should formally state your disagreement within 30 days if you are requesting an informal review or within 90 days to request a Tax Court hearing and dispute the findings on an IRS examination.
4. Prepare for your appeal by getting your supporting documents together and organizing your records carefully to present your case. If you do not have supporting evidence to back up your appeal you may be quite disappointed with the results of your audit.
5. Make a Freedom of Information Act request to obtain the auditor's records so you are on a level playing field. You need to be able to see what information the auditor is seeing to understand the IRS examination.
6. In order to get a settlement, you must be prepared to show the appeals officer that you have a legitimate chance of winning your argument on the tax issues should you go to court.
7. Upon review of your appeal you will either be relieved of your tax obligations or your tax liabilities could be reduced. Keep in mind that audit reports are seldom reversed completely.
8. Appeal to the U.S. Tax Court if you disagree with the findings of the audit supervisor or the IRS Court of Appeals.
9. Most appeal issues are simple enough to handle on your own. However, if you have a history of procrastination and poor financial management skills you should seek professional guidance to help you with an audit. Sometimes a simple and inexpensive consultation is a good place to start when dealing with an IRS audit.
10. If you choose to use a tax professional to help with an audit you should look for a tax attorney, CPA, or Enrolled Agent with experience dealing with audit issues. Use the same guidelines that you should use when seeking a tax resolution planner. In fact, your tax and financial planning professional may also be able to assist you with an IRS audit.

Offer in Compromise- Doubt as to Liability
An Offer in Compromise allows taxpayers to resolve their tax liabilities for less than the amount originally owed. An Offer in Compromise may be requested based on one of three potential reasons:

- Doubt as to Collectibility
- Doubt as to Liability
- Effective Tax Administration

Doubt as to Collectibility is the most popular type of Offer in Compromise that taxpayers generally pursue when they lack the financial resources to pay their tax obligations. The Doubt as to Liability offer may be requested when the taxpayer doubts that he or she is actually responsible for the outstanding tax liabilities. In order to request an offer for this reason you would be required to submit a written statement that fully explains why you doubt that the tax liability is legitimately your responsibility. This type of offer is used less often than the OIC- Doubt as to Collectibility.

In most cases other tax resolution alternatives are more effective, less costly, and faster to process than an Offer in Compromise- Doubt as to Liability. These alternatives include amending tax returns, requesting innocent spouse relief, or asking the IRS to reconsider their audit findings. In my professional experience, I rarely come across a case where an Offer in Compromise is suggested based on a Doubt as to Liability.

Do you qualify for innocent spouse relief?

The IRS states that taxpayers who file a joint return are jointly and individually responsible, even if they later separate or get a divorce. This remains the case regardless of what the actual divorce decree may state. Relief can generally be found in three different categories: Innocent Spouse, Separation of Liability, and Equitable Relief.

Innocent Spouse Relief may be sought if your spouse (or ex-spouse) improperly reported items or omitted items on a return. You may be eligible for relief for paying the tax as well as interest and penalties on the understatement of taxes. By requesting innocent spouse relief you must prove that you filed a joint return and did not know or have any reason to know there was an understatement of the taxes owed. You must also be able to prove to the IRS that it would be unfair for the unknowing spouse to be held responsible for the tax liability. IRS Form 8857 is required to file for innocent spouse relief.

Separation of Liability applies to joint filers who are divorced, widowed, legally separated, or who have not lived together for the 12 months ending on the date on which the election for this type of relief is filed.

Equitable Relief applies to all joint filers who do not qualify for innocent spouse relief or separation of liability. To qualify for equitable relief you must be able to show that it would be unfair to be held liable for the understatement or underpayment of taxes.

Step # 4- Determining your Ability to Pay

Tax Resolution Analysis

After an estimate of the tax liability has been determined you need to figure out your ability to pay the IRS. This part of the process is the heart of "Tax Resolution Analysis". From a tax planning standpoint you need to look at your current financial resources the exact same way that the IRS will be looking at your assets. In order to determine your ability to pay you also need to examine your available resources from a comprehensive financial planning viewpoint. This will help you guarantee that you are dealing with your tax debt in the most appropriate manner. It is important to choose the best tax resolution alternative and get this decision right the first time. For example, attempting an Offer in Compromise that has no realistic chance of being accepted by the IRS can cost you hundreds to thousands of dollars in additional interest and penalties as you wait for an IRS response to your request.

Most tax representation firms, EAs, and CPAs will use a similar version of the Tax Resolution Analysis. The most common use of a Tax Resolution Analysis is to determine whether or not you will qualify for an Offer in Compromise that would allow you to resolve tax debt for less than the amount originally owed. The Tax Resolution Analysis used in the LifeSpan Process of Tax Resolution and Financial Freedom is designed to accomplish the following:

- Determine if you have the resources available to pay off your tax debt in full.

- Identify all available options to help pay down your tax debt.

- If you are unable to pay off your tax debt in full, complete a Tax Resolution Analysis that will decide whether or not you qualify for an Offer in Compromise.

- Estimate a potential settlement amount for an Offer in Compromise.

- If you do not qualify for an Offer in Compromise and do not have available resources to pay off your tax liability, you can use a Tax Resolution Analysis to estimate your monthly payments to the IRS as part of an Installment Agreement.

- Choose the most effective tax resolution alternative from a life planning standpoint.
  Translation: The tax resolution option that you want may not the one that you need.

Instructions

The net worth analysis and cash flow analysis that you completed during Tax Resolution Step # 3 (Assessing Resources) should have prepared you for the Tax Resolution Analysis. There is a reason that we assessed your internal and external resources prior to fully examining your tax resolution options.

Go ahead and refer to your balance sheet that listed all of your assets and liabilities. Next, go ahead and complete the Tax Resolution Analysis- Equity in Assets worksheet located on page 88.

List the estimated value of your assets under the "Fair Market Value" column. If you have a loan that is secured by the property you should enter the loan information under the "Liabilities" column. Normally we would stop here and the difference between your assets and liabilities would be used to determine your net worth. However, for tax resolution purposes the IRS uses a liquidation value or "quick sale" value that reduces your equity in certain assets. It is important to be as accurate as possible when determining the "available" equity in assets.

Use the following chart as a guideline when determining how much you should reduce certain assets. This chart should provide a basic overview of how the IRS may view the equity in personal assets potentially available to pay off a tax liability:

Personal Asset	Reduce the Fair Market Value by this Percentage Amount
Personal Residence	80%
Cash, checking accounts, savings, CDs, money market accounts	100%
Vehicles, motorcycles, campers	80%
Cash value life insurance	100%
Taxable Investment Assets (stocks, bonds, mutual funds)	80%
Retirement Assets (401k, 403b, annuities)	65%
Other real estate property (second home, timeshare)	80%

For example, if your home is worth $100,000 you take 80% of this amount ($100,000 Xs .80 = $80,000). Then subtract the mortgage ($75,000) from the "IRS Liquidation Value" amount of $80,000. This would result in $5,000 available equity in the home for IRS collection purposes.

Business Assets:

If you own a small business the IRS will need to determine the liquidation value of your business assets. This is a standard part of the collection process. Business assets and liabilities are reported on Form 433-B: Collection Statement for Businesses. In some cases a formal business valuation may be necessary to present a liquidation value for tax resolution purposes.

Business Asset	Reduce the Fair Market Value by this Percentage Amount
Cash and Bank Accounts	100%
Inventory	50%
Accounts Receivables	75%
Fixed Assets	65-85% for tools and equipment, 25% for fixtures
Business ONLY Vehicles	80%

Determine Available Equity in Assets

Note: Do not forget to reduce all assets by the appropriate amount to arrive at the IRS Liquidation Value.

Assets	Fair Market Value	IRS Liquidation Value	Liabilities	Equity in Assets
Home				
Other Real Property				
1st Vehicle				
2nd Vehicle				
Boat/Camper/Motorcycle				
Bank Accounts				
Cash Value Life Insurance				
Taxable Stocks/Bonds/Mutual Funds				
Retirement Accounts				
Business Assets				
Second Home/Timeshare				
Other Assets (specify)				
			Total Equity in Assets	

Analysis of Assets

Add all of the asset amounts together to obtain your total equity in assets for tax resolution purposes. If you have negative equity in a particular asset you should enter "0" for the asset class. Keep a record of this amount because you will need to revisit this amount once you finish the next step.

Total Equity in Assets = $ _____

Tax Resolution Tip: Complete a tax resolution analysis. If the equity in assets is greater than the amount of your tax liability then you can likely eliminate the Offer in Compromise- Doubt as to Collectibility as an option. One exception to this general rule is if you are unable to access the equity in assets. If you have equity in an asset but cannot access it you must be prepared to document your situation.

Tax Resolution Analysis Step # 5: Determine Monthly Disposable Income
Instructions

The IRS uses a system of "allowable expenses" to determine what is generally referred to as your monthly discretionary income. The cash flow analysis and personal spending plan steps should have prepared you for this important step. Go ahead and refer back to your budget or spending plan worksheets. Once you have your personal spending plan information readily available you should use it to help complete the Tax Resolution Analysis. Keep in mind that only basic expenses are used by the IRS in determining your monthly disposable income. The IRS determines if an expense is an allowable expense through National Living Standards. Therefore, on paper you may have more disposable income in the eyes of the IRS than in reality.

Total Income

Determine your total gross income from all sources. Do not deduct any withholding or allotments you elect to take out of your pay, such as insurance payments, 401(k) contributions, savings deductions, car payments, etc.

Wages, salaries, pensions, and Social Security: To calculate your gross monthly wages and/or salaries on a monthly basis you may need to make the following adjustments.

If paid weekly- multiply weekly gross wages by 4.3.
  Example: $500 x 4.3 = $2,150
If paid bi-weekly (every 2 weeks) - multiply bi-weekly gross wages by 2.17.
  Example: $1000 x 2.17 = $2,170
If paid semi-monthly (twice each month)- multiply semi-monthly gross wages by 2.
  Example: $1000 x 2 = $2,000

Net Self-Employment Income: To calculate your monthly net business income you need to keep good business records. That is one reason why the personal spending plan step preceded this section. This is the amount you earn after you pay monthly business expenses. Many self-employed individuals have difficulty understanding the difference between net income and gross income. Do NOT enter your gross income for the net business income. If your net income is a loss simply enter "0".

Net Rental Income: If you have income from a rental property you need to enter the monthly net rental income. This is the amount you receive after paying ordinary and necessary monthly rental expenses. Do NOT enter your gross income for the net business income. If your net rental income is a loss simply enter "0".

Other Miscellaneous Income Sources: If you have additional income from any of the following sources you should enter the estimated monthly amount on the Tax Resolution Analysis:
  • Interest
  • Dividends
  • Child Support
  • Alimony

Total Allowable Living Expenses

Recently the IRS updated the National Standards used to determine taxpayers' ability to pay delinquent tax debts. National Standards have been established for five necessary expenses: food, housekeeping supplies, apparel and services, personal care products and services, and miscellaneous items. The standards are derived from the Bureau of Labor Statistics (BLS) Consumer Expenditure Survey (CES). According to the IRS, "taxpayers are allowed the total National Standards amount monthly for their family size, without questioning the amounts they actually spend. If the amount claimed is more than the total allowed by the National Standards the taxpayer must provide documentation to substantiate those expenses are necessary living expenses. Generally, the total number of persons allowed for National Standards should be the same as those allowed as exemptions on the taxpayer's most recent year income tax return."

Rules of Thumb:
- **Expenses must be reasonable**
- **Documented**
- **Established payment history**
- **Based on National Living Standards**

Food, Clothing, and Miscellaneous: This category includes the total of food, clothing, housekeeping supplies, personal care products and services, and other miscellaneous personal living expenses.

Calculate your actual expenses and compare your monthly amount to the National Standard. If your actual expenses are greater than the National Standard you should enter the larger amount if you can substantiate that your actual living expenses are necessary. Refer to the National Standards chart below:

National Standards for Food, Clothing, and Miscellaneous Expenses

Expense	One Person	Two Persons	Three Persons	Four Persons
Food	$277	$528	$626	$754
Housekeeping	$28	$60	$61	$74
Apparel & Services	$85	$155	$209	$244
Personal Care Products & Services	$30	$53	$58	$65
Miscellaneous	$87	$165	$197	$235
Total	**$507**	**$961**	**$1,151**	**$1,370**

If you have more than four persons	Additional Amount Per Person
For each additional person in your household add this amount to the total allowance:	$262

Source: Internal Revenue Service

Housing and Utilities: Include the total rent or mortgage payments for your principal residence. Add up the average monthly expenses for property taxes, homeowner's or renter's insurance, home maintenance, HOA dues, fees, and utilities. The utilities category includes gas, electricity, water, fuel, oil, other fuels, garbage collection, and telephone and cell phone. Since the housing and utilities standards are obtained from U.S. Census data and Bureau of Labor Statistics information they are based on specific county and state data. Refer to www.irs.gov for the housing and utilities standard for your county of residence and family size. For the purposes of the Tax Resolution Analysis, enter the amount actually spent, or the local standard- whichever is less.

Transportation: Enter the total of lease or loan payments, vehicle insurance, registration, maintenance, fuel, public transportation, parking and tolls for the month. Compare this amount to the Transportation Standard. Again, you will be allowed the amount actually spent, or the standard, whichever is less.

The IRS provides two types of transportation standards for taxpayers that own or lease a vehicle: ownership costs and operating costs. The ownership costs provide maximum allowances for the lease or purchase of up to two automobiles if allowed as a necessary expense. A single taxpayer is normally allowed one automobile. The operating costs include maintenance, repairs, insurance, fuel, registrations, licenses, inspections, parking and tolls. The IRS allows you to use the actual amount spent, or the standard- whichever amount is less. If you attempt to provide the IRS with an amount that is more than the transportation standards you must be able to prove they are necessary living expenses.

The IRS transportation standards for tax resolution purposes are available at www.irs.gov (keyword: transportation standards). Refer to the transportation standards below as of March 1, 2008:

Ownership Costs

	One Car	Two Cars
National Standard	$489	$978

Operating Costs

	One Car	Two Cars
Northeast Region	$235	$470
Midwest Region	$183	$366
South Region	$201	$402
West Region	$211	$422

Note: The information above only provides limited operating cost figures. Please visit the IRS website and obtain more detailed living standard information for your particular city.

The data for the Operating Costs section of the Transportation Standards are provided by Census Region and Metropolitan Statistical Area (MSA). The following table lists the states that comprise each Census Region. Once your Census Region has been ascertained, to determine if an MSA standard is applicable, use the definitions below to see if you live within an MSA (MSAs are defined by county and city, where applicable). If you do not reside in an MSA- use the regional standard.

Health Care:
Include the costs of health insurance for this section of the Tax Resolution Analysis. Out of pocket health care standards have been established for out-of-pocket health care expenses including medical services, prescription drugs, and medical supplies (e.g. eyeglasses, contact lenses, etc.). The out-of-pocket health care standard amount is allowed in addition to the amount taxpayers pay for health insurance.

The following table for health care allowances is based on Medical Expenditure Panel Survey data and uses an average amount per person for taxpayers and their dependents under 65 and those individuals that are 65 and older. Out-of-pocket costs are allowed on a per person basis.

Age	Out of Pocket Costs
Under 65 Years Old	$57
Ages 65 and Older	$144

Taxes (Income and FICA): Include all of the following tax payments on your Tax Resolution Analysis:

- Federal Income Tax
- State or Local Taxes
- FICA (Social Security and Medicare)
- Personal Property Taxes
- Estimated Tax Payments

Court Ordered Payments: Alimony and child support are the most common court ordered payments that the IRS will accept as an allowable expenses.

Child and Dependent Care Expenses: Child and dependent care expenses include expenses related to childcare, daycare, or adult daycare services. To qualify, you must have a dependent child age 12 or younger, or a dependent that cannot care for him or herself. If you have a child age 13 or older, the child must be physically or mentally unable to care for him or herself. You may also claim adult daycare expenses for a dependent age 13 or older or for a spouse, if that person is physically or mentally unable to care for him or herself.

Life Insurance: Term insurance is an allowable expense in the resolution of your tax liability. Provide the monthly premium payments on your tax resolution analysis worksheet.

Other Secured Debt: This category includes any additional loans that are secured by property that you own.

Other Allowable Expenses: Some expenses are occasionally accepted by the IRS on a case by case basis. Examples include charitable contributions (if necessary for the production of income), union dues (if required for your line of work), and student loans (client only).

Expenses Generally Not Allowed: The IRS typically does not allow certain important expenses that many would argue are necessary for personal reasons. This is usually one of the biggest areas of frustration for people engaged in the collection process with the IRS. Many taxpayers are disappointed to realize that the IRS generally does not allow them to claim tuition payments for private schools, public or private college expenses. In addition, charitable contributions are not an allowable expense unless they are required for you to be able to maintain employment (e.g., clergy, ministers). Voluntary retirement contributions (401k, 403b, IRAs) are not allowable expenses. You will not succeed trying to convince the IRS that your retirement savings is more important than your tax obligations. Other non-allowable expenses are payments on unsecured debts such as credit card bills, cable television, and other similar expenses. This can be a huge problem for people with significant credit card debt. IRS analysis of allowable expenses may indicate positive monthly disposable income when in reality little or no discretionary income actually exists. That is a reason the personal spending plan is such an important part of the tax resolution process.

Tax Resolution Analysis: IRS Allowable Expenses

Gross Monthly Income (Before Taxes)	
Gross Salary- Client	
Gross Salary- Spouse	
Other Employment Income	
Net Business Income- Client	
Net Business Income- Spouse	
Social Security- Client	
Social Security- Spouse	
Disability Income	
Alimony	
Child Support	
Pensions/Retirement	
Other	
Total Monthly Income	

IRS Allowable Expenses	Amount	IRS Allowable Expenses	Amount
National Standards		**Health Care Expenses**	
(Food, clothing, misc.)		Health Insurance	
Housing		Medical Service	
Rent/Mortgage		Prescription Drugs	
Property Taxes/Insurance		Medical Supplies	
Maintenance/Repairs		**Court Ordered Payments**	
Utilities:		Child Support	
Gas		Alimony	
Water/Sewer/Garbage		Other	
Electricity		**Child/Dependent Care**	
Telephone (w/ Cell Phone)		Child Care	
Total Housing		Elderly	
Housing Standard (refer to IRS.gov)		Special Needs	
Enter the Lower of the Actual or Standard Housing Expense		**Term Life Insurance**	
Transportation		**Other Secured Debts**	
Ownership Costs- Loan/Lease		**Other Expenses**	
Operating Costs		Accounting/Legal	
Public Transportation		Involuntary Deductions	
Current Taxes		Charity (only if required)	
Federal Income		Student Loans	
State/Local		Union Dues (if required)	
FICA/Medicare			
Personal Property Taxes			
Estimated Tax Payments		**TOTAL EXPENSES**	

Total Monthly Income	_____	- (minus)
IRS Allowable Expenses	_____	= (equals)
Monthly Discretionary Income	_____	

Tax Resolution Analysis: Calculating the Minimum Settlement Amount

Enter the total amount of equity in assets (from page ##): $_____

Enter the amount of Monthly Discretionary Income (from page##): $_____

Offer in Compromise Calculation

If you will be able to pay a potential offer amount in **5 months or less:**

Multiply Monthly Disposable Income by 48 (or the number of months remaining on the ten year statutory period for collection, whichever is less)

Enter the Monthly Disposable Income: $_____   X's 48 = _____

Add the Total Amount of Equity in Assets: +   _____

Estimated Offer Amount: =   _____

If you will pay the offer amount in **more than 5 months but less than 2 years:**

Multiply Monthly Disposable Income by 60 (or the number of months remaining on the ten year statutory period for collection, whichever is less)

Enter the Monthly Disposable Income: $_____   X's 60 = $_____

Add the Total Amount of Equity in Assets: + $_____

Estimated Offer Amount: = $_____

Estimated Amount of Tax Liability: = $_____

*Tax Resolution Tip: If the estimated offer amount is less than your actual tax liability you should consider requesting an **Offer in Compromise** with the IRS. If the Tax Resolution Analysis indicates that you have equity in assets and monthly discretionary income that is sufficient to pay off your tax liability you should pay down your tax debt as much as possible and setup an **Installment Agreement** to pay your tax debt over time. The Monthly Discretionary Income amount is a likely amount that the IRS will require you to pay on a monthly basis. If paying your tax debt using existing resources would create a financial hardship you should consider requesting to be placed on **Currently Not Collectible Status**. Refer to the next step for details on your tax resolution alternatives.*

Tax Resolution Analysis Step 6:

Identify Tax Resolution Alternatives

Now that you have gathered all of the puzzle pieces and defined your goals and objectives, it is time to make sense of your tax and financial information. A detailed analysis of your current situation will help determine what needs to be done to meet your tax and financial planning goals. From a Tax Resolution standpoint, this could include analyzing your assets, liabilities and cash flow to determine the tax strategies available to pay off, reduce or eliminate your tax debt. Tax Resolution Analysis is the formal process of determining which options are available to deal with a tax problem. The evaluation process also looks at "big picture" goals and objectives related to other aspects of your financial life. Depending on your actual goals, this could include analyzing investments, retirement objectives, current insurance coverage, etc. A Tax Resolution Financial Planner also analyzes how tax resolution goals relate to other financial planning goals.

The previous Tax Resolution Analysis step identified your collection potential using IRS allowable expenses. You were able to determine whether or not you are a potential candidate for the Offer in Compromise program. If the Tax Resolution Analysis revealed that you are eligible to resolve your tax debt for less than the original amount you should consider requesting an Offer in Compromise-Doubt as to Liability.

Offer in Compromise

An Offer in Compromise is an agreement between the IRS and a taxpayer allowing the taxpayer's delinquent tax debt to be compromised for less than the amount owed. The offered dollar amount is based on the taxpayer's net worth plus their future income potential.

The IRS will generally accept an OIC when it is unlikely that the full amount of tax can be collected and the amount offered reasonably reflects the amount that the IRS could expect to collect through other means. An Offer is based on a taxpayer's ability to pay and not how much he or she actually owes.

There are three ways to pay the amount due based on an accepted OIC:

Cash/Lump Sum- A 20% down payment of the OIC amount is made when the Offer is submitted, and the remaining balance is paid within 150 days of acceptance.

Short-Term Deferred/Periodic Payment- The Offer amount is payable in monthly installments between 6 and 24 months.

Deferred/Periodic Payment- The Offer amount is payable in monthly installments of at least 25 months, but no longer than the number of months remaining in the collection statute.

There are three bases for which an OIC can be filed: doubt as to collectibility, doubt as to liability, or to promote effective tax administration.

Doubt as to Collectibility: This is the most common type of offer used in the tax resolution process. An OIC based on doubt as to collectibility is used to resolve tax liabilities for less than the original amount owed.

Doubt as to Liability: This type of offer can be submitted when a taxpayer feels that he or she does not owe the tax the IRS is attempting to collect.

Effective Tax Administration: This is very rare. Approximately 400 cases were accepted in 2007 according to the Government Accountability Office report.

A Cautionary Note Regarding OIC's: During difficult economic times when millions of families are struggling financially it is easy to assume that the Offer in Compromise program is the best solution to the majority of tax problems. The opportunity to resolve tax debt for less than the original amount owed is an appealing option. The Offer in Compromise program is not for everyone. Unfortunately, a number of aggressive companies are using deceptive marketing tactics to encourage everyone in tax debt to pursue an Offer in Compromise. The truth is nobody can "guarantee" an OIC acceptance. The IRS makes the ultimate decision to accept or reject an OIC. The fees can be high when using a tax professional to submit an Offer on your behalf. If you are pursuing an OIC you do not want to pay too much for tax representation. However, you do not want "cheap" representation either.

According to a Wall Street Journal report, the IRS only accepted about 12,000 Offers in Compromise during the 2007 fiscal year. The actual number of offers received was approximately 46,000. In addition, based on the latest statistics, the IRS takes an average of 380 days to process an Offer in Compromise application. The length of response times vary significantly. Your processing time may be shorter or longer than this depending on the details of your particular situation.

Do not attempt to request an OIC if you have little or no chance to qualify. The Tax Resolution Analysis is an excellent indicator of your potential ability to qualify for an OIC. Always keep in mind that the penalties and interest will continue to grow and increase the total amount of taxes owed. Therefore, a long shot Offer in Compromise attempt may actually worsen your financial situation as your debt continues to grow while you wait to hear from the IRS.

Offer in Compromise companies are growing in numbers as more and more Americans face tax and financial problems. Beware if a promoter is promising "pennies on the dollar" resolution or makes "guarantees" regarding your case. The IRS makes the final determination. Also, do not allow anyone who calls his or herself a "tax professional" to convince you that they can "take care of everything" on your behalf. You still need to take action and perform important steps during the tax resolution process. There is no magic wand or quick fix to help get you out of debt. However, there are large numbers of tax resolution professionals that will operate in your best interests to help you improve your tax situation. It just takes a little work and planning on your part to research and find a qualified professional.

Best Practices
Seek professional tax representation from a CPA, EA, or tax attorney if you are unable to deal with the issue on your own. Remember that fees are generally negotiable. Try to arrange a flat fee for service and always "read the fine print". Never sign anything without reviewing it. Avoid the use of credit cards, automatic drafts, or retail installment agreements to pay for services. If it sounds too good to be true it usually is. Do not believe a sales representative if they say, "We will handle everything." You are responsible for providing documentation such as proof of income and expenses. Most importantly, you will have to play an active role in the process.

Alternatives to an Offer in Compromise
What happens if you are not eligible for an Offer in Compromise? Resolving a tax liability for less than the original amount owed is not your only option. If you are capable of paying off your tax debt using available assets or discretionary income, then you need to review all of your available options. Some additional options such as an Offer in Compromise- Effective Tax Administration, Currently Not Collectible Status, and bankruptcy are available for special circumstances. These options are discussed in greater detail later in the section. The progression of tax debt resolution options will examine each alternative ranging from paying off the tax debt in full to resolving the tax debt for less than the amount owed.

Determining your ability to pay: Available assets
In most cases, if you have the funds available you should go ahead and pay the IRS immediately. Resist the temptation to keep your investments, savings, and liquid assets. The interest rate on any savings account will most likely be significantly less than the total interest and penalties on most tax liabilities.

At this point, if you have the assets available to pay off your tax debt you should go ahead and pay off your tax debt in full. Of course this depends on your ability to access your assets in a timely manner and the potential tax implications related to the sale of certain assets. Some available assets make more sense to use than others when it comes to paying off debt. Keep in mind that the tax resolution process involves paying off tax debt in the most cost effective manner while taking into consideration your life planning goals.

Liquid Assets

Liquidate savings first if you have multiple asset classes to choose from, but be sure to leave some savings for a "starter emergency fund". Liquid assets include checking, savings, money market, and short-term CDs.

Personal Use Assets

Next, consider selling personal assets that you do not need such as boats, motorcycles, investment property, etc. If you are living beyond your means you should consider downsizing your home or vehicles. However, be sure that you get a reasonable price for your property. You would not be the first overly anxious debtor who sold their property below market value in a rush to pay off tax debt.

Investment Assets

If you have investment assets such as stocks, bonds, or mutual funds held in a taxable account you should consider selling these assets and using the proceeds to pay down your tax debt. You will be subject to capital gains (or losses) depending on the performance of your investments. Investment assets held over a year are subject to long-term gains. The capital gains rate is currently 5% for taxpayers in the 15% marginal income tax bracket or lower. The long-term capital gains rate is 15% for everyone else. Short-term capital gains are taxed as ordinary income.

If you decide to sell investment assets, know your cost basis (what you paid for the investment) and have a basic understanding of how it will be taxed prior to any investment transactions. Be sure to have sufficient money withheld from your proceeds to pay the estimated tax. Otherwise you will be subject to future tax problems, and that is what you are trying to avoid with the LifeSpan Process of Tax Resolution and Financial Freedom.

Retirement Assets

Given the fact that there are so many tax debt resolution alternatives available and the real costs associated with doing this are so high, this may not be an advisable method of reducing tax debt. Not only would you be taking money that is meant to be available for your retirement or other life planning goals, but you are liquidating an investment with tax advantages. Retirement distributions are taxed as ordinary income at your marginal tax rate. The tax implications are more severe if your retirement plan withdrawal is deemed an early distribution. If you are under 59 ½ years old you will also be subject to an additional 10% early withdrawal penalty. There are some exceptions to this rule that differ depending on whether the retirement savings account is an IRA or a qualified retirement plan such as a 401(k) or 403(b). Loans against retirement plan assets are a bad idea and can lead to bigger tax and financial problems.

Cash Value Life Insurance

If you have permanent insurance with available cash value you should consider accessing your cash value to help pay off debt.

Tax Resolution Alternatives
Checklist for using Available Assets to Pay off Tax Debt

Source	Amount Available	Is the asset available?	
		YES	NO
Total Amount			

Taking Action!!!
Do you have multiple assets available to pay off or pay down your tax debt? If you are having trouble deciding which set of assets to use to pay off your tax debt then you may need to create a decision tree. Make a brief list of your options and write down the pros and cons of each choice. This is a useful tool in any decision making process and may be able to help you make tough decisions in any aspect of life.

Choosing among available resources: The Decision Tree

Tax Resolution Option	Pros	Cons

Determining your ability to pay: No assets available

If you do not have the assets available to pay the IRS in full, pay down as much as possible and see if you can obtain a bank loan, personal loan, or any other short term loan IF the terms are better than an IRS payment plan. This can get complicated. The interest and penalties on IRS Installment Agreements can often be as high as credit cards and other high interest debt.

If you believe that paying the IRS in full is not possible you should go ahead and complete IRS Form 433-A and 433-B (if a business owner). These forms will use the same information that was needed to complete the Tax Resolution Analysis. The Tax Resolution Analysis follows the same basic structure of an IRS collection statement. Initially the Tax Resolution Analysis was used to see if you qualify for an Offer in Compromise. It will also help you figure out an estimated payment amount for an Installment Agreement (paying your tax debt over time).

Installment Agreements for a tax liability that is less than $25,000 may be set up online or with Form 433-F. This form is less detailed than Form 433-A, but may not take into account all allowable expenses during the Tax Resolution Analysis.

Go ahead and familiarize yourself with these forms if you are planning on requesting an Installment Agreement, Offer in Compromise, Currently not Collectible request, or other tax resolution option that does not involve paying the IRS off in full using existing resources or outside loan options.

> **Taking Action!** If you are unable to resolve your tax debt with the use of existing assets you should go ahead and complete IRS Form 433-A: Collection Statement for Wage Earners and Self-Employed Individuals. Form 433-B: Collection Information Statement for Businesses is required for small business owners. These forms may be obtained at www.irs.gov.

What to do once the amount of the tax debt has been determined

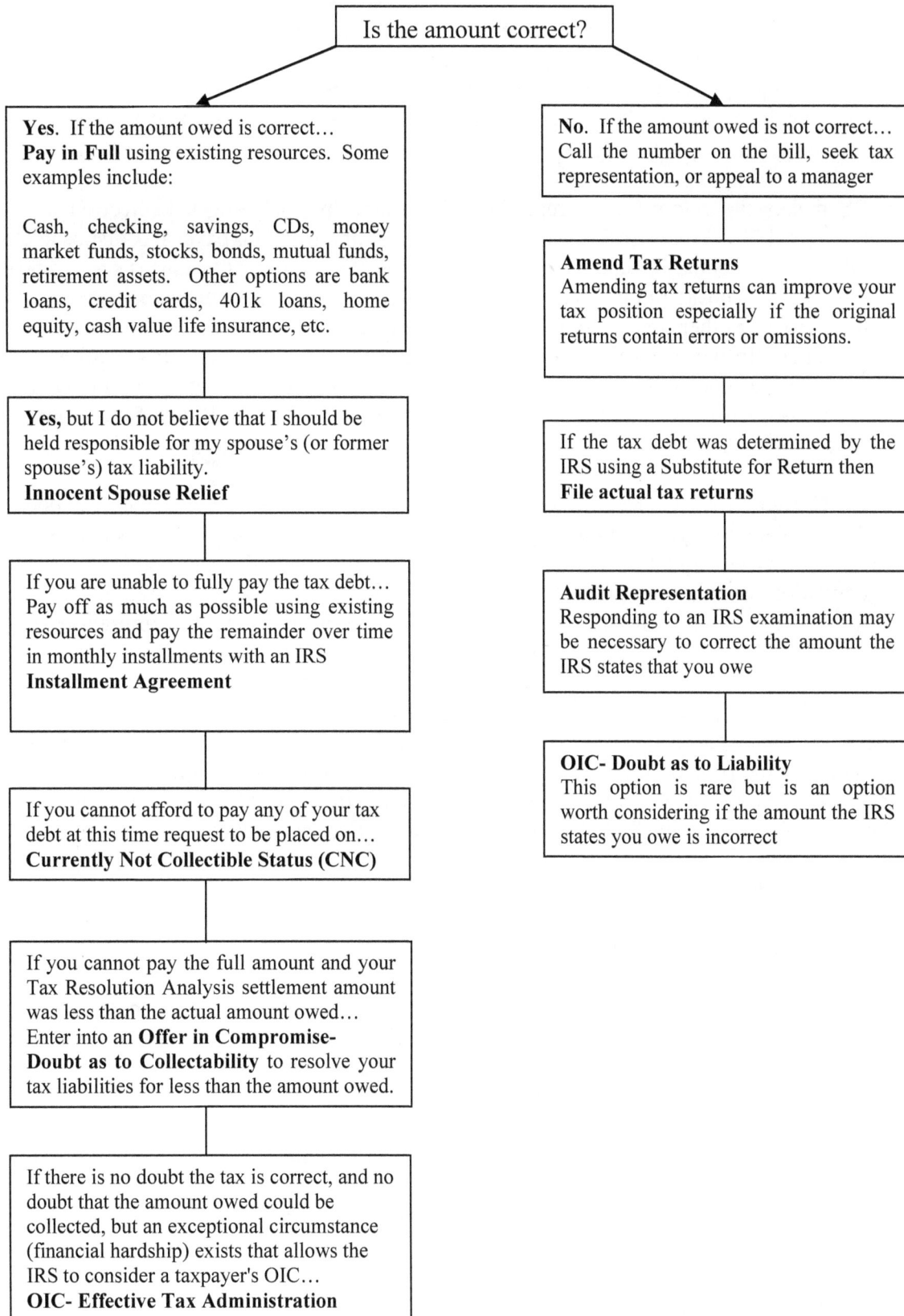

Is the amount correct?

Yes. If the amount owed is correct…
Pay in Full using existing resources. Some examples include:

Cash, checking, savings, CDs, money market funds, stocks, bonds, mutual funds, retirement assets. Other options are bank loans, credit cards, 401k loans, home equity, cash value life insurance, etc.

Yes, but I do not believe that I should be held responsible for my spouse's (or former spouse's) tax liability.
Innocent Spouse Relief

If you are unable to fully pay the tax debt… Pay off as much as possible using existing resources and pay the remainder over time in monthly installments with an IRS
Installment Agreement

If you cannot afford to pay any of your tax debt at this time request to be placed on…
Currently Not Collectible Status (CNC)

If you cannot pay the full amount and your Tax Resolution Analysis settlement amount was less than the actual amount owed…
Enter into an **Offer in Compromise-Doubt as to Collectability** to resolve your tax liabilities for less than the amount owed.

If there is no doubt the tax is correct, and no doubt that the amount owed could be collected, but an exceptional circumstance (financial hardship) exists that allows the IRS to consider a taxpayer's OIC…
OIC- Effective Tax Administration

No. If the amount owed is not correct… Call the number on the bill, seek tax representation, or appeal to a manager

Amend Tax Returns
Amending tax returns can improve your tax position especially if the original returns contain errors or omissions.

If the tax debt was determined by the IRS using a Substitute for Return then
File actual tax returns

Audit Representation
Responding to an IRS examination may be necessary to correct the amount the IRS states that you owe

OIC- Doubt as to Liability
This option is rare but is an option worth considering if the amount the IRS states you owe is incorrect

Currently Not Collectible

Sometimes taxpayers experience extreme financial hardship that makes it impossible to pay any portion of an outstanding tax liability. When financial burdens are too overwhelming the IRS can declare cases as currently not collectible. Currently not collectible refers situations where taxpayers have no ability to pay taxes that are owed. There are a variety of reasons that often lead to being placed on "currently not collectible" status. The most common reason is when full payment would deprive the taxpayer of the basic needs of life such as food, shelter, and clothing. The IRS requires proof that a taxpayer lacks the means to pay anything in order to qualify for currently not collectible status.

The IRS makes the determination regarding "hardship" by analyzing a Collection Information Statement (IRS Form 433-A and/or IRS Form 433-B) to determine if the taxpayer has disposable income or non-essential assets that could be liquidated to pay the taxes. Specific circumstances such as health and age are also taken into consideration. Non-essential assets are things such as investments, savings accounts, luxury items, or other items of value that are not essential to the taxpayer's health, welfare, or production of income. In the event that there is available equity in assets, the IRS requires additional proof that seizing these assets would create additional financial hardship. Therefore, you may have some equity in a personal residence, an automobile or even a retirement plan and still qualify for Currently Not Collectible Status (CNC Status).

While in Currently Not Collectible Status it is important to remember that the debt does not go way. CNC Status means that you cannot afford to pay at the present time. Penalties and interest will continue to be added to the original debt amount. The IRS will receive updates every six months to see if the taxpayer's situation has improved. The 10 year statute of limitations is still in effect meaning the IRS has 10 years to collect the tax. If the IRS is unable to collect before the statute of limitations expiration date then the tax debts will expire.

In summary, Currently Not Collectible Status is a tax resolution alternative that stops collection activities (including levies and garnishments) as a result of financial hardship. Liens may still be filed prior to the account being placed on CNC Status if the Revenue Officer thinks future collection attempts may be successful. If you have absolutely no means to pay the IRS due to financial hardship then being placed on Currently Not Collectible Status with the IRS is an option worth pursuing.

Installment Agreements

An installment agreement is an agreement between the IRS and a taxpayer that allows the taxpayer to pay his or her delinquent debt over a specified period of time.

Guaranteed Installment Agreement: Taxpayers who owe less than $10,000, have been current on the last 5 years returns, and can pay the tax within 3 years may qualify for a guaranteed agreement.

Streamlined Installment Agreement: Taxpayers who owe less than $25,000 of Income Tax or any tax of a business that has been closed may qualify for a streamline agreement. This type of agreement will allow you up to 5 years to pay the delinquent taxes without requiring analysis of financial information.

Partial Payment Installment Agreement: This is a fairly new debt repayment program implemented in 2005 where you have a long term payment plan to pay off the IRS at a reduced dollar amount.

Are you aware that interest and penalties do not stop with an installment agreement/payment plan?
According to the IRS, "You can save money by paying the full amount you owe, as quickly as possible; to minimize the interest and penalties you will be charged. Penalties and interest will continue to be charged

on the unpaid portion of the debt throughout the duration of the installment agreement/payment plan. Remember, the interest rate on a loan or credit card may be lower than the combination of penalties and interest imposed by the Internal Revenue Code." Penalties and interest apply to years in which money is owed. The interest charged on late payments changes quarterly. During the last several years the interest rate has ranged from a high of 9 percent to a low of 4 percent. The interest rate for the calendar quarter beginning January 1, 2009 was 5% for underpayments by individuals. Do not forget to factor in penalties related to the underpayment of your taxes.

Filing Late Penalty
If you do not file your return by the due date (including extensions) you may have to pay a failure to file penalty. The penalty for filing late is generally 5 percent per month, or part of a month, up to 25 percent of the amount of the tax shown due on the return.

Paying Late Penalty
You may have to pay a penalty for each month or part of a month after the due date that the tax is not paid. The penalty for paying late is 0.5 percent per month, up to 25 percent of the unpaid amount due. Typically you can avoid the penalty if you can show good reason for not paying the tax on time.

The Real Costs of an Installment Agreement
Even if a payment plan with the IRS appears to be your best option to get out of tax debt there are definite drawbacks that you need to be aware of. The biggest drawback is that interest and penalties continue to accrue while you still owe taxes. Combined with penalties, the interest rate is often comparable to high interest credit card debt. It is possible to pay for years and feel as if you are making little progress. For planning purposes you can expect the combination of interest and penalties to be comparable to high interest credit card rates.

The purpose of the following example is to illustrate the importance of paying off your tax debt as quickly as possible. As mentioned previously, it is highly recommend that you pay off your tax liability as soon as possible to avoid additional interest or penalties being added to the amount due.

For example, John owes $25,000 to the IRS and has agreed to pay $500.00 a month to the IRS as part of an Installment Agreement. Assuming that his combined interest and penalties are approximately 14%, it could take him 4.5 years to pay off his IRS Installment Agreement. Based on this scenario, he will pay a total of $7,512 in interest and penalties to resolve a $25,000 tax liability.

If John increased his payments by just $200 a month it will take him 2 years and 11 months to pay off his IRS tax debt. The total interest and penalty payments would be $4,977 based on the same scenario (14% combined interest and penalties). An extra $200 payment per month would reduce his total interest and penalties by $2,535. In addition, he could eliminate his tax debt 19 months faster than the original payment plan.

Bottom Line: If an Installment Agreement is your best tax resolution alternative you need to establish a "Personal Spending Plan" that sets aside funds each month to pay off your tax debt as fast as possible. The amount that you send to the IRS should be above and beyond your minimum required Installment Agreement payment. You will always get out of debt sooner by paying off more than the minimum monthly payments required by an IRS payment plan.

Disclaimer: The interest rates used in this analysis are for illustration purposes only and do not represent actual IRS interest and penalties. Refer to IRS.gov or recent Revenue Rulings for more information on interest rates and penalties.

Caution about Installment Agreements

Due to the fact that the interest and penalties on an Installment Agreement can be similar to high interest credit cards, you should always try to avoid paying only the minimum payment amount. However, you should always attempt to establish the lowest required monthly payment as possible to provide a margin of error should you face a cash flow problems. Your primary tax resolution goal with an Installment Agreement is to pay off your liability as quickly as possible to reduce the problems related to compounding interest and penalties.

Abatement of Penalties

An abatement of penalties is a request to the IRS to remove certain penalties that were added to the taxpayer's account for a particular year or multiple years. The taxpayer is required to have "reasonable cause" that is specific for each year when submitting this request and must be able to explain why this reason should grant the penalties to be removed from his or her account.

The IRS has over 100 penalties that may be charged when taxpayers fail to timely comply with the tax laws and regulations. The most common penalties are failure to file, failure to pay, failure to deposit, and accuracy penalties. Most of these penalties can be abated in full or in part if the taxpayer can prove that there was reasonable cause for the delinquency. The IRS has some common reasons for abatement of penalties:

1) Death or serious illness of the taxpayer or a death or serious illness in his/her immediate family.
2) Unavoidable absence of the taxpayer.
3) Destruction by fire or other casualty of the taxpayer's place of business or business records.
4) Taxpayer was unable to determine amount of deposit or tax due for reasons beyond the taxpayer's control.
5) The facts indicate that the taxpayer's ability to make deposits or payments has been materially impaired by civil disturbances.
6) Lack of funds is an acceptable, reasonable cause for failure to pay any tax or make a deposit under the Federal Tax Deposit System only when a taxpayer can demonstrate the lack of funds occurred, despite the exercise of ordinary business care and prudence.

Alternative Methods to Reduce a Tax Liability or Pay it off in Full

Liquid assets such as savings accounts, money market funds, and CDs are generally the first resource to considering using to pay down tax debt. The interest earned on liquid assets is often significantly lower than the total interest and penalties accumulating with tax debt. Next, consider using any investment assets to help pay off a tax liability. The pros and cons of this alternative are specifically tied to the actual investment asset. Potential growth potential of the investment and tax implications related to income taxes and capital gains should be taken into consideration if you are thinking about selling an investment to pay off debt.

Another alternative would be to obtain a loan against any cash value life insurance policies you may have. Loans against retirement plan assets are another consideration when identifying potential ways to raise assets to pay off a tax liability. However, just because you can obtain a loan from your retirement plan does not mean it is always the best idea. I strongly recommend that people only consider a 401(k) loan as a last resort. You should always review the pros and cons of each tax resolution alternative to help guide you through the decision making process. The sale of real estate property or other assets provide another potential alternative to help pay down tax debt. This option again brings up the concern of capital gains.

The previous options considered the use of assets to pay off tax liabilities. If you do not have sufficient assets to pay off a tax liability you should consider other less expensive forms of debt than an Installment Agreement. Some people may be able to borrow from friends or family. This is usually taking a walk on dangerous ground and can have an impact on relationships unless everything happens according to plan. Gifts are usually preferred. You do not want to become a slave to the lender, especially if a friend or family member is playing the role of the banker.

Credit cards can be a potential source of a loan to help pay off tax debt if they are used correctly and the terms are favorable. If you have a good credit score and available credit then you should consider this alternative in certain situations. Be cautious though, credit card companies can offer teaser rates that increase significantly over time. In addition, if you are not able to make payments on time your actual interest rates can go sky high and defeat the purpose of this tax resolution alternative. Your goal is to try to find the lowest interest rate option possible if debt is your only option to pay the IRS over time. With this option you should always seek a fixed rate option over a variable interest rate.

Bank loans from credit unions and community banks should also be considered. Shopping various financial institutions may create lending opportunities that are more favorable than the terms of IRS agreements. As always, do your homework and explore each and every tax resolution alternative to find the most cost-effective alternative that gets you out of debt quickly.

Filing bankruptcy

Eliminating tax liabilities in bankruptcy is an option for people that owe the IRS. The promise of filing bankruptcy and starting over from scratch financially is an option for some to consider. However, the idea of starting over and discharging tax debts only works in certain tax situations. The bankruptcy process is not as easy as it may sound and should be avoided if at all possible. Personal bankruptcy should be viewed as a drastic option of last resort if your tax debts have truly become overwhelming.

Tax resolution and financial freedom emphasizes taking control of your financial life. Bankruptcy is for life and is a tax resolution option when nothing else has worked. Every loan or job application that you complete the rest of your life will ask if you have ever filed bankruptcy. You cannot run from bankruptcy because it is permanent. A Chapter 7 bankruptcy is a total "liquidation" or discharge of allowable debts and will remain on your credit report for 10 years. Chapter 13 bankruptcy is usually a payment plan and remains on a credit report for 7 years.

Most taxes cannot be eliminated by filing for bankruptcy. If you are considering bankruptcy as a tax resolution alternative you should first consider whether or not the income tax debt in question actually qualifies for discharge in bankruptcy. Several factors determine if tax liabilities qualify for discharge or totally wipe out the tax debt during Chapter 7 bankruptcy. Generally speaking, you can discharge federal income tax liabilities if all of the following conditions are met:

- The taxes owed must be individual income taxes. Payroll taxes cannot be eliminated in bankruptcy.
- Tax returns cannot be fraudulent or frivolous in nature.
- The tax debt must be 3 years old or older than the date that bankruptcy was filed.
- Actual tax returns must have been filed at least two years prior to filing for bankruptcy. This means no "Substitute for Returns" are eligible.
- You must pass the "240 day rule". At least 240 days must have passed from the date of assessment to the filing date of the bankruptcy petition.

If bankruptcy is the only option during the tax resolution process you should be aware that bankruptcy will not get rid of federal tax liens. While filing for Chapter 7 bankruptcy may discharge your tax debt a tax lien will remain on your property if the IRS recorded the lien prior to filing for bankruptcy protection.

Consumer bankruptcy laws have changed dramatically since October 2005. I highly recommend that anyone seeking to resolve tax liabilities through bankruptcy seek legal counsel for this option. The process of tax resolution and financial freedom will present better alternatives than bankruptcy in most situations.

Taking Action!!!
What is your tax resolution plan? After reviewing all of your tax resolution options you should have a clear idea of which path to take to conquer your tax debt. In some cases multiple resources may need to be utilized to get out of tax debt. For others tax resolution may require you to follow the steps to request an Offer in Compromise or setup an Installment Agreement.

Go ahead and create a written plan that specifically outlines the steps that you must take and in the order they must occur. Remember that the purpose of the entire tax resolution process is to pay off your tax debt as quickly as possible and in the most cost-effective manner possible based on your own unique financial position.

Summary

The tax resolution process involves a significant amount of work in order to determine the best solution. Prior to reaching this step you need to first understand the details of your unique financial position. The tax resolution analysis step begins following a detailed assessment of available financial resources. Once you have an idea of your actual net worth and cash flow you can begin attacking tax debt in the most effective manner.

Tax resolution analysis follows a progression of steps that are designed to identify the best option based on all available facts. The first step begins with developing an understanding of the tax problem. You cannot identify solutions if you do not understand the actual problem. The initial tax resolution analysis step is used to gain information regarding the type of taxes owed, the years involved, and whether or not there are any past due tax returns that need to filed. All past due tax returns must be filed prior to continuing with the tax resolution process.

The next area of focus involves identifying the reasons for the tax debt. The cause of tax and financial problems may vary greatly from person to person. Identifying the underlying reasons for tax problems is necessary in order to prevent future tax problems. The following step provides us with an estimate of the actual amount owed to the IRS. The more information you have regarding the amount owed the better prepared you will be in choosing among the various tax resolution alternatives.

After obtaining an estimated amount of the tax liability, you are in the position to analyze your ability to pay the tax debt. The next phase of tax resolution analysis builds on the net worth activity conducted during the "Assessing Resources" step. This time you will be looking at your assets and liabilities in the same ways the IRS will be reviewing your net worth situation. The purpose of this net worth analysis is to determine if you have any available equity in assets that could potentially be used to pay off an outstanding tax liability.

Next, you must complete similar activities related to reviewing your cash flow situation. The end result of this cash flow analysis exercise is to determine your monthly disposable income using IRS allowable expenses. This special formula builds on the information you have already gathered regarding your cash flow situation. Monthly disposable income is calculated using an IRS formula that determines your potential cash flow for tax resolution purposes. The IRS formula using allowable expenses that are based on national living standards does not take into account your actual cash flow situation. Certain expenses such as credit card payments and discretionary spending are not included in the IRS formula.

The end result of the tax resolution analysis is to determine your ability to pay the tax liability based on IRS calculations. The IRS formula uses your monthly disposable income and equity in assets to determine your ability to pay the tax debt. The previous steps of the tax resolution process are used to build the foundation for the next important decision on the path to tax freedom, which is determining the best alternative for your situation. The tax resolution analysis generally identifies one of the following alternatives to resolve tax debt:

- Pay in full using existing resources
- Setup an Installment Agreement to pay the IRS over time
- Request to be placed on Currently Not Collectible Status
- Resolve the tax debt for less than the amount owed using an Offer in Compromise
- File for Bankruptcy

The tax resolution analysis step of the LifeSpan Process is designed to help you choose the best form of tax problem resolution. A variety of different solutions exist to resolve tax debt. The greatest challenge of the tax resolution analysis is to pick the best resolution alternative for each unique financial situation. Based on the facts and circumstances you can use the tax resolution analysis to your benefit and identify the best ways to resolve a tax liability. This process helps you save time and money by choosing the most cost-effective alternative. You should maximize your time and energy by avoiding solutions that will not work. Most importantly, you should make sure that your tax resolution options are the best fit for your financial life plan.

Tax Resolution Step #6:
Implementing the Tax Resolution Plan

"I am proud to be paying taxes in the United States. The only thing is, I could be just as proud for half of the money." ~ Arthur Godfrey

Staying Focused, Staying on Track

The proper identification of the most effective tax resolution alternatives allows people with tax debt to establish a plan of action. The previous tax resolution analysis culminated in a written plan of action to provide guidance when dealing with the tax debt situation. However, the journey to tax and financial freedom is not complete until zero taxes are due. Additional work is needed to implement the tax resolution plan.

The concept of "Taking Action" has been a key component of each step from the onset of the tax resolution process. The need for action and goal focused behavior continues as we proceed to follow up on the tax recommendations and make the concept of tax debt freedom a reality. In order to implement the tax resolution plan you must stay focused and stay on track with the LifeSpan Process of Tax Resolution and Financial Freedom.

Tax debt resolution is complicated by the fact that communicating and responding to the IRS can be quite challenging. The IRS requires specific forms, supporting documents, and payment methods. Simply put, you have to play by their rules and get things right the first time if you want to get out of debt as quickly as possible. I often find that this step can be one of the most frustrating steps for my clients due to the significant amount of patience and persistence that is required to implement the tax resolution plan. If you have followed the previous steps, implementing your tax plan will not be as frustrating and you will have a greater sense of control when following through with your action plan.

Getting out of any type of debt situation can be quite difficult. Tax debt is even more challenging due to the complex nature of the tax code and the IRS's authority to take aggressive collection measures. Many people have additional barriers to change related to procrastination and fear that further complicate their journey to tax freedom. If you are following the steps of the Tax Resolution and Financial Freedom process you have chosen a path that overcomes these obstacles. Your mission is to attack this tax debt using the best debt management option available for your financial situation. Staying focused on the immediate goal of tax freedom and the long-term goal of total financial freedom is a necessity.

There will be times that you may question yourself and wonder if you will ever get out of debt. Go ahead and remove any self-doubt. A deep rooted desire to get out of debt should help you stay on track with the commitment and resolve needed to use the positive financial behaviors needed to deal with the tax problem.

How long will the process take? The timing of tax debt elimination varies significantly from case to case and ultimately depends on your financial situation and how long it takes for the IRS to respond to your requests. Some people are able to find solutions that lead to tax freedom in just a few weeks. Other taxpayers may need years to conquer the battle against tax debt. There is simply no right or wrong time frame. But one thing is certain, if you follow the basic tax resolution steps your action plan you will accomplish your goals quicker than you normally would without structured a plan.

This section is designed to provide you with the basic implementation steps to help you completely eliminate tax debt and move toward financial freedom. There are three important components of the implementation stage. They are implementing the tax resolution recommendations, IRS compliance, and income tax planning.

The main goal of the implementation stage is to get rid of the tax problem as quickly and efficiently as possible. Tax resolution should also be done in such a way that smart financial decisions are made to avoid future tax problems from occurring. This is emphasized by the focus on IRS compliance and future tax planning.

Key Elements of Monitoring the Tax Resolution Plan:
- Implementing the tax resolution recommendations
- IRS Compliance
- Income Tax Planning

Implementing the Tax Resolution Recommendations

Now that you have identified the ideal tax resolution alternative (or combination of options) you are ready to follow through with your action plan. You will need to be very detail oriented regardless of the forms of paperwork required for your particular solution. This is an area where tax professionals can be very effective in assisting you through the tax resolution process. Keep in mind that the responsibility lies with you to provide the supporting documentation to process your paperwork with the IRS. You should refer to a CPA, Enrolled Agent, or tax attorney for more specific advice. The IRS website (www.irs.gov) is the source of this information. Refer to the appropriate IRS publications for more detailed information on implementing your tax resolution alternatives.

The most popular tax resolution alternatives include paying the IRS in full, establishing an Installment Agreement, requesting an Offer in Compromise, requesting Currently not Collectible status, or obtaining an Abatement of Penalties. The following guidelines should serve as a basic summary of IRS requirements for the most common tax resolution alternatives.

Tax Resolution Tip: Create a written tax resolution plan. Make a commitment to get out of tax troubles and achieve tax freedom. Put your goals in writing and be sure that if you are relying on a tax professional for guidance they specifically outline the services that will be provided.

IRS Payments

If you are paying in full using existing resources you first need to take the steps to obtain the necessary funds. You may also decide to pay down a portion of your tax debt using existing sources and pay the remaining balance using some of the alternatives listed below. The available resources were explored in detail during the previous tax resolution step. Your best alternative could involve a variety of techniques such as selling investment assets, refinancing a home, applying for a bank loan, or simply writing a check, to name a few. Once you have the funds available to pay the IRS you just need to make your payment to the IRS in a timely manner. The faster you are able to pay off your tax debt the less interest and penalties you will end up paying.

Instructions

When your funds are available you may choose to pay your tax liability electronically or by sending a check or money order made out to "United States Treasury". Electronic payments may be made by using the Electronic Federal Tax Payment System developed by the U.S. Department of the Treasury's Internal Revenue Service (IRS) and Financial Management Service (FMS). This service enables taxpayers to pay their federal taxes electronically online or over the phone. It's convenient, secure, and a timesaver. Log on to https://www.eftps.gov for more information regarding payment options.

Checks or money orders should be made payable to the United States Treasury. Do not forget to provide your correct name, address, Social Security number, daytime telephone number, tax year and form number (i.e., 2006 F-1040) on the front of your payment. If you are making a payment on a joint return provide the Social Security number that was listed first on the return. I should not have to add this final guideline, but you would be surprised what some people actually do. Never send the IRS CASH!!!

If you have a balance due on a recently filed tax return, use Form 1040-V, *Payment Voucher*. Enclose your payment and Form 1040–V with your Federal tax return. Do not staple or otherwise attach the payment or Form 1040–V to your return. Instead, just put them loose in the envelope. If you make a payment in person at an IRS office, keep the date stamped receipt as part of your records.

The IRS also suggests that you never mail estimated tax payments with checks or money orders meant for payment of current year Federal income tax. Mail your estimated tax payments separately to the address shown in the Form 1040- ES, *Estimated Tax for Individuals*.

Requesting an Offer in Compromise- Doubt as to Collectability

Determining whether or not you potentially qualify for an Offer in Compromise is based on the IRS view of your reasonable collection potential. That is the likelihood that they will be able to collect on any of the amount owed. The IRS has the responsibility of accepting or rejecting an offer. Every single Offer in Compromise is evaluated and decided based on the financial status of the individual taxpayer. Therefore, there is never a guarantee that anyone will qualify for an offer. Of course this is usually the option that most every taxpayer would like to be able to qualify for. Be honest with yourself and the IRS. Do not attempt an Offer in Compromise if you do not qualify. The previous tax resolution step (identifying tax resolution alternatives) should have already helped you determine if you are a candidate for the offer to reduce your tax liability.

Forms Required

IRS Form 656
IRS Form 433-A with supporting documents
IRS Form 433-B (Business Owners)

Instructions

Preparing an Offer in Compromise requires great attention to detail and thorough completion of the required paperwork. The OIC is essentially a deal between you and the government. In essence, this should be a win-win situation for both parties involved. The IRS gets a commitment from you, the delinquent taxpayer, to pay a portion of the original amount owed. As a result, they end up with as much of the original tax debt as they possibly can get based on your collection potential. In return you are back in compliance with IRS rules and regulations and have a higher likelihood of filing and paying taxes on time in the future. It is always in your best interests of paying taxes on time and filing future tax returns because the IRS can revoke your offer if you do not maintain compliance with IRS requirements.

On the other hand, as a taxpayer you also benefit by becoming compliant with IRS standards. The weight of a seemingly insurmountable pile of debt has been significantly reduced to a more manageable amount. As a compliant taxpayer you are now able to focus on other financial life planning goals and regain the ability to deal with future tax or financial matters without the fear of aggressive collection measures.

In order to submit an offer that has the highest chance of being accepted you need to follow the required steps. Many people have been rejected by the IRS simply due to the fact that they did not comply with the IRS requirements. Submitting your Offer in Compromise package correctly the first time will save you a significant amount of time and money.

Steps to Submitting an Offer in Compromise

1. **Determine if your offer is able to be processed**
   No open bankruptcy
   If you currently have an open bankruptcy proceeding, you are not eligible to have your offer considered or processed at this time. Any resolution of your outstanding tax liabilities generally must take place within the context of your bankruptcy proceeding.

   File all tax returns
   Have you filed all tax returns that you were required to file prior to submitting your offer?
   The IRS requires that you file all past due tax returns prior to the evaluation of your offer. This includes the following types of returns:
   - All Income Tax Returns
   - Employment Tax Returns
   - Excise Tax Returns
   In addition you must file additional returns required for partnerships, Limited Liability Companies, or closely held S- Corporations.

   Get up to date with employment taxes
   If you own a business with employees you are responsible for paying employment taxes. You must have made all required federal tax deposits for the current quarter. If you have not made your payroll tax deposits already, the IRS will ask you to do so before they will evaluate your offer. In addition, IRS requirements state that you must remain current with all filing and deposit requirements while your Offer in Compromise is being reviewed.

Estimated tax payments must be up to date for the current year

The IRS will not process your offer if you have not made estimated tax payments for the current year's tax liability. The IRS will give you an opportunity to make the required estimated tax payments before they will reject your offer.

2. **Complete Form 656 or Form 656-A (whichever is applicable)**

Form 656 is the official Offer in Compromise agreement. You must complete this form in its entirety and sign it. If you use a tax professional to assist you with the preparation of this form be sure to have your authorized representative complete form 2848, Power of Attorney and Declaration of Representation if you do not already have this form on file with the IRS.

Form 656-A is needed in order to claim to qualify as a lower income taxpayer. According to recent legislation, taxpayers who qualify as low-income or who are filing a doubt as to liability offer are not required to pay the application fee. Low-income taxpayers also do not have to meet the 20% payment requirement or make the initial required payments on a periodic short-term or deferred payment offer.

3. **Include the $150 application fee (or Form 656-A, Income Certification for Offer in Compromise Application Fee)**

The application fee for an Offer in Compromise is $150. As mentioned above, the application fee does not apply if your income falls at or below certain levels. Refer to the IRS Offers in Compromise Monthly Low Income Guidelines to see if you qualify to have your application fee amount waived.

4. **Include complete financial information (Form 433-A or Form 433-B, or both)**

The financial information required on Forms 433-A/B should not be a surprise to you if you thoroughly completed Step #5 of the Tax Resolution process. Since you have already gathered this information to determine if you are an offer candidate you should have a good idea what information is needed to send to the IRS. Complete Form 433-A and B (if needed) as accurately as possible and always have the supporting documentation available to prove your income and expenses.

5. **Attach cash payment and periodic payment offers**

You have three options to choose from when deciding among the potential terms of your offer. The best option for your situation depends on your available resources and the ability to pay the IRS in a timely manner. Be sure to choose the option that eliminates any chance of your offer being revoked simply because you are not able to consistently make timely payments. The three types of offer terms are lump sum cash offers, short-term periodic payment, and deferred periodic payment.

Lump Sum Cash Offer- Do NOT let the name fool you. When the IRS says "cash" they mean check or money order. Never send cash! This type of offer requires 20% of the offer amount to be sent with Form 656. The remaining balance must be paid in 5 or fewer installments. That means you must have the assets readily available to pay off your offer amount in full in less than 6 months time.

For example, if your offer amount was $10,000 you must send in at least $2,000 with your offer and Form 656. Assuming the IRS accepts your offer, you would then need to pay the remaining $8,000 in 5 or fewer installments. This could be done by sending an $8,000 check within 5 months of acceptance. You could even break the payments into $1,600 per month for the next 5 months after acceptance.

Short Term Periodic Payment Offer- This type of offer is paid within 24 months from the date the IRS received your offer. The initial payment must be submitted with IRS Form 656 and you must continue to make regular payments during the review of your offer.

Deferred Periodic Payment Offer- This type of offer allows you to make payments over the remaining life of the collection statute. Similar to the short term periodic offer, you must make regular payments while the offer is being investigated and you need to send in the initial payment with IRS Form 656.

Effective Tax Administration

If you are requesting an Offer in Compromise based on Effective Tax Administration you are stating the following to the IRS:

"I owe this amount and have sufficient assets to pay the full amount, but due to my exceptional circumstances, requiring full payment would cause an economic hardship or would be unfair and inequitable."

Forms Required

IRS Form 433-A
IRS Form 433-B (for business owners)
IRS Form 656 (Section VI)

Instructions

The IRS requires that you must provide accurate financial information when you submit and Offer in Compromise based on Effective Tax Administration. You will need to submit your financial information on Forms 433-A and 433-B (for business owners only). Be sure to send them current financial information that reflects your financial situation for three months immediately prior to the date you send in your offer. Collection information statements must show all assets and income. Any incomplete offer packages will be returned by the IRS. Refer to IRS Form 433-A and 433-B for a list of the required items that must be documented for the purposes of requesting an Offer in Compromise.

Additional Requirements

If you believe that you have special circumstances that affect your ability to fully pay the amount due to the IRS, explain your situation clearly on Form 656, Section VI. This Explanation of Circumstances form is your chance to convince the IRS that you are one of the very few people that actually qualify for an Offer in Compromise based on Effective Tax Administration. Additional sheets may be attached and supporting documentation such as medical diagnoses, disability, and evidence of financial hardship is also suggested.

Installment Agreements

Establishing a payment plan is the most common method of resolving tax debt when you do not have the funds readily available to pay the IRS in full and do not qualify for other tax resolution alternatives. An IRS Installment Agreement allows you to pay your tax debt in smaller, more manageable amounts. Actual Installment Agreement payments are based on the amount owed and your ability to pay that amount within the collection statute expiration date. This is the length of time the IRS can legally collect payment from you. The minimum payment amount is based on your monthly disposable income and the collection information statement (Form 433-A).

One major downside of an IRS payment plan is the tax debt continues to accrue interest and penalties on the unpaid portion of the debt. The trade off for being able to make smaller monthly payments is the fact that you will end up paying the IRS a significant amount of additional interest and penalties. Installment Agreements are still the best option available if you do not have sufficient assets available to pay your debt in full but do have positive monthly discretionary income to make monthly payments on the debt.

From a financial planning standpoint, your ability to make timely installment payments to the IRS depends on how successful you are in managing your day to day finances. Creating a personal spending plan, step #4 of the tax resolution process, is required prior to establishing an IRS Installment Agreement. You have to set aside money each month and plan how you will spend every dollar, including your payments to the IRS.

It is strongly recommended that you attempt to setup the lowest monthly payment possible. This gives you a margin of error should an unforeseen event or emergency occur that stretches your monthly budget too thin. Since you should be working to set aside a starter emergency fund you should be in the beginning stages of establishing and funding a savings account. However, it is always beneficial to have the lowest payment possible should your cash flow situation change.

One of the biggest mistakes that people make with an Installment Agreement is only paying the minimum required amount to the IRS. While you should attempt to setup the lowest monthly payment possible, you should always pay as much as you possibly can per month toward your Installment Agreement. Review your personal spending plan on an ongoing basis (at least once a month) to make sure that you are maximizing your tax debt payments.

The effects of interest and penalties
Are you aware that interest and penalties do not stop with an installment agreement/payment plan? In order to eliminate your tax debt you can save money by paying the full amount you owe as quickly as possible. Not only will you be able to redirect your money to more important life planning goals, but you will also be able to minimize the interest and penalties you will be charged. Penalties and interest will continue to be charged on the unpaid portion of the debt throughout the duration of the payment plan. Remember, the interest rate on some loans or credit card may be lower than the combination of penalties and interest imposed by the Internal Revenue Code.

Penalties and interest apply to years in which money is owed. The interest charged on late payments changes quarterly. During the last several years the interest rate has ranged from a high of 9 percent to a low of 4 percent. The interest rate for the calendar quarter beginning January 1, 2009 was 5% for underpayments by individuals. Do not forget to factor in penalties related to the underpayment of your taxes.

Filing Late Penalty
The penalty for filing late is generally 5 percent per month, or part of a month, up to 25 percent of the amount of the tax shown due on the return.
Paying Late Penalty
The penalty for paying late is 0.5 percent per month, up to 25 percent of the unpaid amount due.

While a payment plan with the IRS may seemingly be the only option to get out of tax debt for some taxpayers there are definite drawbacks. The biggest drawback is that interest and penalties continue to accrue while you still owe. Combined with penalties, the interest rate is often 8% to 10% per year. It is possible to pay for years and owe more than when you started. For planning purposes I generally tell our clients to expect a combined 12% to 14% in interest and penalties per year.

Tax Resolution Tip: If you are establishing an Installment Agreement with the IRS you must first establish a "Personal Spending Plan" that sets aside funds each month to pay off your tax debt. The amount that you send to the IRS should be above and beyond your required minimum Installment Agreement payment. You will get out of debt sooner by paying off more than the minimum monthly payments required by your IRS payment plan.

Installment Agreement Options

Guaranteed Installment Agreement- Your request for an installment agreement cannot be turned down if the tax you owe is not more than $10,000 and all three of the following conditions apply:

- During the past 5 tax years, you (and your spouse if filing a joint return) have timely filed all income tax returns, paid any income tax due, and have not entered into a previous Installment Agreement for payment of income tax.

- The IRS determines that you cannot pay the tax owed in full when it is due, after you have given the IRS any information needed to make that determination.

- You agree to pay the full amount you owe within 3 years and to comply with the tax laws while the agreement is in effect.

In some cases you may be able to setup an Installment Agreement over the phone by calling 1-800-829-1040.

Streamlined Installment Agreement- If you owe $25,000 or less of Income Tax or any tax of a business that has been closed, you may qualify for a streamline agreement. This type of agreement will allow you up to 5 years to pay the delinquent taxes without requiring extensive analysis of financial information.

Online Payment Agreement- According to the IRS about 75 percent of all taxpayers seeking an Installment Agreement can establish one using the Online Payment Agreement Application available at www.irs.gov. This is an extremely simple method of voluntarily resolving tax debt. Online Payment Agreements allows both taxpayers and their authorized representatives a quick and easy method of getting a payment plan approved by the IRS.

Other Installment Agreements – If you do not qualify for one of the above, an agreement may still be appropriate, but the terms will have to be negotiated with the IRS. The monthly payment amount will be based on an analysis of your financial data. The IRS will generally grant an Installment Agreement, but the terms can often be more severe than the taxpayer desires. When necessary, to get lower payments the taxpayer may request that the collection statute be extended for up to 5 years.

Partial Payment Installment Agreement (PPIA) –This type of Installment Agreement is a tax resolution option that allows taxpayers to make monthly payments toward their tax liability for the "life" of the collection statute. This is a different type of installment plan that allows taxpayers to pay what they can afford over their collection statute regardless of whether or not the liability is fully paid off when the statute expires.

Forms Required:
IRS Form 9465 (not required if you choose an online payment agreement or payroll deduction)
IRS Form 433-F or Form 433-A
IRS Form 433-B (Business owners)

Abatement of Penalties
The IRS has a variety of penalties designed to encourage voluntary compliance. Approximately 150 types of penalties exist that range from 5 percent (late filing and failure to pay penalties) to 100 percent (trust fund recovery penalty). It is possible that you could end up owing multiple penalties.

Current tax law allows the IRS to either remove or reduce tax penalties if the taxpayer has an acceptable reason. A penalty abatement request is a written explanation of the particular situation and should include as much supporting information as possible. The burden of proof is on you, the taxpayer, to establish reasonable cause. One common misconception is that the IRS routinely accepts abatement of penalty requests. In actuality, less than 13-15% of all penalties are actually abated by the IRS. If you have a reasonable cause for penalty abatement you should not let this low success ratio intimidate you. The IRS does have a heart and will use common sense if you present a legitimate explanation that falls within their guidelines of reasonable cause for penalty abatement.

If you are considering a request for penalty abatement you should go ahead and make arrangements to resolve your tax debt prior to your request. In most cases you must pay the tax liability in full or establish an Installment Agreement before the IRS will even consider an abatement of penalties request. Penalty abatement does not apply to interest, so do not expect any breaks from the IRS if interest has been assessed on a tax liability that you are legitimately responsible to pay.

If you are considering an abatement of penalties request it is generally advisable that you avoid paying excessive fees for a tax professional to make this request on your behalf. Many times the actual amount of penalties is less than the fees charged by some tax professionals and large tax representation firms to present your request. This is one area where using a professional may be helpful, but you should use caution if you are paying for this service.

Suggested Forms:
IRS Form 843 (Claim for Refund and Request for Abatement)
Instructions:
The IRS provides taxpayers with three different ways to request an Abatement of Penalties:

- IRS Form 843 - Usually a Form 843 is filed with a written "brief" or petition
- A written petition
- Verbally in person or over the telephone

IRS Form 843 is the official form that the IRS accepts for abatement of penalty requests. This form would be followed by a statement of the facts surrounding the case demonstrating the "reasonable cause" and " ordinary business care" and as much third party documentation of the facts.

Typically, a written petition will be comprised of a formally structured letter with an introduction and the request for penalty relief under which type of reasonable cause. This is the most common method, and the request usually goes directly to an appeals officer who generally has a larger scope of influence.

If you submit an abatement of penalty request and it is denied, you cannot make a request on the same grounds again. Therefore it is essential that you present the best case possible the first time around when you submit your request.

Currently Not Collectible Status

If a taxpayer is unable to pay his or her tax liability and collection activity would create an economic hardship, the IRS will consider placing the account in a "hardship", or currently not collectible status. Currently not collectible or "CNC Status" means that a taxpayer has no ability to pay his or her tax debts. The IRS can declare a taxpayer currently not collectible after they receive evidence that the taxpayer has no ability to pay.

In some cases taxpayers may have minimal equity in assets and still qualify for currently not collectible status. For example, a taxpayer could have equity in their home but be unable to access their home equity due to their financial situation. Such evidence is usually obtained from the taxpayer on IRS Form 433-A and 433-B (if applicable). A taxpayer can request "currently not collectible" status by submitting Form 433-A and Form 433-B to an IRS Revenue Officer or the IRS Automated Collection System unit. In some cases the IRS will accept Form 433-F, but I recommend that you send in the most comprehensive financial outlook as possible.

Once the IRS declares a taxpayer currently not collectible, the IRS must stop all collection activities, including levies and garnishments. The IRS must send an annual statement to the taxpayer stating the amount of tax still owed. This annual statement is not a bill.

It is important to note that being placed in "CNC" status is not a permanent solution to a tax problem. A taxpayer that is currently not collectible will have his or her status reviewed every 18 to 24 months by the IRS to determine if "hardship" status is still warranted. While in currently not collectible status, the 10-year statute of limitations on tax debt collection is still running. If the IRS cannot collect the tax within the 10-year statutory period, then the tax debts will expire.

Forms Required:

IRS Form 433-A
IRS Form 433-B (for business owners)
Instructions:
There are basically two different approaches to requesting to be place on currently not collectible status with the IRS:

- Telephone
- Written request

You can request currently not collectible status by telephone or by mailing a written request to the IRS. If you attempt to resolve your tax debt through a currently not collectible request you can call the IRS with your income and expense information readily available. An IRS representative will take your information over the telephone and may have the ability to place your accounts into currently not collectible status. You will most likely be required to send supporting information to the IRS documenting your financial status. You should be sure to write down the IRS representative's name and badge number so you can remember who you talked with about your CNC request.

You can also fill out IRS Form 433-A and send it to the IRS with a letter requesting to be placed on currently not collectible status. The letter should explain why you are unable to make monthly payments towards your tax debt. Send your request to the IRS at the address provided on the last letter that you received. Send your request by certified mail and request a return receipt. Keep these receipts in a safe place for future reference. These receipts are your proof that you mailed your request to the IRS, and that the IRS received your request.

The LifeSpan Process of Tax Resolution and Financial Freedom emphasizes accountability and taking control of your financial situation. Currently not collectible status should not be viewed as a permanent solution to the tax problem. This is based on the fact that interest and penalties continue to accumulate and the tax debt does not disappear. However, for individuals and families experiencing significant financial hardship it is an opportunity to use the tax and financial planning process to get organized and focus on basic living expenses until you are able to aggressively attack the tax debt head on. With our nation's current level of economic uncertainties it is expected that many Americans will need to be placed on currently not collectible status to allow them to regain financial stability.

Tax Compliance

Maintaining compliance with future tax obligations is a must for anyone seeking tax and financial freedom. If your tax resolution plan includes an Offer in Compromise or an Installment Agreement, you absolutely must remain compliant with filing your tax returns and paying your taxes on time for the next five years. Failure to do so may result in the IRS canceling your Offer in Compromise or Installment Agreement and demanding payment in full of your remaining tax liability. This may also result in aggressive collection activity such as wage garnishments, bank account levies and tax liens on your property.

The entire purpose of tax resolution planning is to eliminate tax debt and prevent future tax problems. Each step of the LifeSpan Process is designed to focus on tax and financial freedom. If you only treat the symptoms of tax debt you will never fully address the underlying problem. Thus, you will never truly be free from the cycle of debt until you consistently change your financial behaviors. If not corrected, you will eventually get back into tax or financial trouble.

Tax compliance does not have to be difficult. It basically comes down to two areas of concern-filing all future tax returns on time and paying your taxes on time. For people with a history of tax problems this can still be a major roadblock on the path to financial freedom. That is why you need to be proactive and have an income tax plan in place while you proceed through the steps of the tax planning process. Do not wait to resolve your past tax debt before you start planning to deal with future taxes. The earlier you establish a tax plan the more confident you will be while dealing with your tax problems.

In order to permanently stay out of trouble with the IRS you need to understand your tax compliance requirements. Tax compliance begins with filing your tax returns on time. File your income tax returns prior to the April 15th deadline. Avoid the temptation to file for an extension. There are some extenuating circumstances that require an extension. However, you should actually make an effort to try and file your returns well in advance of the filing deadline.

Pay your taxes on time. If employed you should review your W-4 to determine the proper exemption level for withholdings. Any excess tax withheld that would result in a refund may be applied to your outstanding tax liability. Try to avoid significant refunds. A tax refund may be viewed by some as a type of "forced" savings due to withholding excess taxes from your pay. It is also a quick way to admit that you do not have the ability to plan ahead.

Avoid withholding excessive taxes from your pay. Large tax refunds are not a sign of smart income tax planning. I admit that in the past I received many refund checks and was satisfied with my 0.0% rate of return. After realizing a need to assume total control of my tax and financial situation I began saving and actually started investing that same amount of excess withholdings throughout the course of the year. This is a great way to take control of your financial future. The IRS has a withholding calculator available through their Internet website to assist you with determining the proper exemption level for withholdings. It can be accessed at www.irs.gov/individuals.

Estimated Taxes

If you are self-employed you are responsible for paying the self-employment tax. Any individual who is self-employed, retired, laid-off, or disabled, is responsible for filing and paying Federal estimated quarterly taxes and in states having a state income tax, for filing and paying State estimated quarterly taxes. This can be very different from the taxation that takes place while you are employed. First of all, the term "estimated quarterly taxes" is not exactly accurate. The IRS publishes a schedule that jumps around a little. The first payment for a tax year is due April 15. The second payment is due June 15, and the third payment is due September 15. The last payment is due January 15 of the next year. So the payment schedule is more like 3½ months, 2 months, 3 months and 4 months in making up the Federal estimated quarterly tax payments. The intent, however, is each payment represents ¼ of what you will owe for the year.

It takes discipline to plan and set aside funds for tax payments throughout the year, especially when the individual or married couple is managing their own income. If sufficient funds are not set aside as income is earned, then the individual or married couple will be put in a situation where some assets might have to be liquidated in order to come up with enough money to pay the taxes. An easier method is for the individual or married couple to know what their approximate Federal and State tax rates are and to apply those rates to income as it is earned. The calculated taxes should be set-aside in a separate interest bearing account until it is time to pay the estimated tax payments.

The IRS allows for two basic methods of calculating estimated taxes. An individual or married couple (if filing jointly) can either elect to pay an amount based on the total taxes paid in the previous year or pay at least 90% of the estimated taxes that will be due in the current year. Remember, in either situation, the amounts paid are only for estimated taxes and the actual tax due will probably differ from the total of estimated taxes actually paid. If electing to pay based on the prior year, the IRS allows you to calculate your amount and to then spread that amount into four equal payments, paying them on the estimated tax due dates. Example: A married couple filed a joint return and the previous year's total income was $160,000. The IRS formula is 100% of the prior year income if the income is less than $150,000 or 110% if greater than $150,000. If the couple paid Federal taxes of $42,000 last year on income of $160,000, this year's estimated taxes would be $42,000 X 1.10 = $46,200. The estimated quarterly tax payments would be $11,550 due on each estimated tax installment date.

If you to pay at least 90% of the estimated tax due during the current year, then you must keep track of income received during the year and make sure the total estimated taxes paid by the time the last installment is paid equals 90% of the actual tax that will be due at filing time. (This should be easy to do, even if the first three installments were insufficient, as the last installment date is January of the next calendar year. This allows you to adjust the last payment for any unexpected income.) Failure to pay at least 90% of the tax due will result in a penalty being assessed on the amounts failing to meet the 90%

level. Keep in mind, the 90% option is just that, 90% of the actual tax that will be due by the April 15th filing date. If you just meet the 90% amount, then the remaining 10% due will have to be paid with the final filing.

One surprise people discover when electing the 90% option is that the date of the first payment due in the next year and the annual filing from the last year coincide. Thus, not only is the estimated quarterly payment due for the current year, but any remaining balance owed from the prior year, such as the 10% not paid due to electing the 90% rule, will be due with the year end filing for the prior year. If funds were not set aside coming up with the monies to pay these taxes can be challenging. Keep in mind, these rules apply to both Federal and State taxes if your state has an income tax.

Set up a separate savings or money market account to accumulate funds on a regular basis to pay your estimated taxes. This will help you consistently set aside money to pay your taxes and avoid future tax debt and additional interest and penalties.

Basic Income Tax Planning for the Future

"If you make any money, the government shoves you in the creek once a year with it in your pockets, and all that don't get wet you can keep." – Will Rogers

Income Tax Planning: Understanding the Basics

The foundation of the Tax Resolution and Financial Freedom is financial behavior change and the ability to plan and take positive action. Procrastination and fear related to basic tax and money-related issues are replaced by planning. The tax and financial planning process is designed to help you make the most of your money.

Tax Planning carries an important role in the financial planning process. A solid income tax plan is generally more important for individuals experiencing problems related to past due tax liabilities. Income tax planning should not be confused with the tax resolution process, although the two typically go hand in hand. The biggest difference is the primary focus of tax resolution deals with a past due tax liability. Income tax planning seeks ways to help taxpayers reduce or eliminate their income tax burden for the future.

Once the implementation phase has been reached you should have your tax resolution plan on cruise control. A major life challenge (dealing with tax debt) is now replaced with the need to stay out of tax trouble while remaining compliant with IRS requirements. Another challenge is to minimize your federal income tax liability through proactive income tax planning.

By no means is this section meant to be a comprehensive income tax planning review. You should contact a tax professional or educate yourself about tax planning in general if you need more specific advice. Consider this a starter course that emphasizes the basic foundation. As part of the Tax Resolution and Financial Freedom process it is highly recommended that you have at least a basic understanding of the tax planning process. In doing so you will be able to take control of your future tax concerns and accomplish the following goals and objectives:

- Establish improved confidence in your ability to take control of future tax filing and payment requirements
- Minimize current income tax liability
- Utilize all relevant deductions and adjustments to income
- Invest more money toward life planning goals

- Understand your marginal income tax bracket

Taking Control of Your Income Tax Planning
It is no surprise that most Americans dread April 15th when the deadline looms for filling out federal and state income tax returns. On the surface, learning the tax code can appear more complicated than learning a new language. In fact, sometimes I read the tax code and wonder if the IRS is speaking English. Have you ever vowed to yourself at tax time that you will be better prepared "next year" only to experience the exact same frustration when next year arrives? It is becoming a popular New Year's resolution for people to promise themselves that they will do a better job at maintaining accurate records and getting organized, or that they will pay closer attention to possible tax-saving measures. Unfortunately, many people simply do not follow through with that commitment.

Experiencing a tax problem and seeking redemption through the tax resolution process provides taxpayers with an opportunity to take control of their income tax planning. Instead of being a typical taxpayer and waiting for the deadline to arrive, you should plan ahead and file your tax returns prior to the April 15th deadline. Most importantly, you should file those tax returns with confidence that you are in control of your financial destiny. You may even decide to go ahead and schedule your own deadline of March 15th or April 1st and hold yourself accountable to a self-imposed deadline to defeat the temptations of procrastination. If everything goes smoothly you should celebrate your step toward total tax freedom.

Whether or not you choose to use the services of a tax professional is a personal decision and depends on your individual level of confidence with tax matters. For most taxpayers with a history of recent tax problems I suggest the use of professional tax preparation services for at least a couple of years. At a minimum you should at least use some type of tax preparation software to assist with the process. Turbo Tax, Tax Wise, and Tax Cut are some of the most popular software programs that my clients have used successfully to help prepare tax returns.

Tax planning is more than just trying to reduce your overall taxes. Income tax planning decisions should always be part of your overall financial life plan. Always coordinate tax planning with your comprehensive financial planning goals and objectives. Holistic tax planning requires a deeper focus than just trying to lower taxes. Tax reduction is great. However, it is more meaningful when used in conjunction with bigger picture planning.

Income Tax Planning Is a Year-Round Effort
Preparing income tax returns and following an income tax plan are two separate things. Focusing on filing deadlines is essential to maintain compliance with IRS requirements. What most people forget to realize is the fact that income tax planning is a year-round effort. The April 15th filing deadline is only one day of the year. Tax planning is more than just filing a tax return. The goal of income tax planning is to take control of your finances while minimizing the impact of taxes. There are basic steps of the income tax planning process that you should focus on.
- Get Organized
- Reduce Taxable Income
- Understand your Marginal Income Tax Rate
- Maximize Deductions
- Claim available tax credits

Get organized

For many taxpayers this is the hardest part of the tax planning process. It is very difficult to manage your taxes and money if you have no clue where your most important financial documents are located. Go ahead and create a file for records you will need at tax time. Many stationery or office supply stores sell notebooks with separate pockets for various tax-related items. You can also be creative and save some money by creating your own categories. Start by filing your pay stubs from work. Do not wait until your employer issues a W-2 income and withholding statement at the end of the year to determine your taxable income. Track your income as the year progresses by keeping your own running total of all income and withholding. These figures will provide a general idea of your projected taxes at the end of the year.

Remember to include all sources of income such as dividends, bonuses, stock sales and any part-time earnings when computing income. A quarterly review of your tax situation will allow you to see where you stand from a tax standpoint. At a minimum you should at least review your tax plan midway through the tax year at the end of June. If you are on track to earn more, or withhold less taxes than the previous year, it could mean that you will owe more money at tax time. If you catch any withholding issues early during the tax year there might still be time to adjust your withholding at the company where you work. On the other hand, a big refund means you have given the government an interest-free loan all year.

Get in the habit of saving and filing receipts for your purchases and charitable contributions. If you have any dependent care expenses you should also keep those records. Contributions to qualifying charities will probably be deductible. Be sure to keep track of your non-cash donations of clothing and household goods. Medical and dental costs, including prescription medicines, may qualify for tax deductions, depending on the amount. Similarly, other types of expenditures may be deductible if they meet specific criteria. Keeping track of what you spend will help in setting up a personal spending plan, even if expenses are not deductible.

If you are self-employed or earn 1099 income as an independent contractor you need to have an understanding of your net self-employment income throughout the tax year. Getting organized as a self-employed individual requires tracking all business income and expenses. I highly recommend using professional bookkeeping software such as QuickBooks to organize business finances. At a minimum you should at least set up a spreadsheet on Excel or other software programs to track your income and expenses related to self-employment. A separate banking account for business transactions is also highly recommended for anyone who is self-employed.

Understand Marginal Income Tax Rate

There are two types of tax rates you need to be aware of. They are the average tax rate (also called the effective rate) and the marginal income tax rate. The effective tax rate is the average tax that you pay based on your total taxable income. This figure is calculated by dividing the total amount of taxes paid by your taxable income. For example, if a married couple paid $15,000 in taxes with taxable income of $100,000 they would have an effective tax rate of 15% ($15,000/$100,000 = .15)

The marginal income tax rate is the percentage of tax that you pay on the last dollar of taxable income. For example, let's say the same married couple filed jointly with $100,000 taxable income owes $15,000 in federal taxes. Their average tax rate is 15%. However, the marginal income tax rate would actually be 25% meaning that any additional income would be taxed at that level.

Reducing Taxable Income

One of the easiest ways to reduce your income taxes is to reduce taxable income. For tax planning purposes you need to be aware of your Adjusted Gross Income (AGI). This is your income from all sources minus certain adjustments. Never overlook adjustments to your income. Some of the most common adjustments to income include deductible IRAs, tuition and fees, student loan interest, and alimony paid. Other adjustments to income include educator expenses, health savings account deductions, moving expenses, self-employed health insurance deductions, and one-half of the self-employment tax. These deductions do not have to be itemized to lower your taxable income.

The concept is fairly straightforward. The less money you make, the lower taxes you will have to pay. Therefore, it only makes sense that lowering your income through various financial planning techniques will help your tax situation. Some tax reduction techniques should be viewed as long-term goals as you progress through the steps of tax resolution. Others can be taken advantage of immediately.

Flexible Spending Arrangements

One example of a tax reduction technique is called a Flexible Spending Account (FSA). Employers have the option of providing this valuable feature to their employees as part of a cafeteria plan. FSAs allow people to set aside money for qualified expenses such as medical, dental, or dependent care. If you are already spending out of pocket money on health care or dependent care and your employer offers an FSA, then you should participate in this tax-advantaged account. The contributions are made with pre-tax money and will lower your taxable income. For example, if someone with a 25% marginal income tax rate makes a $2,000 annual contribution to a health care FSA they could reduce their taxes by $500.

Be careful when choosing how much to contribute to an FSA. These accounts have a use it or lose it feature that requires plan contributions to be used by March 15th of the following year. As always, budgeting and following a spending plan is important when determining how much should be contributed to a Flexible Spending Account for health care or dependent care expenses.

Save for Retirement

Contributing to a retirement savings plan at work or through your own business is an excellent way to reduce your taxable income. Unfortunately, saving for retirement generally should not be done until tax resolution has been achieved. This also means that you should not aggressively set aside funds for retirement until all tax debt has been eliminated, you have zero high-interest consumer debt, and an emergency fund is in place. There is one exception to this general rule. If your employer offers matching contributions for 401(k) or other retirement plan contributions you should contribute up to the matching amount (but no more). The final stages of the Tax Resolution and Financial Freedom Process will explain more about retirement savings options. Needless to say, pre-tax retirement contributions are an excellent tax reduction strategy that should be part of a long-term tax plan.

Keep in mind that you are not escaping taxation. You are only postponing it until you make retirement withdrawals. There is a good possibility that you may be in a lower tax bracket by then, and often more important, tax-deferred accounts can grow faster than comparable taxable investments.

Sell losing investments

If you have any investments that have lost money during the course of the year consider selling them. Capital losses from one investment gain can be used to offset any gains from another investment. You can use up to $3,000 ($1,500 for married persons filing separately) in capital losses to reduce your income. Based on the recent performance of the stock market most people with stock market investments have experienced losses. If you are selling investments to help pay down tax debt you should consider taking advantage of the capital loss rules to reduce your future income taxes as much as possible.

Shifting Income
Another method of reducing taxable income is to shift income from taxable investments to tax-exempt investments such as municipal bonds. The use of this strategy must make economic sense as well as be a smart decision from a tax planning standpoint. If you are self-employed or own a business you can shift income from a higher tax bracket to a lower tax bracket by hiring your children (they must actually perform work).

Maximizing Deductions
Nearly two out of three taxpayers take the standard deduction on their tax returns. If you are able to itemize deductions then do so because it will reduce your taxes. Be sure to take advantage of all potential itemized deductions. This is where good recordkeeping and getting organized is important. For the 2008 tax year the standard deduction is $10,900 for married taxpayers filing jointly ($11,400 in 2009). Single taxpayers have a standard deduction of $5,450 ($5,700 in 2009). Taxpayers filing head of household use a standard deduction of $8,000 ($8,350). Mortgage interest, charitable deductions, taxes paid, and health care expenses are some of the most common itemized deductions.

Claiming all available tax credits
Tax credits reduce the tax liability (rather than taxable income) dollar for dollar. Thus, a $500 tax credit saves $500 in taxes. Each tax credit is computed differently. To find out about credits that may affect your taxes, consult a tax professional or research the availability and computation of any credits you may be eligible to use. During the tax planning process you should identify whether or not you are eligible for any of the following tax credits:

- Child and dependent care credit
- Child tax credit
- Earned income credit
- Education credits
- Adoption tax credit
- Tax credit for the elderly or the disabled
- Foreign tax credit
- Tax credit for IRAs and retirement plans
- Tax credit for health insurance costs (qualifying individuals only)
- Alternative fuel (or clean fuel) vehicle credit
- Tax credits for making energy-efficient improvements to a primary residence (or for the purchase of a qualified energy-efficient property)
- First time home buyer tax credit (currently set to expire June 30, 2009)

For more information on the requirements to qualify for these tax credits you should visit www.irs.gov or contact your tax and financial planning professional.

Tax Saving Tips for Small Business Owners

If you own a small business or are self-employed as an independent contractor you need to make the most of your business planning opportunities. This list is intended to help self-employed people take advantage of as many tax saving opportunities as possible.

1. Mileage
   Self-employed people can claim vehicle mileage on personally owned vehicles that are used for business purposes. The mileage deduction during the 2009 tax year is 55 cents per mile. Always keep accurate records that include the beginning and ending odometer readings, total miles driven, and business purpose of the trip.

2. Home office deductions
   If you use a home office and do not have another office location available you can use many utility expenses as business expense deductions.

3. Travel, Meals, and entertainment
   A portion of travel, meals and entertainment expenses can be written off as long as they are for valid business purposes.

4. Vehicle and equipment depreciation
   Most business equipment must be depreciated over either five or seven years. However, there is a special break available to most small business owners. The section 179 deduction allows for an immediate write-off for up to $250,000 of equipment purchases during the 2009 tax year.

5. Self-employed health insurance
   Certain small business owners may qualify for the self-employed health insurance deduction. This enables you to deduct up to 100 percent of the cost of health insurance payments for yourself, spouse, and dependents. This is an above the line deduction which means that it is available whether or not you itemize deductions.

6. Health Savings Accounts (HSA)
   An HSA is a tax-exempt account that is used in conjunction with a high deductible health insurance plan. Contributions to a health savings account reduce your taxable income while setting aside tax-free funds to cover health care expenses. HSA contributions are also deductible as "above the line deductions" on your federal Form 1040.

7. S Corporation
   Structuring a business with an S Corporation taxation election can potentially lower taxes. Using this structure you could pay yourself a reasonable salary that is lower than your net self-employment income. The remainder of your income could be taken as dividends, which are not subject to the self-employment tax.

8. Telephone, cell phones, and pagers
   Many small business owners overlook these expenses. If you use qualifying forms of communication equipment in your business you should include them when calculating business expenses.

9. Tax Planning and Professional Fees
   Legal, tax resolution, and tax preparation fees are potentially deductible business expenses.

Income Taxes: The Basics

Three Types of Income

Earned Income	Portfolio Income	Passive Income
• Salary, Bonus • Commissions • Business Income • Up to 85% of Social Security	• Dividends • Interest • Royalties • Capital Gains or Losses on Portfolio Assets	• Limited Partnership Income • Rental Income • Capital Gains on Passive Activities

Adjustments

Contributions to FSAs Student Loan Interest Alimony
Contributions to IRAs One-half of SE tax Early withdrawal
SEP/SIMPLE Plans SE Health Insurance penalty
Tuition and Fees Moving Expenses Educator Expenses

Adjusted Gross Income

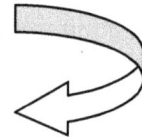

$_____

Itemized Deductions (Subtract from AGI)

$_____

- Medical expenses over 7.5% of AGI
- State and local property taxes
- State income or sales taxes
- Mortgage interest on 1st and 2nd residences, investment interest
- Charitable contributions
- Miscellaneous deductions (most must exceed 2% of AGI)
- OR, use the standard deduction

Minus

Equals

Less: Available Credits

Tax Due

Personal Exemptions

$_____

Taxable Income

$_____

Tax Determined From Schedules

$_____

$_____

$_____

Federal Income Tax Tables- 2008

Filing Status	Taxable Income is Between		Taxes Owed	Plus	Marginal Tax Rate on Excess over 1st Column
Single Taxpayers	$0 -	$8,025	$0.00		10.0%
	8,025 -	32,550	802.50		15.0%
	32,550 -	78,850	4,481.25		25.0%
	78,850 -	164,550	16,056.25		28.0%
	164,550 -	357,700	40,052.25		33.0%
	357,700 -	Higher	103,791.75		35.0%
Married Filing Jointly	$0 -	$16,050	$0.00		10.0%
	16,050 -	65,100	1,605.00		15.0%
	65,100 -	131,450	8,962.50		25.0%
	131,450 -	200,300	25,550.00		28.0%
	200,300 -	357,700	44,828.00		33.0%
	357,700 -	Higher	96,770.00		35.0%
Married Filing Separately	$0 -	$8,025	$0.00		10.0%
	8,025 -	32,550	802.50		15.0%
	32,550 -	65,725	4,481.25		25.0%
	65,725 -	100,150	12,775.00		28.0%
	100,150 -	178,850	22,414.00		33.0%
	178,850 -	Higher	48,385.00		35.0%
Head of Household	$0 -	$11,450	$0.00		10.0%
	11,450 -	43,650	1,145.00		15.0%
	43,650 -	112,650	5,975.00		25.0%
	112,650 -	182,400	23,225.00		28.0%
	182,400 -	357,700	42,755.00		33.0%
	357,700 -	Higher	100,604.00		35.0%

Example: John and Elizabeth are married filing jointly. Their taxable income is $75,000. The marginal income tax rate is 25%.

Married Filing Jointly

Taxable Income: $75,000
Tax on the 1st Column: 65,100   is $8,962.50
Tax on the Remaining Amount: 9,900   x 25.0% =   2,475.00
                                                  11,437.50

Federal Income Tax Tables- 2009

Filing Status	Taxable Income is Between		Taxes Owed	Plus	Marginal Tax Rate on Excess over 1st Column
Single Taxpayers	$0 -	$8,350	$0.00		10.0%
	8,350 -	33,950	835.00		15.0%
	33,950 -	82,250	4,675.00		25.0%
	82,250 -	171,550	16,750.00		28.0%
	171,550 -	372,950	41,754.00		33.0%
	372,950 -	Higher	108,216.00		35.0%
Married Filing Jointly	$0 -	$16,700	$0.00		10.0%
	16,700 -	67,900	1,670.00		15.0%
	67,900 -	137,050	9,350.00		25.0%
	137,050 -	208,850	26,637.50		28.0%
	208,850 -	372,950	46,741.50		33.0%
	372,950 -	Higher	100,894.50		35.0%
Married Filing Separately	$0 -	$8,350	$0.00		10.0%
	8,350 -	33,950	835.00		15.0%
	33,950 -	65,725	4,675.00		25.0%
	68,525 -	100,150	13,318.75		28.0%
	104,425 -	186,475	23,370.75		33.0%
	186,475 -	Higher	50,447.25		35.0%
Head of Household	$0 -	$11,950	$0.00		10.0%
	11,950 -	45,500	1,195.00		15.0%
	45,500 -	117,450	6,227.50		25.0%
	117,450 -	190,200	24,215.00		28.0%
	190,200 -	372,950	44,585.00		33.0%
	372,950 -	Higher	104,892.50		35.0%

Example: John and Elizabeth are married filing jointly. Their taxable income is $75,000. The marginal income tax rate is 25%.

Married Filing Jointly

Taxable Income:	$75,000		
Tax on the 1st Column:	67,900	is	$9,350.00
Tax on the Remaining Amount:	7,100	x 25.0% =	1,775.00
			11,125.00

Summary

Comprehensive tax and financial planning is a year round effort. When working with a financial planner you need to agree in advance who will monitor the progress toward your goals. You also need to determine how often you should review your financial situation. Some important areas of concern include income tax planning, IRS compliance, monitoring savings and investments, asset allocation reviews, and debt management. Periodic reviews will allow you to make adjustments to your plan as is needed. Monitoring the tax resolution recommendations can provide assurance that you are moving toward your life goals as they relate to your finances.

The primary objective during the tax resolution process is to get out of tax debt using the most cost-effective method. The previous steps of the tax and financial process led to a thorough tax resolution analysis. This helped us identify the best alternatives to deal with the tax liabilities. A tax resolution plan would be meaningless unless it actually leads to real results. The end result that everyone should be seeking is tax resolution (or freedom from tax debt). It is no surprise that the final step focuses on implementing the tax resolution plan.

Throughout the tax resolution phase we have discussed the "process" of dealing with tax and financial problems. The process takes time and patience to see real results. Just how long the process will take you depends on your unique financial position. It also depends on how much work you put into your financial life plan. If you are seeking tax freedom you must be 100 percent committed to changing how you deal with taxes and money. Being proactive and following a plan to the best of your abilities will undoubtedly lead to financial success.

Tax resolution planning requires more than simply focusing on eliminating past due taxes. The best tax resolution strategy is to stay on track with future tax obligations and maintain compliance with future filing and payment requirements. Future tax compliance requires a basic understanding of income tax planning. From the beginning we explored the importance of replacing problematic financial behaviors with positive ones. Following through with an income tax plan puts you in control of your finances. A holistic plan will also help you see the "big picture." Every financial decision you make can potentially affect other aspects of your financial life. Most importantly, the tax and financial plan will help you get out of tax debt and stay out of debt while allowing you to pursue the ultimate goal of financial freedom.

Starting the Transition- Tax Resolution to Financial Freedom

The tax resolution process often requires a great deal of planning and persistence. An incredible amount of patience and commitment is also necessary. It usually takes months to years to completely get out of tax debt. The timing depends on the actual amount of your tax debt and the resources that you have available. Tax freedom is the result of changing your approach to money and taxes. When you have finally eliminated tax problems from your life you will find yourself in an excellent position to start taking the next steps to total financial freedom.

The lessons and behaviors that are used during the six steps of the tax resolution process should prove to be a strong foundation for the journey to financial freedom. This is a reason why most traditional financial planning approaches should not be used until a tax resolution plan is in place and tax problems have been dealt with in the most effective manner possible.

You have to follow the steps to tax freedom before you can begin concentrating on the financial freedom process. It does not hurt to go ahead and start thinking about long-term financial life planning goals. In fact, establishing financial life planning goals and objectives gives meaning to the entire tax resolution process. Dealing with IRS tax problems is only one part of a bigger challenge. You can use these objectives to provide the motivation needed to continue along the path to tax resolution. The end result will be a newfound sense of confidence as you deal with future tax and financial issues.

By now you should have adopted new financial behaviors that will serve as the building blocks for your journey to financial independence. Let's review these action steps before we continue to the next stage of financial freedom. The primary action steps are included on the next page. Remember to follow each step one at a time and stay committed to the pursuit of tax and financial freedom. Following the steps of the LifeSpan Process of Tax Resolution will enable you to take control of your financial future and eliminate tax debt from your life. You should also be able to manage your personal finances with more confidence and prevent future tax problems from occurring. The pursuit of financial independence begins after you deal with the IRS and resolve your tax problems with a plan.

Tax Resolution Action Steps

		Task Completed	Target Date	Date Done
1.	Take control of your tax problems and your financial future by making a commitment to change. Take action!	❑		
2.	Establish financial life planning goals that define the purpose of your tax resolution journey.	❑		
3.	Assess your own ability and desire to improve your financial destiny. Identify personal strengths and weaknesses.	❑		
4.	Determine whether or not you will be using the services of a tax resolution professional.	❑		
5.	Complete a cash flow analysis.	❑		
6.	Complete a net worth analysis.	❑		
7.	Establish a personal spending plan	❑		
8.	Establish a starter emergency fund of at least $500-$1,000	❑		
9.	Discontinue any current savings or investment plans until your tax debt has been resolved (Note: If you participate in a retirement savings plan at work and your employer matches contributions you may still contribute up to the matching amount.)	❑		
10.	Determine the actual amount of your tax debt. File any past due tax returns (if needed).	❑		
11.	Complete a Tax Resolution Analysis to determine the best solution to pay off your tax liability.	❑		
12.	Implement your tax resolution plan. Pay off your tax debt as quickly as possible.	❑		
13.	Stay compliant with IRS requirements by filing all future tax returns on time, paying the amount due, and staying current with any estimated tax or payroll tax obligations.	❑		
14.	Minimize the impact of current and future taxes by following an income tax plan. Take control of your taxes and your money through the consistent us of a comprehensive tax and financial plan. Enjoy Tax Freedom!	❑		

Part III: Financial Freedom

Tax Planning for the Future
Starting the Transition- Tax Resolution to Financial Freedom

Part III: Financial Freedom

Step 1: Eliminate Consumer Debt

Step 2: Establish an Emergency Fund

Step 3: Review Life Planning Goals and Objectives

Step 4: Protect Yourself, Property, and the Ones you Love: Life Insurance and Estate Planning

Step 5: Investment Planning: Reaching Life Planning Goals
Retirement Savings
Education Planning

Step 6: Eliminate all Forms of Debt

Step 7: Identify Other Financial Planning Opportunities
Planned Major Purchases
Business Planning
Charitable Giving

Financial Freedom
Step #1: Eliminate Consumer Debt

The only man who sticks closer to you in adversity than a friend is a creditor. ~ Author Unknown

The rich ruleth over the poor, and the borrower is servant to the lender. ~ Proverbs 22:7

Today, there are three kinds of people: the have's, the have-not's, and the have-not-paid-for-what-they-have's. ~ Earl Wilson

Tax resolution refers to resolving tax problems the most effective way possible based on each person's unique financial position. Tax freedom is the ability to not only resolve a tax problem but to deal with the underlying problems related to the past history of ineffective tax planning.

The previous section was solely dedicated to dealing with tax problems. That high level of attention is due to the fact that IRS and state tax liabilities are barriers that block the ability to achieve important life planning goals. If someone owes back taxes they cannot truly reach a state of financial freedom until they have freedom from their tax problems. Therefore, the comprehensive financial planning process cannot begin until the tax resolution process has been completed.

What does the term "financial freedom" mean to you? The LifeSpan Process of Tax and Financial Freedom is designed to empower smart financial decision making. The concept of tax and financial freedom has a different meaning for every individual that decides to follow the tax resolution process. It is up to each individual to define what freedom means to him or her personally. The LifeSpan Process simply defines financial freedom as the ability to take control of your financial life and to integrate current and future financial resources into your overall life plan.   Every individual going through the tax resolution process is encouraged to come up with his or her own unique definition of "financial freedom".

The tax resolution process can be a difficult and time consuming task to undertake. Once you have accomplished the initial goal of tax freedom you can take the next step toward financial freedom, however you choose to define your financial freedom. Use the same positive financial behaviors that you are working on developing to guide you through this next phase of the tax and financial planning process. The same passion and motivation that was needed to eliminate tax debt needs to be harnessed in order to attack other forms of problematic debt. As we transition from tax resolution to focusing on financial freedom we immediately continue our quest to attack the issue of debt in general.

Continuing the Journey
The steps of the tax resolution process follow an overall plan that leads to tax freedom. Financial freedom is accomplished in a similar manner. By taking a step by step approach you can assume complete control of your life as it relates to money. It is much easier to reach important life goals with a plan. Staying focused and on track will allow you to reach your tax and financial planning goals as quickly as possible. The next part of the journey to financial freedom focuses on establishing a debt reduction plan.

Getting Started
You must achieve tax freedom before proceeding with the first step of the financial freedom process. This means you need to be 100% tax debt free and have a plan in place to stay out of tax troubles. A personal spending plan should already be in place, and you must also have a starter emergency fund of at least $500-$1,500. If you do not have at least $500 in a starter emergency fund you need to make this a top priority prior to starting an aggressive debt elimination plan.

As a note of warning, it is important to realize that many people with tax problems end up getting back into tax troubles or have other financial struggles because they fail to follow a financial plan once their tax debt has been resolved. Tax resolution is part of a bigger life challenge. Avoiding the temptation to skip a step will keep you on track to reach both tax and financial freedom. You will walk on dangerous ground financially if you do not have a plan to eliminate other forms of problematic debt after your tax liabilities have been resolved.

Debt Reduction Planning

Tax debt really does not like to travel alone. Usually it is accompanied by other forms of debt such as credit cards, vehicle loans, installment loans, and student loans. Remember the motto that we discussed during the tax resolution section. "Debt is dumb. Tax debt is dumber. Dealing with tax debt without a plan is pure stupidity." Similarly, dealing with other forms of debt requires a well thought out action plan.

The primary reason to focus on resolving tax debt in the first place is because the IRS is generally the most important creditor to pay off. Tax debt is one of the most problematic types of debt. The IRS has the ability to take aggressive collection measures and can make your life miserable if you do not address tax debt. Interest and penalties related to tax debt are often more punitive than most credit cards. When the IRS actually tells taxpayers on its website to use alternatives to Installment Agreements it is usually a sign that you need to be careful when selecting among tax resolution alternatives.

Other forms of debt such as credit cards, installment loans, and high interest consumer debt (e.g., vehicle loans) can be just as damaging financially speaking as tax debt. Once you have eliminated tax debt you need to determine which form of debt to payoff next. You also need to have a written plan in place to guide your efforts to get out of debt. The written document that is used to guide the debt reduction process is generally referred to as a debt elimination plan.

Disturbing Statistics about Credit Use
- On average, today's consumer has a total of 13 credit obligations on record at a credit bureau. These include credit cards (such as department store charge cards, gas cards, and bank cards) and

installment loans (auto loans, mortgage loans, student loans, etc.). Not included are savings and checking accounts (typically not reported to a credit bureau). Of these 13 credit obligations, nine are likely to be credit cards and four are likely to be installment loans. (Source: myfico.com)

- 55 percent of credit card users keep a balance on their credit card, up 2 percent from 2007. (Source: ComScore, September 2008)

- The average American with a credit file is responsible for $16,635 in debt, excluding mortgages, according to Experian. (Source: U.S. News and World Report, "The End of Credit Card Consumerism," August 2008)

- According to Experian, the average American with a credit file is responsible for $16,635 in debt, excluding mortgages.

- Approximately 51 percent of the U.S. population has at least two credit cards. (Source: Experian national score index study, February 2007)

- The average family today carries $8,000 in credit card debt according to the American Bankers' Association.

Choosing your priorities

Financial uncertainties are not uncommon during the course of the planning process. Be prepared for setbacks and frustration as you embark on the important mission of eliminating debt from your life. If you are struggling to get on track financially it can be difficult to determine who to pay first if you have multiple creditors knocking on your door. Some forms of debt are higher priority items that others. If you are overwhelmed by debt and your expenses exceed your income, you may find yourself in a difficult position of trying to choose who to pay off and who to put off until later. There are some basic guidelines that you should follow until your cash flow situation improves.

One basic rule of thumb is to always pay off creditors who can take the quickest action to damage you, not those who are calling you the most often. Pay your basic expenses such as mortgage or rent first; worry about credit card or doctor bills later. Once your financial situation stabilizes you will be in the position attack your debt. It is important that you understand the debt hierarchy when determining which debts to focus on first.

Choosing who to pay off first

If you have multiple creditors (and most people do) you may need to prioritize which creditor to pay off first. This is especially important if your expenses currently exceed your income. Income tax debts are almost always top priority. Other forms of high priority debt include housing expenses (rent or mortgage), basic utilities, car loans, and child support payments. Next on the list of priorities are court judgments, and student loan payments. Finally, lower priority debt generally includes loans without collateral. Most credit card debts, attorney, doctor and medical bills, and other debts to professionals, and similar debts should be treated as a lower priority if you are struggling making payments to all creditors. Ideally you will be in a position to pay off all of your creditors. During difficult financial times you may be forced to make some difficult decisions.

Establishing a debt hierarchy or priority of payments should be based on your needs and realistic ability to pay off debt. Do not move a debt up in the priority list just because a creditor threatens suit. Usually the debt collectors that make the most noise and call more frequently are the lowest priority. This does not mean you should ignore them. Many threats to sue are not carried out. Even if the creditor does elect to sue, it will take a while for the collector to be able to reach your property, and some of your property may be protected from seizure by law. On the other hand, non-payment of rent, mortgage and car debts may result in immediate loss of your home or car.

What defines "problematic debt"?
In order to create an effective debt elimination plan you need to first identify the types of debt that need to be dealt with immediately. The tax resolution process focused on tax debt because that is one of the most problematic forms of debt. For the purposes of the LifeSpan Process problematic debt is defined as debt that has no value or is used to obtain something that immediately decreases in value upon purchase. Vehicle loans, credit cards, personal loans, installment loans, and boat loans are some examples of problematic debt.

Less problematic forms of debt include investment debt that has the potential to increase in value. Home mortgages, business loans, student loans, and other real estate loans are some examples of better forms of debt. Unless the actual interest rate and terms on these debt forms are excessive they should not be included in this debt elimination step. Instead, concentrate on eliminating all forms of problematic debt from your life.

A few thoughts about Debt Consolidation, Credit Counseling, and Debt Management Companies:
The LifeSpan Process uses a debt reduction plan that is for people who have the ability to make minimum monthly payments (or more) on all forms of debt. Financial mistakes and poor decision making will most often result in debt problems. Many people continue to make mistakes when choosing among the alternatives to get out of debt. The debt reduction plan that I recommend requires hard work and basic financial sense. The continued emphasis on taking action and making a commitment to change works with all forms of debt.

Effective debt elimination plans do not use a quick fix approach. Debt consolidation and debt management programs are generally not the best alternatives to get out of debt if you have the ability to meet your monthly obligations. Debt management companies will help you manage debt by working out lower payments and interest with your creditors. You make one payment to the debt management company who in turn works out a payment plan with your creditors. There is a cost for this type of service. This system typically has a drastic impact on your credit score and is viewed by some lenders as negatively as Chapter 13 bankruptcy. My biggest argument against this approach is that you are not taking control of your financial future if you rely on debt management or credit counseling.

Debt consolidation is essentially a loan that is used to pay off debt. With this approach you may actually end up with a lower interest rate and lower monthly payment. The sad reality is that you will stay in debt longer and usually pay more to the lender over time. If you follow the steps of the LifeSpan Process and take control of your money related behaviors you can avoid the urge to rely on quick fixes to resolve high-interest debt.

There are other debt elimination alternatives that you should avoid in addition to debt management and debt consolidation plans. Credit card balance transfers and 401(k) loans generally led to other tax and financial problems. They only provide temporarily relief from debt and do not address the real problem. Avoid making bad debt elimination moves and instead concentrate on establishing a plan that works.

Establishing a Real Debt Elimination Plan

The main purpose of the debt elimination plan is to completely pay off potentially high interest consumer debt such as credit cards and vehicle loans. A secondary goal is to eliminate all other forms of debt (other than the mortgage). The reward is unmistakable. Debt elimination frees up monthly discretionary income that can eventually be redirected to more important life planning goals. You will never be able to achieve a complete sense of financial freedom until you eliminate problematic debt from your life.

Here are the basic steps of the debt elimination plan:

1. **Understand the Cause of Debt**
   Now is the time to start thinking about how you got into debt in the first place. Since the tax resolution process included a similar process of self-exploration you likely will not need to dwell on this step too long. However, you should not neglect the need to understand why you ended up accumulating debt. Treating only the symptoms of debt will usually result in a continued pattern of financial problems. From a psychological standpoint you must address problematic financial behaviors and fix the underlying problems that lead to debt.

   The debt elimination process uses the same fundamentals that were used during the tax resolution process. Debt can occur due to countless reasons. Some of them may have been preventable and others are not. Life events such as the loss of a job, medical problems, and economic downturns are some events that can lead to debt. Other examples include living beyond ones means, buying more house than is realistically affordable, or living off gross income rather than net income after taxes. Whatever situation may lead to debt problems there is always a solution. The key is to take control of your financial situation and take action. You may not always have complete control over past events that contributed to debt problems. However, you do have control over how you choose to deal with debt.

2. **Set Measurable Goals**
   If you simply want to get out of debt desire alone is not enough to get the job done. The difference between wants and needs is discussed frequently during the tax and financial planning process. When it comes to debt reduction there is a relationship between wants and needs. If you WANT to get out of debt you NEED to have a realistic plan that is measurable.

   Go ahead and establish a target date to eliminate all forms of debt other than home mortgages. Be sure to set goals that you are capable of reaching. You may have to adjust your initial goal once you complete the other steps. I still find it quite helpful to go ahead and set a realistic timeframe for debt elimination. The key point to remember is the sooner you are out of debt the better.

   For example: I want to be debt-free in 18 months. This includes paying off my car loan, credit cards, and bank installment loan.

3. **Assess the Situation**
   In order to determine the best approach to reduce your debt you need to assess your debt situation. Start the debt reduction process by revisiting your net worth analysis. When you originally assessed your resources with a net worth analysis you completed an important building block for this step of the debt elimination process. Take a moment to record all of your liabilities. A debt reduction worksheet is also located on the next page (or appendix).

   Make a list each of your debts. Include the amount owed, minimum monthly payment, and interest rate. Then rank your debts in order based on their interest rate. This should be done from highest to lowest. You should attack the account that has the highest interest rate by paying more to it, and making the minimum payment to the others. Once the debt with the highest interest rate is paid in full, allocate the payment you were making on the now paid account along with the regular monthly payment to the account with the next highest interest rate. This will help start eliminating your debts and allow you to be debt-free as quickly as possible.

Attack the Debt with the Highest Interest First: This strategy always results in the lowest total interest paid over time. Simply put, this is the smartest debt elimination program from a pure numbers perspective. Depending on the balance of your highest interest rate loans it may take you longer to see your first forms of debt completely paid off. In the event that the difference in the total interest is not significant, you may actually gain more satisfaction and a stronger feeling of immediate success if you focus on eliminating the debt with the lowest balance owed first.

Another alternative that some financial counselors advocate is to pay off the debt with the lowest amount owed first. This approach may seem counterintuitive but it generally works for people that need to see immediate results to stay focused. The argument for this approach is based on the idea that most people do not make rational decisions when it comes to money. Paying off the highest interest rate debt first is a rational choice and will end up saving you money in additional interest.

My take on this decision is that the tax resolution and financial freedom process is based on changing financial behaviors and making smart financial decisions. If you have any forms of debt with a small balance, feel free to go ahead and pay off that debt first if you want to see immediate results. In my opinion this is a personal decision and should be based on your unique psychological makeup. However, in general you should usually stay focused on eliminating high interest debt first. Use the following debt elimination worksheet to write down each and every form of debt. List them in the order of priority according to interest rate.

Debt Elimination Worksheet

Debt	Balance	Interest Rate	Minimum Payment	Due Date
Total Amount of Debt		**Total Monthly Payments**		

4. **Maximize Monthly Payments**
   Paying off the minimum amounts is a guaranteed way to stay in debt for as long as possible. This is a fact of life when it comes to any form of high interest debt. Similar to the approach that it recommended to attack IRS payment plans, you should make every effort to maximize your monthly debt payments. This requires the revisiting the Personal Spending Plan. As you can imagine, those words spending plan and budget keep coming back up.

It is no surprise that the spending plan is a critical element of the debt elimination plan. The tax resolution planning process is based on the personal spending plan. Financial freedom requires this same essential building block for success.

The personal spending plan should be reviewed on a monthly basis. It is especially important to update your spending plan once all tax debts have been paid off. The personal spending plan will help identify how much you can afford to pay toward debt above and beyond your minimum required payments.

When you complete your updated personal spending plan you should allocate the funds that were being used to pay off any back taxes to pay off consumer debt. That should be automatic.

5. Rate Reduction

Credit card companies are in business to help you make that special purchase and make all your wildest dreams in life come true. Yeah right! Their mission is to charge you high interest and rake in hundreds and thousands of your hard earned dollars. Just because you have credit card debt does not mean you have to always accept the rates they apply to your balances.

If you have a consistent payment history you should attempt to negotiate lower rates with your credit card companies. Persistence can really pay off in the event you have high interest debt that is negotiable. Any interest rate reductions could significantly speed up your debt elimination plan because a bigger chunk of your payments will be applied to your actual balance (rather than just paying interest).

You should also consider refinancing debt or consolidating debt with a lower interest rate alternative. If you are considering debt consolidation or refinancing you need to be aware of the associated costs. You also need to avoid adding any additional debt to your personal balance sheet. Cut up your credit cards and avoid making any purchases with the use of credit.

6. Change Financial Behaviors

The greatest debt reduction plan will always fail unless you change the financial behaviors that are related to debt. Remember that previously we established the recipe for financial freedom was 75% behavioral and 25% intellectual knowledge. This means you must take control of your financial situation by passionately following the steps of tax and financial freedom. Replace your negative financial behaviors with the positive alternatives that have been discussed throughout this book. The self-awareness process should have helped you identify your problem areas financially.

Establishing a personal spending plan and following it every month is one of the most important financial behaviors that you have control over. Do not lose focus and review your plan every other month or when it is convenient. Consistently follow your spending plan and the other positive financial behaviors such as spending less, earning more, and selling assets that you do not need to help aggressively reduce your high-interest debt.

7. Improve Credit Score

A good credit score is the key to lower interest payments. The concept is fairly simple, lower interest rates mean more of your monthly payment is being applied to principal. While improving your credit score does not happen overnight it is an important part of the debt elimination process.

In a perfect world you should not need a good credit score. Why? Because ideally when you achieve financial freedom you will not need to finance any planned major purchases. This is a difficult concept to understand in our consumer driven society.

It is highly recommended that you obtain a copy of your credit report and review it for any errors or adverse entries. Recent studies indicate that between 30% to 40% of all credit reports contain errors that may impact your ability to obtain credit or lower your credit score.

If you find an error on your credit report you should write to the credit bureau detailing the errors in your report. Send your correspondence by certified mail with a return receipt requested as you work to clean up your credit report. This will provide you with a documented proof of your request and help you remember when and how to follow up with the reporting agency.

Here are just a few ways you can help maintain a good credit score:

- Make your payments on time. This is the best way to improve your credit score.
- Pay off debt rather than shuffling it from one credit card to another.
- Keep your credit card balances low--creditors like to see that you can manage credit responsibly.
- If you are shopping around for credit (such as a mortgage), you can shop around for up to 30 days before your credit score is affected. During that time, multiple lenders can pull your credit and it will only count against your credit as one pull.
- Never live beyond your means or overextend yourself financially.

8. Track Progress Regularly

The only way to assess how well your debt elimination plan is working is to track your progress regularly. Spend time each month reviewing your personal spending plan to make sure that you are applying as much money as possible toward your consumer debt. You can also use a debt reduction planner such as the worksheet provided (on the next page, appendix, etc.). Similar to the tax resolution process, the more active you become during this stage of debt elimination the more motivated you will be.

It is essential that you stay on track with your debt reduction plan. Eliminating debt can be a life changing process. Keep track of your balances and watch them gradually dwindle down to nothing as you aggressively pay off each creditor in a systematic fashion from the highest to lowest interest rate.

9. End the Cycle of Debt

Eliminating debt will do you absolutely no good unless you are able to stay out of debt. Many people who get out of debt only temporarily find themselves free from the stranglehold of debt. This is most likely due to the fact that they only addressed the symptoms of the problem and did not make any changes in how they handle their everyday finances. The tax resolution and financial freedom system requires you to change your financial behaviors. Negative financial behaviors must be replaced by more positive and forward looking actions. A tax and financial plan can ultimately end the cycle of debt if implemented appropriately.

Behavior change often starts with an attitude change. We live in a society that encourages debt and promotes instant gratification. Our government has recently incurred an unprecedented amount of debt. Consumer debt levels are also reaching dangerous levels. Do not expect to get any help from external forces such as government, media, or corporate America when it comes to dealing with debt. Your friends and neighbors may not be the best source of financial guidance. Millions of Americans are struggling with debt and simply do not understand just how much trouble debt is creating in their lives. Even if they see the problem they lack an actual plan to get out of debt and stay out of debt.

While many excellent resources actually exist to help individuals manage debt, the ultimate source of an attitude adjustment rests on each person's shoulders.

It is difficult to change a lifelong process of learning. It is even more challenging trying to change negative financial behaviors that are often associated with past lessons regarding money. Many of us have grown accustomed to messages that debt is good. We are conditioned to focus on monthly payments and interest rates. The focus is often on "how much house or car can I afford" rather than "how much do I really need". If you have a longstanding relationship with debt it may be difficult to accept the motto that "debt is dumb, tax debt is dumber, and dealing with debt without a plan is pure stupidity." The elimination of debt from your life will undoubtedly give you a new sense of freedom and allow you to focus on more important goals and objectives.

Summary

The basic premise of financial life planning is to find ways to make the most of your money. Eliminating high interest consumer debt is the first step on the path to financial freedom. An incredible amount of effort is usually required to reach the initial goal of tax freedom. The tax resolution process usually takes time and a great deal of planning. The positive financial behaviors that were developed during the process of eliminating tax problems also can be used to reach other financial goals. The initial step of eliminating other forms of problematic debt builds on the momentum of the tax resolution process with financial freedom as the primary objective.

Getting out of debt is a cognitive and behavioral process. You need to change your thoughts about money and recognize the true meaning of wealth. Financial behaviors also need to be changed. In the grand scheme of things eliminating tax problems is most relevant when you use tax resolution as an impetus for total financial change. Many people who get out of tax debt never truly find freedom because they simply transfer debt problems to other areas of their lives such as credit cards, car payments, and other loans. The LifeSpan Process recognizes this risk factor and focuses the initial pursuit of financial freedom on the elimination of all forms of debt (excluding mortgages and student loans).

There are many common financial roadblocks that stand in the way of success. Some of the biggest debt issues that people are faced with today include owning more house than they can afford, excessive car payments, painful leases, having too many toys with payments (motorcycles, boats, RVs), not enough savings, borrowing money to meet everyday living expenses and bad spending habits. Smart financial life planning helps prioritize goals and uses the planning process to navigate around potential obstacles.

In order to make your money work as hard for you as you work for it, you need to stay active with your plan to eliminate debt. Attacking your debt with an aggressive debt elimination plan is the best approach when it comes to making the most of your money. Follow this step and you will take control of your financial future. If you are lazy, procrastinate, make excuses or try to hold onto the old financial behaviors that did not work in the past and resulted in tax problems and other debt, you will stay in the cycle of debt.

Ways to Stay Out of Debt:
- Do not incur any additional debt during your debt elimination plan
- Avoid installment loans
- Only use credit cards if you pay them off monthly(NO EXCEPTIONS)
- Pay cash for used cars
- Do not lease vehicles

- Always follow a personal spending plan

Following the resolution of tax debt you should devote 100% of your planning efforts to eliminating potentially high interest consumer debt. Avoid the temptation to return to the cycle of debt. You have to completely change your approach to financial matters in order to stay out of debt. This requires a disciplined approach and spending with a purpose. If you have been living beyond your means in the past new financial behaviors must be used to replace the old bad habits.

Paying off your highest interest debt first is the fastest way to get out of debt while reducing the total interest that you have to pay. Continue to track your progress by reviewing your net worth on a regular basis. Most importantly, you should follow a personal spending plan that creates as much money as possible per month to pay down your problem debt. The personal spending plan should be used as your guide throughout the debt reduction process. Once you have eliminated your problem debt you will be positioned to proceed to the next step- establishing an emergency fund.

When you reach this point you may feel a great sense of relief being able to focus on life after the tax problem. The tax resolution process provides many rewards to the people that make an effort to change their financial lives. If finding a solution to tax debt feels so great, imagine what life could be like without other forms of problematic debt creeping into your daily routine and holding you back. Eliminating consumer debt puts you in complete control of your total financial situation, not just your tax situation. Make it your top priority once your tax liability has been resolved. Holistic tax and financial planning focuses on more than just dealing with tax problems. Financial freedom is the primary goal, and removing problematic debt from your life is the first step on the path to independence.

Financial Freedom Step #2:
Establishing an Emergency Fund

""Gloom, despair and agony on me-e!
Deep dark depression, excessive misery-y!
If it weren't for bad luck I'd have no luck at all!
Gloom, despair and agony on me-e-e!"
~ from Hee Haw

Life is unpredictable. Most people reading that statement would likely agree this is a major understatement. If I asked most people I work with that have tax problems if they actually planned on being in debt to the IRS, not many would say that was part of their life plan. Sometimes it is difficult to convince a person who has never been faced with a life emergency that they need to prepare for the unexpected. Going through the tax resolution process likely indicates that something happened in life that was unexpected and did not fit into the original game plan. Life emergencies and financial surprises are realities that we all need to be prepared for as best as possible.

For some people the source of the tax crisis could be related to a period of living beyond their means and financing a lifestyle that was unaffordable at the time. Other people may have experienced medical emergencies, disability, layoffs, and other personal crises that led to tax debt and other forms of debt. The bottom line is we cannot predict the future. However, we can always have a plan for it. The LifeSpan Process of Tax Resolution and Financial Freedom concentrates on planning for life beyond tax debt. Establishing an emergency fund is part of the financial planning process that should be a top priority once you have eliminated tax and consumer debt.

According to the National Foundation for Credit Counseling, one third of all Americans do not have any emergency savings- zero savings. Of those households that do have an emergency fund in place, only 43% have adequate savings available for emergencies. If you genuinely want to reach a state of financial liberation then you need to be different from the average person. As indicated above, the majority of people in this country have no emergency savings. We already discussed during the previous step how most people are drowning in debt. Financial freedom requires being a renegade who approaches money matters in a unique way. Planning for unforeseen events and the unpredictable in life is not unique. However, in this day and age of negative savings rates and growing debt an emergency fund will go a long way in separating you from others who are content living in a world of debt.

Establishing an emergency savings fund is another important step toward taking control of your life as it relates to money. Most financial planners agree that an emergency fund is needed prior to beginning any long-term savings or investment plan. The recommended amount is generally between 3-6 months basic living expenses. No matter how hard you may have worked to get out of tax and consumer debt you should not skip this step. It is easy to get distracted and the desire to go ahead and start funding other financial goals can be powerful. I urge you to resist this temptation and systematically begin funding your emergency fund.

When you initially created a personal spending plan you began funding a starter fund of between $500-$1,500 depending on the size of your family and other variables. Following that recommendation should have put you on the fast track to success. If you successfully followed that step you are now one step ahead toward the goal of fully funding your emergency savings account. In the event you had to use the "starter" emergency fund you should work to replace it as soon as possible.

Emergency savings funds are an absolute necessity during the process of achieving financial freedom. The lack of a savings fund may lead to additional debt problems when you are faced with an emergency that requires financial resources to deal with. Do not forget that the underlying problem that you are trying to avoid is debt. Protect yourself by figuring out how much you need to save and find a safe place to keep your savings.

How much savings do you need?
The actual target amount for an emergency fund depends on the stability of your income. Each person is different and has unique issues such as job security and lifestyle situations that must be taken into consideration. If your income is unpredictable or heavily relies on commissions or bonuses you should strive to save at least 6 months worth of living expenses. On the other hand, if you are married and you both have stable income sources then 3 months' savings should suffice. During uncertain financial times when unemployment is high and economic recession is a major concern it is wise to consider increasing your emergency fund to 6 months' living expenses.

Calculating the amount needed to fund your emergency savings account is a relatively simple process. You do not need an advanced degree or a financial guru to tell you why an emergency fund is so important. What you do need is the discipline to follow through with this important step on the path to financial freedom.

When you initially set up the personal spending plan you listed all of your living expenses. Simply take the monthly amount and multiply it by the number of months that is typically recommended for your situation. For example, if you are married and you both are working three months should be sufficient assuming you both have relatively stable sources of income. If you are self-employed, have only one spouse working, or have an unstable job you should work to build up an emergency fund that consists of 6 months living expenses.

Use the general rules of thumb below to help you determine how many months worth of living expenses you should strive to maintain in your emergency fund:

- Single no children (3-6 months)
- Single w/ children (4-6 months)
- Married, dual incomes (3 months)
- Married, dual income sources w/ children (3-4 months)
- Self-employed or unsteady income source (4-6 months)

How do I figure out where my emergency savings will come from?

Use your personal spending plan to figure out how much you can set aside for your emergency fund each month. The Personal Spending Plan Worksheet will help you identify areas of your budget that you need to be saving for on a regular basis. Your personal spending plan will also help you figure out just how much you are capable of saving each month.

Financial Freedom Tip: Establish an emergency savings account and fully fund it with 3-6 months living expenses. Use your personal spending plan to determine how much you are capable of saving each month.

Refer to your personal spending plan or budget worksheet to establish a specific plan to fund your emergency savings. Enter a specific amount that you will be capable of setting aside each month for your emergency fund. Plan to set aside your emergency savings before the month begins rather than saving what is left at the end of the month. You will not be as effective if you simply wait until the end of the month to fund your emergency savings. Consider using direct deposit or a systematic savings plan to deposit funds into your savings account.

Your emergency savings is for emergencies only. Protect yourself and keep your fund in a safe place that is easily accessible during an emergency or unforeseen event. This does not mean digging a hole in your backyard or taking over your child's piggy bank. You need your money to work for you and earn as much interest as possible. Most importantly, you need to keep your funds separate from your day to day finances. This means do not use your everyday checking account as the source of your emergency savings.

If you have experienced discipline problems in the past by accessing your savings for routine purchases you should use a separate financial institution. Your emergency fund needs to be readily accessible. However, you need to make sure that accessing it does not become too much of a routine. Always ask yourself whether or not you should tap into your emergency savings fund. Many credit unions, local banks, and online financial institutions have highly competitive savings or money market rates. Using these types of accounts may help you avoid the temptation to tap into your savings for non-emergencies.

How long will it take to establish an emergency fund?

The length of time involved in creating a fully funded emergency savings account varies. It is up to each individual to stay focused and follow the disciplined approach outlined in the Tax Resolution and Financial Freedom Process. The following formula may be used to help calculate how long it will take to fund your emergency safety net. Keep in mind that this does not take into account interest earned on your savings.

Amount needed (minimum 3 months expenses): _____

Current Savings: (Minus) _____

Emergency Fund Shortfall: (Equals) _____

Monthly Savings Amount (from budget): (Divided by) _____

Months Needed to Reach Goal: (Equals) _____

Where do I keep my emergency savings?

Liquidity is the key when selecting an appropriate place for your emergency savings. Liquidity refers to your ability to access your money in a relatively short amount of time. In general, this is measured by how fast it can be converted into cash.

You should be less concerned with the rate of return than you are with the ability to consistently set aside money to fund your emergency fund. If an emergency does occur you should work hard to replace the amount that was withdrawn as soon as possible.

These are the most common liquid savings vehicles that you should consider:

Checking Accounts- generally have low interest, not usually the best choice

Savings Accounts- higher interest rate than checking, normally no fees, many have high yield options available

Money Market Deposit Accounts- held at bank, higher interest rate with limited number of transactions

Money Market Mutual Funds- an open-ended mutual fund that only invests in money markets

Certificates of Deposit- less liquid, penalties normally associated with early withdraw

When choosing the best emergency savings option for your situation you need to do some research and shop around. Websites such as Bankrate.com, money-rates.com, and bankaholic.com allow you to comparison shop money market and high yield savings rates on both a local and national basis. Also be sure to check with community banks and local credit unions to see what type of rates you can get locally. Avoid accounts with minimum deposit requirements and monthly service fees.

Debt Alternatives to Avoid

We have already established the belief that debt is dumb, tax debt is dumber, and dealing with them both without a plan is pure stupidity. Well one part of your plan is to avoid returning to revolving cycle of debt. An easy way to find your way back into debt is to operate without an emergency savings fund in an uncertain world that is always full of surprises.

Avoid these emergency fund alternatives:
- Home Equity Line of Credit (HELOC)
- Unsecured Bank Line of Credit
- Overdraft Protection
- Pay Day Loans
- Personal Loans from Friends and Family

What do all of those items have in common? They are all liabilities. DEBT! All of these so called "safety nets" provide a false sense of security. Do not fall for the trap. You will only get sucked into the world of debt that you worked so hard to get out of in the first place. Using these liabilities for emergencies decreases your net worth and increases your overall debt obligations.

The Key to Saving
Establishing an emergency fund is a building block step that serves a dual purpose. The primary purpose is to prepare for the unexpected in life and to avoid getting sucked into the cycle of debt should an emergency occur. Another purpose is to help you develop a positive financial behavior- saving. Keep in mind that you are learning how to consistently set aside funds for the greater purpose of financial freedom however you choose to define your sense of freedom.

> **Taking Action!!!**
> Establish an emergency that consists
> of at least 3-6 months living expenses.

Summary

A fully funded emergency savings account is a necessary step on the journey to financial freedom. This step requires the ability to stay focused on the ultimate reward, which is financial freedom. If you practice positive financial behaviors such as spending wisely with a plan and routinely saving money for the unknown you will be prepared for potential obstacles along the way. Minor financial setbacks and unforeseen events are a part of life. Emergencies always seem to happen at the worst possible times. An emergency fund is a critical part of staying on track financially and will help you avoid future problems with debt.

The emergency fund step is often overlooked as many people try to skip ahead to other financial planning steps. Most people with or without a history of tax problems do not have adequate savings. I strongly urge you to avoid letting impatience get in the way of making smart financial decisions. Following this step will undoubtedly give you a greater sense of control over your financial life. Now if your car's transmission blows up, the heating unit gives up the ghost mid-winter, or the doctor recommends an expensive procedure, you will be in a better position to deal with the financial ramifications.

Emergencies and their unexpected costs still remain unpleasant. However, they are much more manageable financially speaking with a savings plan ready and available "just in case". We all know that surprises occur in life. Prepare for emergencies with a plan. Set aside your emergency funds as quickly as possible using the discipline required through a personal spending plan.

The easiest way to identify the source of your emergency funding is to look back at the previous step. After you pay off your problematic debt you should redirect those debt payments to your emergency fund. Do not put yourself in a position of having to decide whether you should save or spend this extra money. Pay yourself first by funding your savings at the beginning of the month. Always keep in mind that the sooner you have an emergency fund in place the sooner you will be able to start building real wealth through an investment plan.

Financial Freedom Step # 3:
Reviewing Life Planning Goals and Objectives

"Life happens- all during the time you're trying to plan for it."- Unknown

The Tax Resolution and Financial Freedom Process will allow you to take a proactive role in planning your life. While no one person is in complete control over all of life's events, we are not subject to fate or chance alone. Everyone has the ability to positively influence the course of their own unique life path.

Money is merely a tool and has no intrinsic power, meaning, or value by itself. A million dollars sitting in a bank account would change nothing in your life if it just sat in an account. However, if money is used wisely as part of a financial life plan it has more meaning and purpose.

What do you want from your money? This is your life and your money that we are talking about. Why not create a plan to guide you along the journey? Life is without a doubt the great unknown. Life planning can help people to prepare for its many potential outcomes. Life planning has been defined as a comprehensive approach to the planning process that is appropriate and useful across the lifespan. A financial life plan is essentially a master plan for your whole life as it relates to money. Rather than immediately dive into some of the most popular financial planning topics such as retirement planning or education funding it is more appropriate to revisit life planning goals and objectives.

Financial freedom and security is only a part, albeit an extremely important part, of the entire life planning process. The life plan as a whole comprises the values, visions, and dreams of people both now and in the future. There is a direct relationship between money and how you plan your life. A holistic or "whole is greater than the sum of its parts" approach to understanding specific financial goals will increase the likelihood that you will plan and implement your financial strategies related to these goals. Individual personalities, family dynamics, social structures, and countless other factors work together to shape important financial objectives. Therefore, a one size fits all cookie cutter approach to tax and financial planning will not fully address the life planning process.

What was your original intent when you first committed to engage yourself in the tax and financial planning process? Did you simply begin the Tax Resolution and Financial Freedom Process to get the IRS off your back and satisfy other debt obligations, or did you realize that enough was enough and you were tired of feeling helpless and out of control when it comes to the topic of managing your money?

Most likely the driving force behind the pursuit of tax and financial freedom is the ultimate desire for freedom itself. Freedom and financial independence rely on the planning process to guide the forces of positive financial change. This stage of reviewing life planning goals is essential. The tax resolution process included this important step. Once tax freedom has been accomplished life planning goals become more realistic and achievable. The binds of financial slavery that once held you back from even contemplating important long-term goals such as putting a child through college or funding retirement dreams can now be removed. Tax freedom is a precursor to financial freedom. The elimination of debt and creation of an emergency fund set the stage for the real fun of building wealth. It is a great relief to focus on creating wealth rather than eliminating debt.

Establishing goals and objectives are such important parts of the LifeSpan Process of Tax Resolution and Financial Freedom that there are two steps devoted to goal setting. During the tax resolution process goals and objectives are needed to provide meaning, purpose, and focus to the pursuit of tax freedom. Financial life planning starts with understanding what is important to you. Financial stress and anxiety related to tax problems can make it difficult to think about any goals or dreams beyond getting out of debt. The reality is that people who take the time to look at the big picture of their tax and financial problems are more successful when it comes to improving their financial future.

Eliminating tax debt alone will not improve your quality of life. However, it will give you more time and energy to focus on other aspects of your life. Remember the word "balance" that we discussed in the context of characteristics shared by financially successful people. Tax debt can throw off your balance in life if not dealt with effectively. The goal setting stage of the financial freedom process recognizes that things change in a good way once tax problems have been eliminated. Financial life planning goals must be revised as you get closer to being able to turn your dreams into reality.

The next step on the path to financial freedom includes a focus on insurance planning, estate planning, and investment planning. Before we really jump into these steps of the wealth building process we need to figure out the purpose of insurance, estate, and investment planning. Take a moment to revisit your life planning goals and objectives. Let's start by reviewing the three questions that were presented during the tax resolution process. You may be surprised that some of your life planning goals changed. Hopefully some goals have become clearer and are well defined at this point.

1. Imagine that you have paid off all of your tax and consumer debt. You owe absolutely nothing and have enough money to take care of your needs, now and in the future. How would you live your life? Would you change anything?

2. Imagine that you visit the doctor and she says you have only five to 10 years to live. You will not feel any pain or sickness, but you will never know when death will actually come. What will you do? Will you change your life? How?

3. Finally, now try to imagine that your doctor says you have only one day left to live. Ask yourself: What did I miss? What did I not get to be or do? Do I have any regrets?

> **Taking Action!!!**
> Refer back to Step #2 of the Tax
> Resolution Process. Review your life
> planning goals and objectives. Has
> anything changed since you originally
> completed the exercise? Refer to pages
> 36-39 if you do not fully recall your
> previous responses.

Have your life planning goals changed now that you have started taking control of your financial life?
□ Yes □ No

If so, how have they changed? _____
_____
_____

What are your top three financial concerns at this time?

1. _____
   _____
   _____

2. _____
   _____
   _____

3. _____
   _____
   _____

Revisit Life Planning Goals
It is not uncommon for your priorities in life to shift over the course of time. This revised goal setting step allows you to revisit your life planning goals and objectives. You may even find that your life goals are easier to define now that the weight of tax debt has been lifted.

During the tax resolution phase we identified the seven major goal areas of the life planning process. Each of these goal areas are related to the others in one way or another. Take a moment and think about your life planning goals.

Financial Freedom Tip: Revisit your life planning goals after you have resolved your tax liability and eliminated problematic consumer debt from your life. Write down your goals and objectives for the seven major goals areas of the life planning process.

Seven Major Goal Areas of a Life Plan
- Financial
- Physical
- Career
- Family
- Social
- Intellectual
- Spiritual

Self-Assessment

As people with tax debt begin the tax resolution process they have varying levels of financial literacy. Some people may feel extremely comfortable dealing with financial matters while others fall into the category of financially ignorant (somewhere between the two). Combining the financial planning process with tax resolution places the emphasis on financial behavior change. The primary goal of this process is to do more than just resolve a tax liability. It is to entirely change the approach to tax and financial matters. Rather than treating the symptoms (tax debt) you are now in the process of treating the underlying disease (lack of a well-designed financial life plan). As you progress through the stages of the LifeSpan process and transition from tax resolution goals to financial planning goals you should assess where you are in your financial life. You also need to assess how taking control of your taxes and your money has an impact on your overall life.

As you progress through the steps of the tax resolution process do you feel more empowered to manage your personal finances?

How confident are you in your own ability to make smart financial decisions?
    (1- Low Confidence, 10- Highly Confident) _____

Life planning involves the explanation of possibilities and the purposeful process or prioritizing these potential outcomes in life. That may be a mouthful of P's, but each word represents an essential component of the tax resolution and financial freedom process.

Planning- An effective plan is the key to making financial life planning goals become realities.
Possibilities- Use the planning process to discover your endless possibilities in life. Establish realistic goals, put them in writing, and use a financial life plan to make your dreams become possibilities.
Purposeful- Financial life planning is about more than just taxes and money.
Priorities- Effective goal setting requires taking action. It also forces you to establish priorities in life and use these priorities to determine how to best allocate your time and money. Take action by doing the right things at the right time. Work smarter not harder.
Potential- Everyone has the innate ability to become self-actualized, or like the old Army slogan says, "Be all that you can be." Live up to your own potential and use the tax resolution and financial freedom process to discover yourself.

Process- Financial life planning is a journey and the challenges go far beyond the topics of debt and taxes. Have the patience to realize that tax and financial freedom take time to accomplish. Those who follow the step by step process and commit to take control and stay in control of their tax and financial plan are destined to succeed.

Summary

Financial life planning undoubtedly deals with so much more than taxes and money. It can be difficult to focus on the big picture when tax problems are present. During the beginning of the tax resolution process goals are set to provide direction and meaning. You must begin the tax resolution process with the end goal of financial freedom in mind. Initially most goals and objectives may appear to be too difficult to achieve or simply appear unattainable due to the heavy burden of tax debt.

Tax problems can have a significant emotional effect on people if they do not confront the tax problem with a healthy attitude and a plan of action. The positive factors of dealing with tax problems far outweigh the negative. By taking control of your tax and financial situation you assume control of your financial destiny. The IRS, credit card companies, and the bank that offered you a high interest car loan cannot control your life once you get them out of yours. Getting out of debt frees up your available resources to focus on what is most important to you in life. Since we all have a limited amount of time and resources during the life experience you should make the most of what you have.

Establishing well-defined goals helps provide direction during everyone's unique financial life planning journey. By putting your goals in writing and reviewing them on an ongoing basis you will put yourself in the best possible position to attain your objectives in life. Life planning goals should be used to make sure they manage your life resources such as time, money, energy, talents, and relationships as effectively as possible.

Financial Freedom Step #4:
Protecting Yourself, Property, and the Ones You Love

"Live as if you were to die tomorrow. Learn as if you were to live forever." ~ Mahatma Gandhi

"According to most studies, people's number one fear is public speaking. Number 2 is death. Death is number 2. Does that sound right? This means that to the average person, if you go to a funeral, you're better off in the casket than doing the eulogy." ~ Jerry Seinfeld

"I'm going to a special place when I die.
I want to make sure my life is special while I'm here." ~ Payne Stewart

Insurance planning is one of those things in life that you never want to use but always need to have ready just in case you do need it. The entire purpose of insurance is to transfer financial risk from you to the insurance company. Making insurance payments can often feel like you are simply throwing your money away. Insurance planning is an essential part of an overall financial plan.

Life Insurance
Although death and taxes are essential parts of the financial planning discussion, they are not the easiest topics to discuss. My faith has taught me to live by the motto that "I know that I am going somewhere special when I die. I just want my life to be as special as possible while I am still here." On that same note, I also want my wife and children to be taken care of and live comfortably in my absence.

Life insurance is an essential part of a comprehensive financial plan. It helps protect against the financial devastation that can be caused by an unexpected or early death. At some point in life we all must realize the inevitability of death. The realization that loss of life results in loss of income and a change in lifestyle also occurs and should guide the insurance planning process.

Life insurance planning does not have to be confusing. At this point in the Tax Resolution and Financial Freedom Process you need to address these basic questions:

1. **Do I need life insurance coverage?**
   Yes, in most cases you will need some type of life insurance coverage. As your wealth grows and your debt decreases, the need for life insurance will likely decline. In most cases you will be able to self-insure your life as you achieve financial freedom. Until then you will need to share your risk with others. That is the general premise of life insurance.

2. **How much coverage do I need?**
Determining the recommended coverage amount is critical. You do not want to go underinsured, and you should not pay any more in life insurance premiums than is necessary. Many insurance professionals and financial planners recommend that you have life insurance coverage of 7-10 times the amount of your income. This multiple of earnings approach is easy but is flawed.

A needs-based approach to estimating the amount of life insurance coverage required is a better alternative. This approach takes into account the actual amount of income that needs to be replaced and the length of time your survivor needs the income. You also need to include whether or not you would like to pay off debt such as a home mortgage or other loans. Final expenses and burial costs must also be included in determining the amount of coverage needed. Also, include education expense needs or other special needs when determining the dollar amount needed.

If you have any questions regarding how much coverage is needed you should consult a fee-only financial planner or life insurance broker that has your best interests first.

3. **What type of life insurance should I obtain?**
There are two basic types of life insurance plans available: term life insurance and cash-value life insurance. Term life insurance provides death benefits only if the insured person dies within a specific time period or term. Cash-value life insurance provides benefits at death but also includes a savings or investment component.

If you follow this simple recommendation you will save yourself a significant amount of money: Buy term and invest the rest on your own. Cash-value life insurance is considerably more expensive than term insurance. In addition, many people are mistakenly misled to believe that the savings or investment aspects of cash-value insurance make it a better option. This assumption is incorrect and is usually "sold" by insurance professionals that make more money recommending cash-value life insurance over term.

Cash-value or permanent insurance does play an integral role in many complex financial planning scenarios. However, 99.9% of the people taking part in the tax resolution and financial planning process need only focus on term life insurance. This will allow you to make the most of your money and separate life insurance decisions from investment planning. As you follow the Tax Resolution and Financial Freedom Process you should only seek to obtain term life insurance coverage.

Financial Freedom Tip: When seeking life insurance you should only focus on term insurance. Do not purchase cash-value life insurance since there are better investment alternatives.

Health Insurance
Adequate health insurance coverage is a must for any financial plan. Everyone needs health insurance-without exception. Health insurance protects you from the potentially devastating high costs of medical care. If something happens to you or a family member you need to be prepared to pay for health care costs. Without health insurance you could easily accumulate thousands of dollars in medical bills caused by illness or injury.

In fact, medical debt is often cited as the number one cause of bankruptcy in this country. You need to be prepared for the high cost of medical care and include health insurance as a vital part of your financial plan. The cost of insurance itself is not cheap and continues to be a subject of great debate in our country. If you do not currently have health insurance coverage you should not wait on the government to fix the situation. Take action and protect yourself and your family. The cost for health insurance is significantly less than out of pocket health care costs should you need medical care!

Consider yourself fortunate if you work for an employer than provides a good health care plan. Many Americans do not have access to group health insurance coverage. If your employer does not offer health insurance (or if you are out of work) you should try to purchase an individual policy. Shop around for the best alternatives. If you are self-employed consider joining a group policy. Many trade associations and professional organizations offer some type of group coverage depending on your profession or line of work. Finding affordable health insurance can be a significant challenge. Shop around and consider all available options.

Consider a health savings account if your insurance plan qualifies as a high-deductible plan. Contributions to an HSA are above the line tax deductions. Most importantly, you can use funds in an HSA to pay for out of pocket health care expenses tax-free.

Homeowners, Renters, and Automobile Insurance
Homeowners, renters, and automobile insurance policies are also important areas of the financial planning process. You need adequate protection against the possibility of unexpected and costly damage or loss to property. You also should protect against the possibility of injury or harm to people. If you own a home you should have homeowners insurance. Renters should also protect your property with a renter's insurance policy.

Disability Insurance
One of your greatest assets is your ability to work and earn an income. If you are unable to work due to illness or injury you will have trouble paying bills and following through with financial planning goals and objectives. An emergency fund helps minimize the financial impact of disability and other unforeseen events for a relatively short period of time.

Disability insurance provides you with income replacement when your income is either reduced or eliminated altogether. The statistics on disability can be downright scary. More than 2 out of 3 people between the ages of 35 and 65 will face a disability of 3 months or longer in their lifetime. Additionally, there is a 1 in 3 chance that you will experience a long term disability (average of 5 years) before reaching typical retirement age. Unless you know how to defy the odds there is a good chance that you will experience some type of disability. Seek an affordable long-term disability policy.

Long Term Care Insurance
Protect your assets and make sure that you are taken care of in the event you need long-term care. Begin the process of obtaining long-term care between the ages of 55-60 years old. When you reach this period of your life you should begin to consider long-term care insurance. At this stage in life you must start thinking about the financial consequences of a prolonged disability or chronic illness that requires long term care at home or in a nursing home. The cost of long-term care can be overwhelming and can deplete income and assets very quickly. Figures from the U.S. Department of Health and Human Services in 2008 indicate that annual nursing home costs for a semi-private room average $68,000 per year. One year of periodic personal care at home from a home health aide would cost approximately $18,000 per year.

Recent statistics indicate that about 70% of all people at age 65 and older will need some type of long-term care during their lifetime. Many people mistakenly believe that Medicare will cover long-term care costs. Medicare only pays for long-term care in a skilled nursing facility for a short period of time (up to 100 days). Home health care costs are only covered by Medicare under limited circumstances.

Long-term care helps protect your personal assets and reduces the risk that you will need to use retirement savings and investment assets to cover the potentially high costs of long-term care. Every person should begin considering long-term care when he or she reaches the mid 50's. Long-term care is an important part of the financial planning process that should not be overlooked.

Personal Umbrella Coverage

Consider an umbrella policy if you have significant assets. We live in a litigious society and some lawyers and people are constantly looking to sue. Umbrella insurance coverage is designed to provide added liability protection above and beyond the coverage limits of homeowners or automobile policies. Umbrella policies generally provide between 1-5 million dollars in additional liability protection.

Insurance Checklist

The following insurance checklist provides a list of the major types of insurance that may be needed for your financial plan. Review your current level of insurance coverage and indicate whether or not you have adequate coverage. If you have no clue or are not sure whether or not you need a specific type of insurance, or if your current level of coverage is enough you should contact an insurance professional in that particular area.

Type of Insurance	Yes	No	Need to update or contact an insurance professional? Explain.
Life Insurance			
Homeowners (or Renters)			
Health Insurance			
Auto Insurance			
Disability Insurance			
Long-Term Care Insurance			

Protecting Yourself and the Ones You Love

Basic Estate Planning

No matter what your actual net worth is you need a plan in place to make sure that your family financial goals can be accomplished after your death. A common mistake that many people make is assuming that they do not have an "estate" or enough assets to have an estate plan. Everyone needs an estate plan. An effective estate plan has several different elements. At a minimum you should have a will, durable power of attorney, healthcare power of attorney, and living will.

Wills

A will is a simple document that determines how your property is distributed in the event of your death. Your desires and wishes for the distribution of your estate may conflict with state intestacy laws. If you die without a will, you die "intestate" and state law determines how your assets and possessions are distributed among your heirs. Allowing the courts to decide who gets your assets can lead to countless problems, family dissent, and unnecessary stress among survivors. You do not want complete strangers making important decisions on your behalf.

Establishing a will is extremely important if you have young children, special needs children, or adults who would need to be provided for in the event of your death. If you have minor children the state will also determine who will become their guardian. The only way to be sure that your final wishes for the care of your children are carried out is to make a will.

It should go without saying that the preparation and maintenance of a valid will is an important planning matter. If you do not have a will, I strongly recommend that you have a will prepared as soon as possible. Surprisingly, over 70% of adults in our country do not have a valid will. Some of the most common reasons people do not have wills are procrastination, denial, cannot afford an attorney, not enough time, or lack of education on the importance of estate planning.

Do not procrastinate with your estate plan. Go ahead and make arrangements to have a will prepared if you do not already have one in place. If you are married you both need a will. When you have your wills prepared, you should ensure that your will is properly attested in accordance with state law. The best way to do this is enlist the help of a local estate planning attorney. If costs are a concern and you have a fairly simple estate you should consider using online legal services and will preparation from companies such as U.S. Legal Forms or LegalZoom. The respective websites for these companies are www.uslegalforms.com and www.legalzoom.com.

A typical will includes the following components:

- A statement by you that the document is your last will and testament, and that you were of "sound mind and body" when you prepared it;
- The name of the executor, the person you designate to ensure that your wishes as expressed in the will are actually carried out;
- A list of who you want to receive your money, personal possessions, and other assets;
- The name(s) of the person(s) you want to become the guardian(s) of your minor children;
- The signature of two witnesses who are not beneficiaries of the will.

Be sure that your heirs or attorney know the location of important documents, financial records, and your inventory of personal property. We recommend that you keep original vital documents in a safe deposit box and keep copies of those documents in a different, yet safe and readily accessible location. Most importantly, be sure to provide instructions to your family or friends to direct them to your important financial documents if needed.

Periodically review the provisions and your selection of executors and beneficiaries. Have your attorney review and update your will as necessary. When you obtain life insurance and establish retirement accounts, keep in mind that these assets pass to the designated beneficiaries outside of probate by contract law and there is no need to specify beneficiaries for these assets in your will.

Financial Freedom Tip: Make arrangements to have a will prepared immediately if you do not have one in place already. Be sure to name a guardian for any minor children. Review your will on a regular basis and have your will updated as significant life events occur (birth of a child, divorce, inheritance, etc.).

Will Substitutes
Not all of your property and assets will actually pass through your will. Property that transfers outside of the probate process is called a will substitute or "non-probate transfer". Will substitutes purposefully avoid the probate process and make sure that your property is transferred to your beneficiaries in accordance to your wishes. Avoiding probate helps speed up the distribution process and also can reduce the costs associated with the probate process.

Common will substitute techniques include titling property as joint tenancy with right of survivorship (JTWROS) or tenancy by entirety (tenancy in common). Designating beneficiaries for certain accounts or property types is another form of a will substitute. This includes payable on death (POD) accounts and transfer on death (TOD) accounts.

The proper designation of beneficiaries is also important for other contracts such as life insurance policies and annuities. Retirement assets such as qualified plans, 403(b) tax deferred annuities, 457 plans and Individual Retirement Accounts (IRAs) also allow you to determine how to transfer property to your beneficiaries in the event of death. Trusts are another popular way to avoid probate that is discussed in greater detail below.

The most important features of will substitutes are as follows:

- They help to avoid probate
- Fairly easy to make changes to and amend
- You maintain control since they are generally revocable until death
- Many of these planning tools are free and easy to implement

Financial Freedom Tip: Review your beneficiary selections for all of your bank accounts, investment accounts, life insurance policies, and retirement accounts. Make sure that you update your beneficiary selections as needed.

Durable Power of Attorney

Consider executing a durable power of attorney for financial affairs. A durable power of attorney grants to another person the right to act on your behalf to pay your bills, make investments, and to make key financial decisions such as buying and selling property. It may be used if you become unable to handle your own affairs for reasons of age or health. This is an important consideration should you lose the ability to control your financial life.

Advanced Health Care Directives and Living Wills

You should also consider establishing a healthcare durable power of attorney and living will (also known as advanced health care directives) for you to take effect in the event of physical or mental incapacity. Advanced health care directives make your medical wishes known in advance of potential decisions that family members may be faced with regarding life-sustaining medical interventions.

A living will generally refers to a written directive by you, addressed to another person, who would be making decisions concerning your medical care and treatment in the event you are so totally incapacitated as to require life-support or other extraordinary measures in order to keep you alive.

Trusts

As your wealth grows you should explore the use of the various types of living and testamentary trusts. Consulting with a qualified estate planning attorney is highly recommended as your estate planning needs change and become more complicated. Trusts can be arranged to accomplish the following:

1. Reduce the delay, expense, and publicity of probate.
2. Provide income to survivors from all assets, including those of the trust.
3. Assure competent management of trust assets.
4. Provide an efficient means of distribution to your heirs.
5. Allow you to keep full investment control of the assets.
6. Enable you to make changes or cancel the trust any time prior to your death.

Estate Planning Checklist

Place a check mark next to each estate planning item that you currently have setup:

Which of the following do you have?	Client	Date Last Reviewed	Spouse	Date Last Reviewed
Last Will and Testament				
Durable power of attorney for business affairs				
Durable power of attorney for healthcare				
Living will				
Advanced healthcare directive				
Grantor of a trust or trusts				
Beneficiary of a trust or trusts				

Summary

No matter what your net worth situation may be, it is important to have a plan to protect yourself, property, and the ones you love. Every comprehensive tax and financial plan should include insurance and estate planning. If you are just starting the process of climbing out of debt and building wealth you still need to have adequate insurance and a basic estate plan. This step can often be placed higher in importance due to individual circumstances. In fact, some insurance planning recommendations may actually have a positive impact on the outcome of the tax resolution process. For the purposes of the tax resolution and financial freedom process it is most relevant to place this section after the goals and objectives step.

Insurance protects you against the risk of loss. If something happens to your life, health, or property you need to have basic protection in place to reduce the financial impact of the loss. Insurance helps offset the costs by sharing your risk with others. Always work with an insurance professional to determine the appropriate level of coverage for your various insurance policies. Be concerned about more than just the cost of insurance. You should always think about the potential cost of financial freedom should you ever need to use certain types of insurance.

The estate planning process has several basic elements. A will should be at the core of your estate plan. Without exception, everyone needs a will. If you die without a will you have no control over how your assets are distributed. This can have a costly impact on your family and leave important decisions about the transfer of your assets to potential strangers. If you have minor children or dependents that you care for you need to provide instructions for their care. Shockingly, many families with young children still do not have a guardian appointed for their children in the event of an early death. This is inacceptable during this day and age of affordable wills. Everyone should make arrangements to have a will in place.

Other estate planning elements include a power of attorney, living will or healthcare proxy (medical power of attorney). In certain situations trusts may also make sense. Estate planning needs vary from person to person. The most important thing to focus on during the financial freedom process is the fact that an estate plan is not just for the wealthy. Start the planning process early. Dealing with the idea of death and taxes is not an exciting endeavor. Leaving your family without a solid plan is even worse.

Financial Freedom Step #5:
Reaching Life Planning Goals Through
Investment Planning

"Life is full of uncertainties. Future investment earnings and interest and inflation rates are not known to anybody. However, I can guarantee you one thing... those who put an investment program in place will have a lot more money when they come to retire than those who never get around to it." ~ Noel Whittaker

"An investor without investment objectives is like a traveler without a destination." ~ Ralph Seger

Financial Planning Tip: In general, investing should be a long-term goal after you resolve your tax liability. Keep in mind that the expected long-term rate of return of investments is probably much less than the total interest and penalties on any tax liability or high-interest consumer debt. Therefore, it usually advisable to resolve any tax liabilities and pay off all consumer debt before beginning an investing program suited to your risk tolerance. The main exception to this rule is a retirement savings plan with matching contributions. It is okay to fund a retirement plan up to the match amount as long as doing so makes sense based on your cash-flow situation.

If you have a tax liability with the IRS or a state taxing authority it does not make much sense to begin the discussion of investments until a game plan has been established to eliminate tax debt. Everyone has heard the saying that you have to learn how to crawl before you can walk. In the context of this book, that is the primary reason that investment planning is discussed after tax resolution planning. The tax resolution steps were the foundation for success. By the time that you have reached this point you should be ready to work towards the ultimate goal of financial freedom. Now is the time to start building true wealth.

The financial planning process is often used to increase your net worth through savings, investments, and debt reduction. This investment planning section is designed to provide you with the basic tools necessary to build wealth through proper investment planning. As you begin (or resume) the investment planning process you should continue to use the same positive financial behaviors that got you to this point. Establish and review life planning goals. Follow a spending plan. Avoid debt. Always have an emergency fund in place. These steps sound very simple in writing. Putting these financial behaviors into action is the real test.

Once your tax liability is resolved, you have eliminated debt, and you have an emergency plan in place you are truly ready to start reaching your life planning goals through an investment plan. Focus your efforts on developing a systematic investment philosophy and well-allocated portfolio to increase your net worth and obtain your life planning goals. No matter how much knowledge you have about investing you can still succeed. Tax resolution requires the elimination of fear and anxiety in order to eliminate the tax debt. Fear, anxiety, and financial ignorance also need to be eliminated when it comes to the topic of investing.

The investment planning process should be kept as simple as possible. Financial success does not have to be complicated. Some investment professionals may attempt to complicate the process and try to convince you that you cannot invest on your own. Have the courage and confidence that with some guidance you are capable of changing your financial destiny.

Certain investors are capable of using a do it yourself approach while others need professional guidance along the way. Be honest with yourself when determining whether or not to use a financial planner or investment adviser to assist you with an investment plan. Using a professional or not still requires work on your part to implement the investment plan. This step of the financial freedom process should give you the basic tools and guidance to develop a successful plan. If you get stuck or need professional guidance you should follow some basic words of advice:

- Always have a written plan or investment policy statement to guide your decisions.
- Do not focus on picking individual investments.
- Stick with no-load index mutual funds and exchange traded funds (ETFs).
- Be well diversified
- Asset Allocation will drive investment performance.
- Avoid the temptation to try to time the market.
- If you need investment planning advice use a fee-only financial planner who can provide comprehensive tax and financial planning advice and will always act in your best interests.

These basic investment planning tips are explained in greater detail throughout the chapter. The main point to emphasize when selecting investments is that portfolio selection or asset allocation is the most important factor when it comes to future investment returns. Portfolio or asset allocation refers to the mix of investments that you utilize, including stocks, bonds, CDs, cash, and real estate. Every investor needs to set realistic expectations for performance and commit to an investment discipline that meets their own comfort level. Dollar cost averaging into qualified retirement plans, Roth and traditional IRAs, annuities, and/or mutual funds can be an excellent way to achieve this goal. These techniques will also be explained in greater detail.

Putting an Investment Plan in Motion
Why do some people fail on the journey to financial independence? In most cases it is because they did not take the important first step of the planning process- getting started. Many people fail to have a plan in place that is both easy to implement and simple to track on a regular basis. Besides procrastination and fear, other common excuses that inhibit financial freedom are misconceptions that investing is too risky, too confusing, too difficult or time consuming, and only for the wealthy.

In reality, there is absolutely nothing complicated about basic investment principles. If you simplify the process and eliminate the distractions and noise that often gets in the way of individual investors you will realize that investing is for everyone and not just the wealthy. The biggest investment risk that you face during the financial freedom process is not educating yourself about investing.

There is a significant difference between saving and investing. Previously we discussed the importance of establishing an emergency fund. This is a form of savings and not a long-term investment. An emergency fund should be in place and all high interest debt should be eliminated prior to beginning an investment plan. It is important to realize the difference between savings and investing. They both have important roles in your financial life plan. But they serve two different purposes.

Investing helps you prepare for the future. Unfortunately the future is expensive due to inflation and increased life expectancies. It is up to you to prepare for your future. During the tax resolution process you were faced with the challenge of taking action and assuming control of your tax situation. On a similar note you are accountable for your own financial future looking beyond the tax and debt issues. Do not rely on the government. Plan on being self-reliant and do not rely on social welfare programs. Social Security will likely be changed significantly in the coming decades and play a less significant role in your life than it did for previous generations. Likewise less corporations offer pension plans. This leaves the burden of responsibility for retirement savings on you the individual.

Investment Goals

Investment planning starts with a purpose or vision. You need to have a general idea of why you are investing in the first place. Whatever your reason is for investing (retirement, education, funding a dream) you need to have an investment plan to reach these important life goals. When it comes to the subject of financial freedom you need to make smart financial management decisions in order to enjoy a comfortable life. Your life planning goals most likely include the ability to enjoy a future full of financial security for you and your family.

Common investment techniques are not overly complicated. Unfortunately, it is human nature to make things more complicated than necessary. Personal finance is based on the premise that human beings will behave rationally when it comes to money and investing. It is hard to eliminate emotions and irrational thinking. That is why many people become overwhelmed by the investment planning process and make bad investment decisions.

With countless elements of distraction and information available to potential investors it can be difficult to figure out the best way to start an investment plan. Many individuals with tax debt share a strong misconception that investing is just for the wealthy or their tax debt will prevent them from being able to start or continue an investment plan. If you follow the steps of the tax resolution financial planning process, you may be surprised to find that you can start an investment plan now. If not, go ahead and create a game plan for future investments. This will enable you to be prepared to begin a structured investment plan after the resolution of your tax debt.

Saving versus investing

Savings and investing are two important aspects of every tax and financial plan. But these two financial terms should not be confused with one another. With savings, your principal does not typically fluctuate in value and earn interest or dividends. Savings is usually used for emergencies and unforeseen events. Savings also may be used to fund short-term financial goals such as purchasing an automobile or taking a vacation. Checking accounts, money market accounts, savings, and certificates of deposit (CDs) are the most popular savings vehicles. In comparison, investments typically fluctuate in value and may or may not pay interest or dividends to investors. Stocks, bonds, mutual funds, and real estate are a few examples of popular investment vehicles.

Why do people invest in the first place? You must invest for the future, and the future is expensive. For example, college expenses are increasing at double the rate of inflation, and people are retiring earlier and living longer. You have to take responsibility for your own finances--nobody else is going to. Government programs like Social Security will probably play a less significant role in your life than they did for previous generations. Corporations are switching from guaranteed pensions to plans that require you to make contributions and choose investments. The better you manage your dollars, the more likely it is that you'll have the money you want for your retirement.

Because everyone has different goals and expectations, everyone has different reasons for investing. However, it simply comes down to managing your money in order to provide a comfortable life and financial security for you and your family. This leads us to our next Financial Freedom Tip. This is also one of the most important financial planning steps on the path to financial independence.

Financial Freedom Tip: Establish an investment plan that routinely sets aside 15-20% of your total household income. Revisit your personal spending plan and set aside money for investing before the month begins.

Imagine how difficult this desired savings objective would be with excessive debt and tax liabilities. Saving this amount would appear to be virtually impossible. However, once the layers of debt are removed your cash flow begins to increase and this money can actually start working for you and your financial goals. If you cannot contribute 15-20% of your total household income initially you should set aside as much as possible according to your personal spending plan. If you can only afford 5% at first that is okay. Use this shortfall as your motivation to increase the amount of your investments over time. Review your budget regularly and replace your former debt payments with investments. Constantly seek ways to increase your investment contributions to the 15% target and beyond.

How do I invest?
It is easy to make mistakes or get sidetracked when setting up an investment plan. There is no shortage of opinions from friends, family, and the media as to how people should invest. Avoid the distractions and keep your investment plan simple from the start. There are some basic investment techniques that you must follow in order to succeed:

- The tax resolution and financial freedom process heavily emphasizes the need to change financial behaviors. One important behavior change is getting in the habit of saving. You must set aside a portion of your income as often as possible. As mentioned numerous times throughout this book, following a personal spending plan is the key to making sure that you focus on saving and investing.

- After you have established a fully funded emergency fund you are in a position to start seeking higher investment returns. In order to achieve higher investment returns than are possible with savings or money market accounts you must invest in other financial markets so your money can grow at a meaningful rate. Equity or stock market investments should be a core element of your long-term investment strategy.

- Investment planning requires patience and planning. Avoid making emotional decisions regarding your investments. Ignore short-term price fluctuations in the stock market. Always focus on long-term potential.

- Ask questions and become educated before making any investment. One educated approach is to use a passive approach using no load index funds or exchange traded funds.

- Always invest with your head and use an investment policy statement to guide your current and future investments. Investment policy statements help eliminate emotional decision making. Never invest with your stomach or heart. Avoid the urge to invest based on how you feel about an investment or what a friend or colleague says works for them. What is right for someone else is not necessarily right for you.

Seven Keys to Successful Investing

A successful investment plan is needed to achieve financial freedom. Smart investors always try to maximize their gains and minimize losses. A plan will help guide your investment decisions. As discussed previously you need to first set life planning goals in order to make your financial dreams a reality. Use the following investment planning tips to guide your decisions.

- ➢ Establish a Solid Financial Base
- ➢ Save for retirement first (maximize the use tax advantaged investments)
- ➢ Long-Term Compounding: Allow Time to be on Your Side
- ➢ Understand Risk
- ➢ Choose the Right Asset Allocation Mix
- ➢ Put Your Spending Plan on Cruise Control: Dollar Cost Averaging
- ➢ Review Your Progress

Establish a Solid Financial Base

Before you start an investment program you need to establish a solid financial base. Every step of the tax and financial planning journey has been designed to create that solid fundamental base. During the tax resolution and financial freedom process this means resolving tax problems, eliminating high interest debt, and establishing an emergency fund.

At this point in the tax resolution and financial freedom process you should have already organized your finances and have a stronger sense of control over your money. Taking action and assuming control helps anyone with or without tax problems manage their money more efficiently. Remember, investing is just one component of an overall financial plan. Once you have developed positive financial behaviors such as the use of a personal spending plan, avoidance of problematic debt, and an understanding of your overall net worth you should have a clear picture of where you are today. The investment plan will be built on solid ground. Investors who make the mistake of investing prior to establish a solid financial base are at a greater risk for tax and financial problems.

Continue to take the necessary steps to stay out of debt and make the most of your money. Review your personal spending plan on a monthly basis and make sure that you spend your money before the month begins. Review your net worth on an ongoing basis. Maintain an adequately funded emergency fund. Avoid high interest consumer debt.

Financial Freedom Tip: Review your personal spending plan and determine exactly how much you are capable of investing each month. Invest in your own financial freedom prior to paying other monthly expenses. This requires you to set aside investment money before the month begins. Giving and saving/investing should always come first with your personal spending plan.

Save for Retirement First with Tax Advantaged Accounts
Now that you have determined exactly how much you can comfortably set aside you need to figure out in what type of account to invest your money. There are essentially three main options to consider. Investment accounts can be classified as taxable, tax-deferred, or tax-free. When choosing where to invest you should maximize the use of tax advantaged investments within retirement accounts first. This means participating in pre-tax retirement accounts such as 401(k), 403(b), 457, Keogh, SIMPLE IRA, and SEP IRA plans through your employer.

Pre-tax retirement accounts allow you to set aside money for retirement that will not be taxed until distributed during retirement years. If your employer offers a matching contribution you should participate in this plan at least up to the matching contribution amount. This is free money from your employer that will disappear if not used. Use it to your advantage. After you have maximized any matching contributions, you should consider contributing to other tax-deferred retirement accounts. Pre-tax savings or tax-deferred savings refers to the fact that the money you are investing is reducing your taxable income. This is a good thing! However, your pre-tax investments will be taxed as ordinary income once withdrawn during your retirement years. When you eventually withdraw your retirement investments you have more control over how your distributions will take place. Your marginal income tax rate may even be lower during retirement.

After taking advantage of any employer matching contributions you should consider tax-free retirement savings vehicles such as a Roth IRA or Roth 401(k). Contributions to tax-free accounts such as a Roth 401(k) or Roth IRA are never deductible. However, if certain requirements are met these accounts will continue to grow tax-free if held until normal retirement age (59 ½ years of age).

If you are self-employed you should set up a retirement account for your business if you are able to contribute above the maximum amount to a Roth or traditional IRA. Individuals who are married but only one spouse is working should consider a Spousal IRA. Income limits apply, so be sure to check with a financial planner or a reliable resource to find out if you are eligible.

Retirement Accounts
Let's review your retirement savings options in greater detail. If your employer offers a retirement savings plan you should contribute the maximum amount that you can comfortably afford to your employer's retirement plan (e.g., 401(k), 403(b), Thrifts Savings Plan, 457, SIMPLE IRA, or SEP plan). The maximum IRS allowed contribution to a 401(k) or 403(b) plan in 2009 is $16,500 ($22,000 for ages 50 or older). Your employer may have its own contribution limit, so be sure to comply with its rules. Retirement plan contributions give you tax savings in the calendar year you contribute and provide additional funding for life planning goals such as retirement. If your employer's plan includes a matching program make sure you maximize the benefits of matching before considering any other investment vehicles. This is essentially free money from your employer towards your retirement and should be taken advantage of before considering any other investments.

In the event that your employer does not offer a retirement plan such as a 401(k) plan you could establish and fund a traditional IRA up to the maximum amount per year. You should do this in order to take advantage of the tax savings for the calendar year in which you contribute and to supplement your retirement income. The annual limit on contributions for traditional IRAs in 2008 and 2009 is $5,000 ($6,000 for ages 50 or older). An additional benefit is that your earnings will grow tax-deferred. Keep in mind that there are certain income limitations if one spouse is covered by an employer's retirement plan and the other spouse is not.

An excellent alternative to a traditional IRA is a Roth IRA. You may want to establish a Roth IRA and contribute up to the maximum amount per year. You can do this in addition to contributing to your employer's retirement plan, i.e., 401(k) plan. The annual limit on contributions for Roth IRAs in 2008 and 2009 is $5,000 ($6,000 for ages 50 or older). Be mindful that a contribution to a Roth IRA is phased out for taxpayers with adjusted gross income above certain limits. The most important thing to remember is that Roth IRA contributions are non-deductible, but you will receive tax-free distributions during retirement after age 59 ½ and as long as you have had the account for at least five years. Unlike traditional IRAs, individuals are allowed to make contributions after age 70 ½ and are not forced to take at least the yearly minimum required distribution by the age 70 ½.

The traditional vs. Roth IRA decision depends on your particular financial situation. Your decision when choosing between a traditional IRA and Roth IRA should be based on which tax bracket you will be in when the funds are taxed. If you presume you will be in a lower tax bracket when you decide to withdraw the funds it would be beneficial for you to invest within a traditional IRA. If your tax bracket will be higher when you withdraw your funds it would be best to invest within a Roth IRA.

After you have maximized contributions to qualified retirement plans or IRAs, consider using other tax-favored investment vehicles. Vehicles such as annuities, municipal bonds, growth stocks, or tax-efficient, low turnover mutual funds can improve your after-tax return.

Education Accounts

Saving for a child's education is a common life planning goal for many families with children or grandchildren. The vision of helping the next generation try to live up to their fullest potential is a noble endeavor. Unfortunately, many people with a history of tax problems and other financial setbacks may feel like they are playing a game of catch-up trying to overcome years of debt problems. If you have children with future college plans, education planning should be a part of your financial plan. However, you need you have your own investment plan in motion prior to considering investing in a college savings plan for your child or grandchild. This means you should direct at least 15% of your investment money into tax advantaged retirement savings accounts before funding an education plan.

This is a hard pill to swallow for many and does not mean that you love your children any less just because you cannot afford to fully fund their future education costs (or have to delay education funding). The reality is that you can find other ways to fund a child's education such as borrowing, paying out of pocket, scholarships, work-study programs, etc. You will not be able to borrow for retirement, and your children should not be expected to help fund your retirement dreams. Financial freedom requires courage to make hard decisions. Choosing between retirement and education is a difficult choice for parents. By taking the steps outlined in the financial freedom process you may be able to achieve both goals.

Education Savings Accounts

If your retirement savings are sufficient and you have already maximized your retirement investments you should go ahead and establish a college savings plan. Set aside up to $2,000 per year into an Education Savings Account (ESA). These accounts are structured similarly to IRAs.

529 College Savings Plans

If you are married filing jointly and your income is above $200,000, or you are able to participate more than the $2,000 annual limit to an ESA, you should consider participating in a 529 College Savings Plan. A 529 plan allows your college savings to grow tax-free as long as the gains are used to pay for qualified education expenses. Some states even offer income tax deductions for certain contributions to a 529 Plan. There is no income limit in order to participate, and the contribution amounts are extremely high.

Long-term Compounding: Allow Time to be on your Side

You must understand the impact that time has on an investment plan. Take advantage of the power of compounding and let the impact of time work in your favor. The power of compounding works when you have a solid financial base to build upon. Compounding is basically defined as the earning of interest on interest, or the reinvestment of income. For instance, if you invest $10,000 at 8 percent, you will earn $800. By reinvesting the earnings and assuming the same rate of return, next year you will earn $864 on your $10,800 investment. The following year, $11,664 will earn $933.

Use what is referred to as the Rule of 72 to calculate the potential growth of an investment. Divide the projected rate of return into the number 72. The resulting answer is the number of years that it will take for the investment to double in value based on the projected rate of return. For example, an investment that earns 8 percent per year will double approximately every 9 years.

The Rule of 115 works the same way and may be used to help determine how long it will take to triple your investment. If the number 115 is divided by an expected rate of return the result is the approximate number of years it will take for the investment to triple in value. For example, at a 10% rate of return it will take only 11.5 years for the investment to triple.

With the concept of long-term compounding on your side the nest egg may get bigger and bigger over time. The debt snowball approach to paying off debt used the momentum of payments to eliminate high interest debt. The "rolling snowball" effect also works for investing.

Historical Rate of Investment Returns

While we are on the subject of investment returns it is necessary to establish the reason why some asset allocation classes are better than others when designing an investment portfolio. Understanding expected rates of returns for investments will help you set realistic expectations and evaluate performance over long periods of time. Remember that the following figures are based on historical data. The popular disclaimer within the investment world is "past performance does not guarantee future returns". You cannot predict the actual return of any investment with any accuracy over time. Investment professionals can only make educated guesses. However, you can make long-term strategic investment decisions based on average annual returns over long periods of time. Here is a general idea of the expected rates of return for major asset classes. Keep in mind this information is based on the historical performance of various asset classes. The underlying index that tracks the asset class is also provided.

Expected Rates of Return Based on Historical Performance:

Asset Class	Underlying Index	Rate of Return
U.S. Large Company Stocks	S&P 500	10%
U.S. Small Company Stocks	Russell 2000	10-11%
International Stocks	MSCI EAFE	9-10%
Fixed Income	Lehman Brothers Aggregate Bond Index	5.5-6%
Money Market	Citigroup 3-month U.S. Treasury Bills	5.5%
Inflation	Consumer Price Index	3.0%

Understanding Risk

After discussing the amount to invest and the type of accounts to invest in, our next step is to figure out which type of investments are a best fit. This leads us to the discussion of understanding risk as it relates to an investment plan. One of the biggest risks that we have discussed up to this point is not being in control of your financial future. Becoming an active participant in the tax and financial process helps eliminate that risk. Once you make the decision to set aside funds for retirement or other life planning goals you will be faced with the question of where to place your investment money. Do not take this decision lightly. Prior to selecting your investments you need to understand the meaning of risk as it applies to investments.

One of the most frequently used financial planning terms is risk. Risk has a variety of meanings in the area of personal finance. Most often the term "risk" refers to the price volatility of specific asset classes or investments. Your tolerance for risk is an important factor in deciding what financial products you will be comfortable including in your investment plan.

A special relationship exists between risk and reward. Generally speaking, the more risk that you are willing to assume the higher your potential investment returns. Similarly, higher risk also leads to higher potential losses or declines in the value of investments. It is common sense to avoid higher risk investments without the prospects of higher returns. Your goal during the investment planning process is to maximize your investment returns while assuming an appropriate amount of risk. Each individual has a personal tolerance for risk that must be taken into account during the investment planning process.

Understanding your own tolerance for risk is a critical step when choosing investments. The amount of investment risk that you are willing to accept is directly related to your investment time horizon. This is the length of time for which you are investing your money.

Determine your individual risk tolerance
Everyone has their own tolerance for risk when it comes to investing. Risk tolerance is defined as the degree of uncertainty that an investor can handle in regard to a negative change in the value of an investment portfolio. Risk tolerance helps determine which investments are most appropriate for your investment plan. Your risk tolerance depends on when you will need the money you are investing, your financial life planning goals, and if you will be able to sleep at night if you choose a risky investment that has a potential for loss.

Your overall investment objectives and age have a significant influence in determining your risk tolerance. Younger investors have more time on their side to weather poor market conditions (such as our market decline- currently 38% decline in the S&P 500 during 2008). As investors get older and approach life planning goals the focus should be on more conservative investments.

The possible risk profiles are generally broken down into the following categories:

- Conservative (risk-adverse)
- Moderately Conservative (willing to assume a modest level of risk)
- Moderately Aggressive (willing to assume higher risks)
- Aggressive (highly risk-oriented)

Many investment risk tolerance profiles are available on the internet or through various financial institutions. I encourage you to explore your own risk tolerance level. Do not rely solely on a risk tolerance questionnaire to determine your actual tolerance for investment risk. Risk profiles are excellent tools to help start the risk tolerance discussion. They should never be used as the sole determining factor in how to invest your money. Taking multiple risk tolerance profiles may reveal somewhat different results. You should be able to identify a pattern in your responses and have a better understanding of your tolerance for risk.

Reducing risk through diversification

By now most everyone has heard the old saying, "do not put all of your eggs into one basket." This is referring to the concept of diversification. This leads us to the next basic investment concept of asset allocation. The asset allocation process is designed to help investors avoid putting all of their eggs in one basket through diversification. It determines which baskets to use and how many eggs to put into the basket.

Asset Allocation

Asset allocation is one of the most important components of a solid investment plan. Research indicates that over 90 percent of investment returns are determined by how investors allocate their assets. Individual security selection, market timing and other factors are less important determinants of investment returns. Therefore, in order to maximize returns and minimize risk it is necessary to spread the wealth across different asset classes. If diversification is the process of not putting your eggs in one basket, asset allocation is the process of determining which baskets to put them into with the highest probability of a successful outcome.

Asset allocation allows you to spread your investment money over several categories of assets, usually referred to as asset classes. These classes include stocks, bonds, cash (and equivalents), real estate, precious metals, collectibles, and insurance products. Asset classes involving stocks (or stock mutual funds) can be further broken down into more specific categories such as large cap stocks, small cap stocks, international equities, government bonds, other fixed income investments, and cash or money market.

The general idea of asset allocation is that different types of assets carry different levels of risk and potential for return. Different asset categories typically do not respond to market forces in the same way at the same time. Therefore, when one asset class is experiences declining returns, another asset class may actually be growing (though there are no guarantees). If you diversify by owning a variety of asset classes, a downturn in one asset class will not necessarily spell disaster for your entire investment portfolio.

Using the following asset allocation models and your own risk tolerance, you can identify the asset classes that are appropriate for your investment plan:

Conservative

Large Cap Stocks	25%
Small Cap Stocks	5%
International Equity	10%
Fixed Income	50%
Cash or Money Market	10%

Time Horizon: Approximately 5 years
- Mostly seeking current income with relative stability
- Want an opportunity to increase the value of investments

Historical Returns (1970-2007):
- Average annual return: 9.7%
- Best year: 27.1%
- Worst year: -6.6%

Moderately Conservative

Large Cap Stocks	35%
Small Cap Stocks	10%
International Equity	15%
Fixed Income	35%
Cash or Money Market	5%

Time Horizon: Approximately 10 years
- Mostly seeking solid growth with relative stability
- No need for current income
- Willing to tolerate some fluctuations or volatility but less than the overall stock market

Historical Returns (1970-2007):
- Average annual return: 10.4%
  (Moderately Conservative continued)
- Best year: 30.9%
- Worst year: -12.9%

Moderately Aggressive

Large Cap Stocks	45%
Small Cap Stocks	15%
International Equity	20%
Fixed Income	15%
Cash or Money Market	5%

Time Horizon: At least10 years
- Mostly concerned about the growth of investments
- No need for current income
- Willing to tolerate fluctuations or volatility but seeking slightly less risk than the overall stock market

Historical Returns (1970-2007):
- Average annual return: 10.9%
- Best year: 34.4%
- Worst year: -19.2%

Aggressive

Large Cap Stocks	35%
Small Cap Stocks	10%
International Equity	15%
Fixed Income	35%
Cash or Money Market	5%

Time Horizon: At least 15 years
- Mostly seeking investment growth
- No need for current income
- Willing to tolerate volatility and have

a high tolerance for risk

Historical Returns (1970-2007):

- Average annual return: 11.2%
- Best year: 39.9%
- Worst year: -23.8%

Source: Schwab Center for Financial Research with data provided by Ibbotson Associates, Inc.

Financial Freedom Tip: Determine the target asset allocation mix for your individual risk tolerance level.

Passive versus active investing

If you are a sports fan or enjoy competition in general, the following statement may make you a bit uncomfortable. When it comes to choosing your investments, do not try to beat the market- go for a tie (or as close to a tie as possible). Research studies indicate that passive investors tend to outperform active investment strategies over long-term holding periods. A market index is a group of stocks that represent the market performance of specific asset classes. The most popular market indexes are the Dow Jones Industrial Average, the Standard and Poors 500 (S&P 500), the Russell 2000, and the FTSE.

Many fee only financial planners recommend that you invest in index mutual funds or exchange traded funds (ETF's) rather than "actively managed" mutual funds or individual stocks. ETF's are relevant for lump sum investments, while index mutual funds are ideal for systematic investment plans due to lower costs. Index mutual funds provide valuable diversification to a portfolio and outperform most comparable investments. Studies show that to obtain the same amount of diversification available through a low-cost stock index fund (such as the Vanguard 500 Index Fund), you would need to own over 50 individual stocks. These days there are index funds and ETF's for every major asset class.

Financial Freedom Tip: When creating an investment portfolio use low cost index mutual funds as the core holdings across your target asset allocation categories.

Dollar Cost Averaging: Put Your Investment Plan on Cruise Control

Financial success requires developing positive money management behaviors and repeating them over and over again until they become a way of life. Budgeting for investments uses the personal spending plan to your advantage by allowing your money to work hard for you. Placing investment money aside and actually having a plan before the month begins is an easy way to get on the fast track to financial freedom. The practice of dollar cost averaging helps you routinely invest for future goals.

Dollar cost averaging is a method of investing consistently and often. This method of systematic investing allows you to accumulate shares of a mutual fund or stock by purchasing fixed dollar amounts of these investments over long periods of time. When prices are high your investments buy less. When prices are low the same fixed dollar amount buys more shares. This is a much better approach than trying to time the market. Very few investors can actually time market highs and lows. A popular saying in the investing world is "time in the market not timing the market".

No-load mutual funds are the ideal investments for dollar cost averaging. No load refers to the fact that no sales commissions are built into the price of mutual funds. This puts more of your investment dollars to work for you and eliminates sales commissions. I recommend that investors use no-load index funds when using a systematic investment plan. More information regarding index funds is provided in this chapter.

It is no surprise that the key to a successful dollar cost averaging approach lies with a personal spending plan. The budgeting process helps ensure that adequate funds are available each month to put into a systematic investment plan. You can essentially put your investment plan on cruise control with a dollar cost averaging plan. Routine investments eliminate the urge to try to time the market. Dollar cost averaging can actually help reduce market risk. This approach cannot guarantee profits or insulate your investment portfolio against losses in a down market. However, dollar cost averaging into no load index funds is a cost effective way to invest over long periods of time.

Review Your Progress

Review your investment progress on a regular basis, but do not feel like you have to track your investments daily if doing so will keep you up at night. Remember that a solid investment plan is the best way to reach long term life planning goals. This means that short term increases and declines in investment prices are less relevant than the historical positive performance of stocks and bonds over long periods of time. It is important to understand how your investments are performing in comparison to the market in general. Know the underlying index performance for each asset class in your portfolio. Track your performance at least annually to see where your investments stack up as a whole.

It is essential to review your portfolio and game plan consistently. I recommend a buy and hold, but this does not mean you should buy and forget. Investments will perform at different rates over time. While some asset classes are performing well others may be underperforming. That is the idea of asset allocation. Over time it is likely that your asset allocation mix will change. You will need to rebalance your portfolio at least once a year (or more frequently during periods when the market experiences greater short-term volatility). Significant shifts of 5 percent or more may also serve as a trigger for rebalancing. However you decide to monitor your investments, you should always have some type of rebalancing plan. Rebalancing will help restore your original asset allocation mix.

Create an Investment Policy Statement

Now that you have reviewed the Seven Basic Steps of Investment Planning it is time to take action and put that knowledge to work. An excellent way to make sure that you follow an investment plan and have a measurement stick in place to track your progress is the setup an investment policy statement. A solid investment plan requires proper direction and guidelines that will help any investor stay on track regardless of the situation. Plans will frequently change or be altered over time, but if you have a plan in place from the beginning you can always figure out whether or not you are on track to meet your financial goals. That is why you need to put your investment plan in writing and create an investment policy statement to guide your investment decisions. An investment policy statement is a written document that defines how an investment portfolio should be managed.

An investment policy statement typically answers the following questions:

- How much do you intend to invest each month?
- How many years will you be investing?
- What is the expected rate of return for the portfolio?
- What is your target asset allocation mix?
- What are your allowable assets?
- Which no-load index mutual funds fit into those asset categories?
- What are the benchmarks for the portfolio (DJIA, S&P 500, FTSE, etc.)?
- How often will you review your investment plan?
- When will you rebalance your portfolio?

> **Taking Action!!!** Create a written investment policy statement that defines your investment plan.

Use professional guidance as needed
Consider working with a financial planner to help review your asset allocation mix and investment performance. Professionals are available to track progress toward financial goals and provide unbiased support along the journey to financial freedom. Many fee-only planners are available on an hourly as needed basis to provide investment advice. Always keep in mind that your investment plan is just one aspect of your overall plan for financial freedom.

Summary
The entire purpose of the financial freedom process is to turn financial life planning goals into realities. Investing is the best way to establish sufficient funds to pay for long-term goals and objectives such as retirement, education, or funding a business. A solid investment plan is needed to fund financial objectives and make sure that your investment money is working hard for you. A well-designed investment strategy must always be appropriate to your individual risk tolerance.

The investment planning step puts every previous step to work for your financial future. In order to begin an investment plan you must first have a solid foundation in place. You cannot owe any taxes or high-interest consumer debt and invest at the same time. It does not make any sense to earn lower historical returns in the stock market or other classes than the interest that is generally charged by the IRS and other creditors. Getting out of debt and establishing a fully funded emergency fund of between 3-6 months basic living expenses is your prerequisite to begin an investment strategy. A clear idea of your financial goals and objectives must also be in place prior to beginning an investment plan.

Most people fail to follow these basic steps of creating a solid financial foundation. The eagerness to make money in the stock market and save for long-term goals can often overshadow the need to fully complete the steps that lead to investment planning. Once you are ready to begin investing you must make sure that you follow the basic principles of investing.

Start by saving for retirement first. Set aside as much investment money as possible into tax advantaged retirement accounts such as a 401(k), 403(b), Thrift Savings Plan, SEP IRA, SIMPLE IRA, traditional IRA, or Roth IRA. If your employer sponsored retirement plan offers a matching contribution feature you should maximize these contributions. After you have taken advantage of any available retirement plans at work you should consider a traditional or Roth IRA. If you are self-employed you should also consider establishing a retirement plan for your business.

Set your contribution goal as high as possible. Your goal should be to invest as much as 15-20% of your total household income. Your ability to invest is based on your cash flow situation. It should come as no surprise to realize that following a spending plan allows you to plan your investments. Investing always comes at the beginning of the month. It does not matter when your investments actually take place, go ahead and invest the money on paper before the month begins so it is not available for other potentially less important goals. Saving/investing and giving should come first and appear at the top of your spending plan worksheet.

After you determine how much to invest you need to figure out what type of investments in which to put your hard earned dollars at work. The LifeSpan Process advocates a passive investment strategy that primarily uses index mutual funds. Depending on your actual risk tolerance you may have some exposure to fixed income investments such as bonds. However, the core of your investment portfolio should always be centered with stocks. For the long haul stock market returns provide the best opportunity to create wealth and have historically been the top performing asset class. Build your investment plan with an asset allocation strategy that matches your individual tolerance for risk. There is not a right or wrong answer when it comes to deciding the investment portfolio that is best for your situation. If you need any help designing an investment portfolio you should use the services of a fee only financial planner who does not receive commissions for the sale of investment or insurance products. Fee only planners have the fiduciary responsibility to act in their clients best interests and provide an excellent source of objective investment advice.

Similar to resolving tax and consumer debt problems, investment goals take time to achieve. Allow time to be on your side and invest with long-term objectives in mind. If you review your investment portfolio on a regular basis and use portfolio rebalancing strategies to make sure that your strategy is always on track, you will succeed in reaching your life planning goals. Try to keep in mind that investments will fluctuate over time. The asset allocation process uses multiple asset classes such as stocks and bonds to minimize risk and maximize investment returns. Always strive to invest with proper asset allocation in mind and eliminate the urge to try to time the market or be a stock picker. The most successful investment plans are always more concerned with asset allocation. Yours should be as well.

If you are starting to invest for the first time or resuming an investment plan that was sidetracked due to tax problems, you need to constantly keep in mind the reasons you are investing in the first place. The development of positive financial behaviors is the key to financial freedom. Investing is one of the most important financial behaviors you can display as part of your tax and financial plan. An effective investment plan can do more than reduce taxes. It can increase the likelihood you will reach your financial objectives. Never lose sight of your visions and dreams as you continue to follow the investment planning step toward financial independence.

Financial Freedom Step #6:
Consider Eliminating all Forms of Debt

*"A bank is a place where they lend you an umbrella in fair weather
and ask for it back when it begins to rain."* ~ Robert Frost

*"Always bear in mind that your own resolution to succeed
is more important than any other one thing."* ~ Abraham Lincoln

The process of becoming debt free requires focused intensity in order to reach financial goals. Eliminating tax liabilities and other types of problematic debt relies on the ability to replace negative financial behaviors with smart decision making that is guided by a plan. Financial freedom also requires an attitude change toward debt. What is once a way of life will eventually become a way of the past once you reach the wealth building stage of the LifeSpan Process of Financial Freedom.

Once you make it to this point on the journey to financial freedom you should have already eliminated bad debt, established an emergency fund, and started investing at least 20% of your total income into retirement or other tax advantaged investments. Accomplishing those tasks takes courage and hard work. If you look back to the first step of the entire tax resolution process you realize that the concept of "Taking Control " and "Taking Action" describes this process perfectly.

It is no surprise that getting out of debt has a psychological component to it. Debt affects our thoughts, actions, and behaviors. It also brings up a variety of emotional responses. With all of the action steps that need to be completed to get out of debt, it easy to develop a complete aversion to all forms of debt (including "good" debt). The temptation to slide back into debt can be a difficult obstacle to overcome. Many people counter the temptation to fall back into the cycle of debt with a plan to eliminate all forms of debt from their lives.

The first step on the path to financial freedom used positive financial behaviors such as planned spending to eliminate problem debt as quickly as possible. This leads us to another debt elimination step that may be used to get rid of so-called "good debt" such as mortgages, other real estate loans, student loans, and business loans.

Eliminating good debt is a debatable concept among financial planning professionals and everyday people faced with the option of investing versus paying off debt. Most financial planners will generally advise against paying off a mortgage rather than investing the money. The argument against paying off other forms of debt such as mortgages primarily focuses on the higher potential rate of return from long-term investments in comparison to current low mortgage interest rates. Stock market returns have historically outperformed the guaranteed savings of paying off mortgage interest.

The guaranteed feature is a big component in this debate. Mortgage interest rates are a known factor. You can determine exactly how much you are saving when you pay off mortgage debt. In order to calculate the after tax cost of debt you multiply the interest rate by one minus your marginal tax rate. For example, if someone in the 25% marginal income tax bracket has a mortgage with a 6% interest rate, his or her after tax cost of debt would be 4.5% (6.0% x (1 - .25) = 4.5%). Do not forget to add the state income tax rate to this calculation. Paying down mortgage debt in this example would essentially be equivalent to a 4.5% fixed interest investment.

Financial life planning uses the wealth building process to help fund important goals such as retirement. Stock market investments play a significant role in building wealth. Over long periods of time the investment planning techniques used in the LifeSpan Process are based on the expectations of at least 9-10% average annual returns. This is a huge difference in comparison to the fixed rate return of paying off a mortgage.

Some people still prefer the psychological benefit of completely eliminating debt over maximizing the use of their money. Rather than fall back on the rational argument that you can improve your returns by investing rather than paying off good debt I suggest that you consider paying off all forms of debt. The elimination of mortgages, student loans, and business loans may be a goal worth considering if you meet certain qualifications.

In order to consider eliminating all forms of debt you should have accomplished the following:

- You must already be setting aside a minimum of 20% of your total household income into retirement savings plans or other tax advantaged investments.
- You need to have a conservative risk tolerance.
- Your current interest rate must be higher than current national averages.
- You must be willing to accept the fact your actual savings may be lower than potential investment returns.

If you still have the desire to eliminate good debt then by no means should you allow me to stop you on your quest to be completely debt free. As long as you do not ignore the need to aggressively save for retirement and other life planning goals I will never criticize someone who is passionate about getting out of debt. There is a great sense of security in having a paid off mortgage or student loan. This is indeed an excellent way to gain a true sense of the term financial freedom.

Consider focusing on dual objectives

If you are in a position to start thinking about paying off a mortgage, student, or business loan but are torn between the investing vs. pay off debt debate you may want to consider doing both. You can accomplish both objectives by continuing to invest as much as possible while increasing your regular debt payments. This will help you to reduce your overall interest payments. This requires the use of good discipline to accelerate your debt elimination plan.

Summary

Always make sure that you are maximizing the funding of your financial life planning goals prior to shifting your focus on eliminating all forms of debt. This means that at least 20% of your total household income should be going toward long-term investments prior to considering paying off mortgages, student loans, or business loans. The elimination of all debt forms is an optional goal during the financial freedom process.

If you decide that paying down your mortgage and other acceptable forms of debt is in your best interests then you should follow an action plan. Use the same basic principles that were discussed during the first step on the path to financial freedom. Make the use of a personal spending plan, a habit that you follow regularly to maximize your monthly spending.

The decision to pay down acceptable debt (a.k.a. "good debt") should be based on the actual interest rate for the liability. If the interest rate on your loan is high and you have a fairly conservative investment risk tolerance you may benefit from paying down the good debt. Otherwise, continue to focus on using the investment planning process to create wealth. You can achieve dual objectives by accelerating your debt elimination plan and continuing to set aside investment money to reach your life planning goals.

Avoid paying for debt acceleration programs or bi-weekly mortgages. If a financial company tries to sell you these services be very wary. You can always accelerate your debt payments on your own and get rid of mortgages and student loans with discipline and a solid tax and financial plan.

Being an active participant in the tax and financial planning process will change your approach to taxes and money. It will also change your attitude toward debt. Debt was once normal part of everyday life. Now it should become something that you work hard to stay away from in your new financial life. It is not uncommon to develop some strong aversions to debt as you follow the steps of tax resolution and financial freedom. The desire to completely eliminate all forms of debt is a real and attainable objective. In no way is it unreasonable to imagine a life completely free from the burden of debt.

Financial Freedom
Step 7: Identifying Other Financial
Planning Opportunities

"We are all faced with a series of great opportunities brilliantly disguised as impossible situations." ~ Charles Swindoll

"Life is a gift, and it offers us the privilege, opportunity, and responsibility to give something back by becoming more." ~ Anthony Robbins

The existence of significant tax liabilities and bad debt creates a seemingly impossible challenge that is difficult to overcome. In the beginning of the tax resolution process it is difficult to truly understand the impact that debt has on your life. As you progress through the tax and financial planning process you experience the power of change as debt starts to disappear. Completely closing the door in debt's face will open you up to countless opportunities in life. You can accomplish so much more when you no longer have to deal with the physical, emotional, and social problems related to debt. The elimination of debt also allows you to focus on other financial planning concerns that you never thought would be possible with debt problems in your life.

Tax resolution prepares the way for the pursuit of financial freedom. Many financial life planning opportunities are created from the single decision that is made early in the tax resolution process. That is the decision to take control of your financial future. The decision to take action and make a commitment to change has long lasting effects if you continue to make the smart decisions needed to reach a state of tax and financial freedom. Life planning goals become attainable once you get out of tax and consumer debt.

Everyone has their own unique set of goals and objectives. The next step of the process focuses on identifying other financial planning opportunities. For the purposes of the LifeSpan Process of Tax Resolution and Financial Freedom, it is important to review some of the most common goals that many people tend to pursue in life. Some specific examples of financial goals that become more realistic without tax and consumer debt include: planning for major purchases, business planning, and charitable giving. If you have a specific goal that you would like to become a reality, then this step will be your chance to make it happen.

> **Taking Action!!!** Do you have a life planning goal you originally thought would be impossible but would like to strive to achieve? Eliminating tax and problematic debt from your life creates additional financial planning opportunities that would otherwise be difficult or impossible. Take a moment to think about some other life goals that you would like to accomplish once you have resolved your tax problems and started an investment plan for retirement. What else would you like for your wealth to create?

- Are you interested in buying a home, vacation property, or new car?
- Do you want to start a new business or grow an existing one?
- What charitable organizations would you like to donate your time, money, or talents?

Write down any additional financial planning goals that you would like to accomplish once you have resolved your tax problems and completely eliminated high-interest debt from your life.

Planned Major Purchases

Do you have a big purchase that is part of your financial plan? Perhaps it is buying a home, a car, boat, RV, or an expensive vacation. Whatever dreams you may have, you need a plan to help you prepare for a major purchase.

Buying a Home
The American dream has always included the desire to own a home. Unfortunately, many people in our government and financial institutions have sold this idea to people with no business owning a home based on their current financial position. Still, the desire to be a homeowner is real, and the benefits of home ownership make this goal a planned major purchase worth pursuing. The recent housing crisis in our nation has hopefully opened up the eyes of many people thinking about buying a home. The reality of this decision is that buying a home takes a significant amount of planning, and your finances must be in order prior to the purchase. Simply qualifying for a mortgage does not mean that the particular mortgage is right for your situation.

If the purchase of a home or real estate is in your plans you need to first make sure that your financial house is in order. By the time that you reach the seventh step of the financial freedom process you will have eliminated all forms of consumer debt, established an emergency fund, and started investing at least 15% of total income. You also should have a will in place and an insurance plan to protect your health and your wealth. At least 20% of the purchase price should be available for a down payment. If you cannot afford a 15 year mortgage you probably are looking at more home than you can reasonably afford.

Buying a Car
The best way to avoid future debt problems is to stay away from problematic debt. It does not make any sense to work so hard to get out of debt only to get right back into it. Since it is highly likely (almost certain) that you will need another car in your lifetime you should have a plan for this major purchase. The LifeSpan Process uses a simple approach to buying cars that should help you prepare for this future purchase decision.

Always buy "new" used cars and pay with cash.

Automobiles depreciate the second you drive them off the dealership floor. Buying a newer model used car saves you money. According to the experts, new cars depreciate between 15-20% during the first year of ownership. After that they generally lose about 10% in value over the next four years. This is the main reason that purchasing lightly used cars (or "newer" used models) is a smart financial decision.

If you have to finance a car purchase for any reason you should be able to fully payoff the loan in 12-18 months. Stay away from long-term loan deals. Only people with exceptional credit who qualify for incentive financing should even consider a vehicle loan. In most cases I still suggest paying for a quality used vehicle with cash. The absence of a monthly car loan payment provides more money to invest for the future.

Always incorporate a car replacement fund into your personal spending plan. When you created a personal spending plan in Step # 4 you should have noticed the category for car replacement fund. If you plan on replacing a vehicle within the next 3-5 years you should go ahead and begin saving for this purchase (above and beyond your emergency fund). Car replacement funds help keep your emergency fund intact and put you in control of the buying process. The psychology of debt and the related emotions of having a vehicle loan can be avoided by paying cash for future purchases.

Other Planned Major Purchases

The same basic principles of buying a car can be applied to other planned major purchases. If you are considering buying a boat, RV, second home, or a cruise around the world, you should be prepared to purchase with confidence. The best way to make your purchase fit into your financial plan is to save for it well in advance. Many people make the mistake of impulsively purchasing things because they want them now and cannot wait. Lenders make the decision making process more difficult because they tend to only focus on monthly payments and low interest rates. The real question is "do you really need to make the purchase or not".

If you do, then you should make a wise purchase decision as part of your big picture financial plan. Avoid the temptation to purchase non-essential items until you have cash to pay for them in full. Second homes, RVs, and yachts are a few exceptions to this rule due to the deductibility of mortgage interest. If you are considering purchasing these items you should still make at least a 20% down payment and never extend loan payments beyond 15 years.

Business Planning

Everyone should pursue a career that they love and enjoy. There is nothing more meaningful and fulfilling than doing something that you are passionate about in life. Being your own boss is an attractive part of being a small business owner. However, only self-starters and entrepreneurs should apply. As a small business owner or independent contractor you have the ability to take advantage of many additional planning opportunities not available to regular employees. You are also responsible for your own decisions.

Small business is the lifeblood of our nation's economy. The discussion of tax and financial freedom would be incomplete without the discussion of basic principles of business planning. The freedom of self-employment is a blessing for many. It can also become the source of stress and heartache if the business is being operated without a plan or a clear sense of direction. Business planning works hand in hand with personal financial planning. The purpose of this step of the financial freedom process is to outline some tips for current and future small business owners. If you are already self-employed, then you can use this step to confirm that your existing approach to running a business is correct.

Many self-employed individuals get themselves into tax trouble as a result of not running their business in an effective manner. Various cash-flow problems can lead to difficulties paying the self-employment tax and payroll taxes (if the business has employees). If you are a small business owner your self-employment may have actually contributed to the initial tax problem. Whether you are already in business or contemplating becoming your own boss, following basic business planning strategies will help you make the most of the self-employment experience.

- Plan your life first and then plan your business
- Avoid going back into debt to start a business
- Structure your business for success
- Keep good records
- Use a team approach
- Create a marketing strategy
- Understand basic business tax planning

Plan your life first and then plan your business
A solid business plan begins with a well-defined life plan. The financial life plan is designed to help you make the most of your money. If you do not have a clear vision or purpose then your business will likely suffer as a result. Finding happiness and joy in a career can be a challenge. That is why you need to have your life plan in place before you try to plan the future of your business.

It is important to understand the reasons you are in (or want to be in) business for yourself. Define your individual strengths and weaknesses to make sure that they are a good fit for your business. Also, be sure that you have a mission statement that clearly states the purpose of the business. This will help you and your employees have a good idea of what the business stands for and represents. Finally, a written business plan is a must for any business whether it is old or new.

Avoid going back into debt to start a business
The desire to own a business can prove to be an expensive endeavor. You need to have your finances in order prior to starting a new business. According to the U.S. Small Business Administration nearly two-thirds of new businesses survive at least two years, 44 percent at least two years, and 31 percent last at least seven years. The number one reason for small business failure is generally related to cash flow problems. If your business is starting out with debt then you have a higher risk of failure due to cash flow problems.

Fund your business with existing savings or investments that are not tied to other life goals such as retirement or education. Never use a home equity loan or line of credit to fund a business. If something goes wrong and failure is a real possibility, you do not want to lose both your home and your business.

Structure your business for success
It is important to choose the ideal structure for your business. Determining how to structure a business depends on a variety of factors. Some of these factors include the type of business, details regarding ownership, and the number of employees. From a business planning standpoint your basic options are as follows:

- Sole proprietorship
- Partnership
- S Corporation
- C Corporation
- Limited Liability Company (LLC)

Due to the fact that legal and tax considerations play a significant role in selecting the most appropriate business structure, it is generally recommended that you seek professional advice in order to determine the best structure for your business.

Create and follow a budget for your business

A personal spending plan is a positive financial behavior that leads to success. Tax and financial freedom requires you to make the budgeting process a way of life. You should have separate budgets for your business and your personal finances. Small business owners usually have trouble separating business finances from personal finances. They should be treated as separate entities no matter what the circumstances may be. Self-employment can seemingly become part of everything that you do. However, you need to be able to separate your business and personal life to some degree. At a minimum, try to maintain separate budgets.

Keep good records

Business success is also tied to good budgeting and accounting practices. Small business tax and financial problems are generally linked to poor budgeting and improper record keeping. Good organization and bookkeeping will help your business succeed. It will also make your tax returns easier to file and will help protect you from the IRS if your returns are ever subject to examination. Consider the use of accounting software, or use a professional accounting service to track your business income and expenses.

Always have a general idea of where your business stands from a financial point of view. This requires you to have a general understanding of your net self-employment income at all times. Accounting software helps you track your business income and expenses. This enables you to stay current with all of your business obligations (accounts payable, payroll taxes, estimated taxes, etc.). Without exception, you should always maintain separate bank accounts for your business. Do not mix business and personal income or expenses unless you enjoy making your financial situation an organizational nightmare!

Use a team approach

Every small business owner needs a network of professionals to help guide him or her through difficult decisions. Professional help is also useful during positive times to help maximize growth and encourage smart business planning decisions. A team based approach incorporates the knowledge and guidance of various colleagues or professionals into the decision making process of a small business owner. Your team could include a mentor, attorney, accountant, financial planner, or other tax professionals. Different businesses require different types of support. No matter what your career may be, you need a team of professionals and colleagues to support the growth of your business or self-employment.

Create a marketing strategy

An effective marketing plan is useful regardless of the product or service you provide. In some cases you may simply be marketing yourself and skills to others. In others you are marketing an actual business with products and services. Part of the marketing plan involves first determining how much you will charge for a product or service. Do not sell yourself short during this important part of the process.

Understand Basic Income Tax Planning

The structure of your business determines how you will be taxed.

It is important to make estimated tax payments on your total income from your business to avoid getting behind on your taxes and incurring penalties.

You may also want to obtain additional information on operating a small business by visiting the U.S. Small Business Administration web site at www.sba.gov.

Advanced Estate Planning

Step #4 concentrated on protecting your family's assets and financial well-being in the event of your or your spouse's death. When you are just starting the wealth building process basic estate planning techniques such as creating a will and maintaining adequate life insurance is all you should focus on. As your wealth continues to grow your estate planning needs are also likely to change. Creating a more detailed estate plan is another potential financial planning opportunity that you should consider.

The estate planning process will likely become more and more complicated as you start to develop significant wealth. A well-designed estate plan will allow you to determine how your assets will be transferred upon your death. There are many different strategies available to make sure that your estate plan is designed to meet your individual hopes and concerns.

Charitable Giving

"The only thing you take with you when you're gone is what you leave behind." – John Allston

Financial freedom allows you to redirect your time and energy to important life goals. Many people in debt wish they had more financial resources to give to charitable causes. However, tax and financial problems can create major financial roadblocks that limit your abilities to give financial resources to others. Simply put, there is not too much available to give when you are deeply in debt. This does not mean that people with debt should discontinue giving to others; it merely is being stated to point out that with debt there is less discretionary money to give. It can be hard to give to others when there is not much to give.

Financial stress also limits our ability to fully give to others with passion and energy. When you remove the financial stress of debt from your life you allow yourself to give to others more freely. Charitable giving can be good for your heart, soul, and your tax return.

Charitable giving was discussed briefly during Step #4 of the Tax Resolution Process-Establishing a Personal Spending Plan. Saving and giving should always come first when following a spending plan. Determining how much to give to others is a very personal decision. Rather than get caught up in the details of how much to give to the greater good of helping others, I believe it is more appropriate to discuss the various ways to give.

Everyone knows the old saying that it is better to give than to receive. It is even more beneficial to give and see your generosity rewarded. A well-planned gift can play a valuable role in your tax and financial plan. Charitable gifts are capable of producing the following benefits:

- They provide an opportunity to become more involved in church, community, or charitable causes that are close to your heart.
- Charitable gifts can reduce income taxes.
- Charitable giving may also be used to help reduce or avoid estate taxes.

Charitable gifts can provide you with an ability to maintain a sense of financial freedom. Charitable planning can also help you maintain control over your assets during your lifetime and beyond. In addition, your charitable donations may also allow you the opportunity to continue to take care of your heirs while also giving to others. When you reach this stage of the financial freedom process you need an integrated wealth transfer plan that supports your goals of philanthropy and altruism. Since giving to others can also have significant tax advantages you need to use strategies that allow you to enjoy the personal and financial benefits of planned giving. Some examples of popular estate planning strategies that may be used to implement your charitable ambitions include gifts of appreciated property, Charitable Remainder Trusts (CRT), Charitable Lead Trusts (CLT), and private foundations.

Once you reach this final stage of the LifeSpan Process of Tax Resolution and Financial Freedom you will be able to reward others while rewarding yourself for all the hard work and commitment used to reach the ultimate goal of financial freedom. Do not wait until your financial situation improves or you have earned significant sums of wealth to begin giving back to others. There are countless benefits from giving your time and talents to worthy causes. True wealth is not measured by a net worth statement or spending plan.

Summary
It takes a great deal of confidence to attack debt with a plan. People who win the battle versus debt are able to regain control of their lives. They are also in a position where they can finally focus on reaching long-term life planning goals that once appeared impossible. Whether you have aspirations of purchasing a large asset that has been a lifelong dream to own or you are trying to start a small business, you need to be out of debt to move forward with your objective. Similarly, the creation of significant wealth that can be transferred across generations of heirs or donated to charities or other important causes relies on the attainment of financial freedom.

The ability to make smart financial decisions and live a debt-free life presents countless opportunities in life. Tax freedom allows people a chance to redirect their time and energy in areas where they can accomplish great things in work, play, and community involvement. Not having to worry about taxes and other forms of debt means that you get to worry about other areas of the financial life.

Your challenge as you proceed through the steps of the Tax Resolution and Financial Freedom process is to focus all of your efforts on reaching important financial life planning goals. You get to define financial freedom and decide what independence means to you when it comes to the topics of taxes and money. Having a plan that you can follow is always the solution to any tax or financial problem whatever your life planning goals may be.

The elimination of debt from your life will allow you the freedom to be able to identify financial life planning opportunities that would otherwise be impossible to achieve. Without debt, you are able to concentrate on things you would not be able to even think about while living a financially out of control life.

Part IV
A New Beginning: The LifeSpan Plan for Tax Resolution and Financial Freedom

Conclusion

"Outstanding people have one thing in common: an absolute sense of mission." ~ *Zig Ziglar*

Conclusion

The pursuit of tax and financial freedom is a challenging mission with a lot at stake. At the beginning of this mission you are standing in the middle of the road with a big decision to make. You can always turn back in the direction you came from originally. This is the normal way of life you feel comfortable with and is referred to as the "status quo" or the easy road. The old way includes financial behaviors of the past that have not worked, such as spending without a plan, living beyond your means, and not saving or investing enough for the future. Your other option is to charge forward with passion and desire into the direction of financial freedom. This unfamiliar road is not always easy and will challenge your comfort level in life as you learn new financial behaviors and a brand new approach to dealing with life as it relates to money. One major obstacle lies in the middle of this road and may be the biggest financial roadblock that you will ever have to overcome. The financial roadblock that I am referring to is called tax debt. The only way to successfully complete the mission and reach the final destination of financial freedom is to break through the tax resolution barrier.

During these uncertain economic times millions of Americans are struggling financially. Debt in general is already reaching crisis levels throughout the nation. Tax debt is also growing at record levels. Dealing with the IRS should be a top priority for people experiencing debt problems. The IRS is capable of taking aggressive collection measures and should not be ignored. In fact, debt problems in general should never be ignored. Tax liabilities need to be dealt with in a timely manner with a plan.

If you or someone close to you owes back taxes, an action plan is needed to resolve the tax debt with the most effective solution. The ideal plan should be a holistic tax and financial plan that focuses on the total financial situation. I refer to this big picture approach as the LifeSpan Process of Tax Resolution and Financial Freedom. The typical approach to dealing with tax debt tends to focus solely on alleviating the tax problem. While tax resolution is initially a top priority, the primary goal should be to use the occurrence of tax problems as an opportunity to seek meaningful change. The need to take action and assume control over both taxes and money is a common trait shared by most people experiencing tax problems.

Tax resolution should be for life. Once a person gets out of debt he or she needs to stay out of debt. Tax liabilities will occur in the future or simply transition to other financial problem areas if you do not completely change the way you handle personal finances. The lifelong pursuit of "tax freedom" refers to the sense of empowerment that is needed to assume control over future taxes. While nobody should be expected to know everything about income tax planning, it is important to feel like you are in greater control of your tax situation and gain a basic understanding of tax obligations and ways to stay compliant with the tax code.

Tax resolution planning is about living a better life. The most effective tax resolution approaches are the ones that look at the whole person rather than just seeing an individual with tax debt. Since tax liabilities are a sign of bigger problems, they should be viewed as symptoms of a disease. Financial life planning is the best known cure because it seeks permanent change for both the tax situation and the overall problems related to money management.

People get into tax trouble in a variety of ways. The most common characteristic shared by people with significant tax liabilities is that they did not have a tax and financial plan to guide their money related decisions. Changing the tax and financial mistakes of the past is necessary to move forward without any future tax problems. Therefore, an effective tax resolution plan must be put in action to deal with the current tax liability, prevent future tax problems, and provide guidance in other areas of the financial life. Having a tax problem does not define who you are as a person. However, how you choose to deal with the tax problem will define the rest of your life as it relates to money.

Many taxpayers with tax problems challenge the notion that the financial planning process is the answer to their problems. Common misconceptions are shared by delinquent taxpayers such as "planning is only for the wealthy", "financial planning only deals with insurance and investments", or "a financial plan will not help my tax problems". These beliefs are wrong and fail to recognize that financial planning is defined as the process of taking control of your finances. It is also defined as the process of meeting life goals through the proper management of your money. From this perspective the financial planning process is the perfect fit for someone engaged in the tax resolution process.

It is easy to be so overwhelmed by tax debt that the only concern is responding to IRS collection efforts. However, the failure to see the need for comprehensive tax and financial planning is the biggest mistake that a person with tax debt could possibly make. A well-constructed tax and financial plan is not only the best way to deal with tax problem, it is the best path to financial freedom.

The existence of tax problems can prove to be one of the most significant financial challenges that anyone will face during his or her lifetime. The consequences of debt are significant. Debt has an effect on relationships, health, and overall wealth. Procrastination, anxiety, and financial ignorance must all be overcome in order to attack tax liabilities or any other financial problem with a plan. The planning process begins once the taxpayer makes an honest commitment to both self and family to seek tax and financial change.

Seeking change can be a confusing process when tax liabilities are involved. A variety of tax resolution options exist. Finding the ideal solution based on your financial situation can be a challenge. An effective tax resolution analysis is needed to identify the best tax resolution alternative that is based on individual goals and objectives. The tax resolution analysis must be preceded by a thorough self-analysis. This is the defining area that separates the LifeSpan Process from other tax resolution plans. The typical approach with tax problem resolution is to jump right in and try to fix the tax problem immediately. This can lead to poor decisions and does not address overall financial planning goals and objectives. Focusing only on the tax problem does not do anything to correct the cause of the tax problem, nor does it do anything to improve the way that people with a history of tax problems approach tax and financial matters in the future.

Prior to finding the best solution to the tax problem, you need to step back and look at your total financial situation. Completing a detailed cash flow and net worth analysis provides a deeper understanding of where you stand financially. A brief self-assessment will allow you to measure your own ability to change more than just your tax situation. You also need to assess your ability to achieve meaningful change through a financial life planning approach. If you are married or in a committed relationship, you both must become active participants in the tax resolution process to see any lasting benefits. The final assessment that must occur is an honest analysis of whether or not a tax resolution professional is needed to provide additional guidance during the tax and financial planning process.

Once you get organized you need to create a personal spending plan. This is yet another action step that is required before the tax resolution analysis can actually begin. Tax resolution and financial freedom obviously takes a great deal of dedication and desire. It is easy to stray off the path of financial change. The reward of tax and financial freedom lies ahead for those people who follow the step by step process. It takes a solid financial foundation to resolve tax problems in the most effective manner possible. Developing a spending plan before analyzing your ability to pay off a tax liability is of critical importance. You need to resist the urge to be a passive participant in search of tax resolution. Following a spending plan and practicing the positive financial behaviors puts you in control of your financial future.

The tax resolution analysis stage begins after all of the initial steps have been taken to get organized, establish meaningful life goals, assess your resources, and create a spending plan. The developmental steps are geared to create self-awareness and basic financial management skills. You need to have a solid financial base established prior to choosing the best form of resolution for any financial problem. Now that you understand where you are financially you are in a position to look at your finances the same way the IRS looks at them. This process is referred to as the tax resolution analysis. The primary goal of this analysis step is to identify the most effective solution. The IRS provides a variety of tax resolution alternatives. Every single person engaged in the process is faced with the challenge of finding the best solution that fits into his or her overall financial life plan.

Whether your best solution is an Offer in Compromise, Installment Agreement, paying off the debt in full using existing resources, or some other option, you need to make a smart decision. The first big challenge is to decide to take control of the tax problem and take action. The biggest challenge is choosing the best alternative. Following the steps of the tax resolution process will help you make sure that you make the smartest decision possible. By following the tax resolution plan you will find yourself out of debt as quickly as possible and save a significant amount of money in interest and penalties. Most importantly, you will tear down the major barrier known as tax debt on your journey to financial freedom and independence.

The mission begins with tax resolution and culminates with a much bigger and much more important reward. Work the steps of the LifeSpan Process and you will be able take control of your future as it relates to taxes and money. No matter how stressful the tax and financial problems of the day may appear to be, there is always the promise of hope. There is always a solution. With the willingness to take action and seek change there is always the possibility of a better financial future. The ultimate responsibility always is on you to create a better tomorrow and make your life planning goals become reality. Your mission begins with a simple step. A tax and financial plan is the ideal solution as you take the journey in search of tax debt resolution and financial freedom.

Appendix
Tax Resolution Tips

➢ Never let fear guide your decision in selecting a tax resolution specialist. Always complete your homework, ask appropriate questions, and never feel pressured into making any immediate decisions.

➢ If you are currently investing money in stocks, bonds, mutual funds, annuities, or other investment vehicles (including retirement plans) you should STOP your investment plan contributions until your tax liability has been resolved. If you participate in a 401(k) or other retirement savings plan and your employer matches contributions you should still contribute up to the maximum amount your employer will match (if possible from a cash flow standpoint).

➢ The creation of a "Personal Spending Plan" is an essential part of the tax resolution process. The initial spending plan that you create during the tax resolution process begins with a detailed Cash Flow Analysis. Review your current income and expenses using the cash flow worksheet on the next page. Compare your monthly spending to national averages.

➢ Always stay focused and do not get discouraged with process of creating a personal spending plan. This is the key to your financial future. The path to financial freedom starts with a personal spending plan that puts you in control of your money.

➢ Complete a tax resolution analysis. If the equity in assets is greater than the amount of your tax liability then you can likely eliminate the Offer in Compromise- Doubt as to Collectibility as an option. One exception to this general rule is if you are unable to access the equity in assets. If you have equity in an asset but cannot access it you must be prepared to document your situation.

➢ If the estimated tax resolution offer amount is less than your actual tax liability you should consider requesting an Offer in Compromise with the IRS. If the Tax Resolution Analysis indicates that you have equity in assets and monthly discretionary income that is sufficient to pay off your tax liability, you should pay down your tax debt as much as possible and setup an Installment Agreement to pay your tax debt over time. The Monthly Discretionary Income amount is a likely amount that the IRS will require you to pay on a monthly basis. If paying your tax debt using existing resources would create a financial hardship you should consider requesting to be placed on Currently Not Collectible Status.

➢ If you are establishing an Installment Agreement with the IRS you must first establish a "Personal Spending Plan" that sets aside funds each month to pay off your tax debt. The amount that you send to the IRS should be above and beyond your required minimum Installment Agreement payment. You will get out of debt sooner by paying off more than the minimum monthly payments required by your IRS payment plan.

➢ Create a written tax resolution plan. Make a commitment to get out of tax troubles and achieve tax freedom. Put your goals in writing and be sure that if you are relying on a tax professional for guidance that they specifically outline the services that will be provided.

Financial Freedom Tips

➤ Seek the assistance of a tax professional, financial counselor or financial planner who will take the time to understand your tax resolution needs. Choose a professional who is empathic and will take the time to educate you about the tax resolution process. You are seeking someone with the heart of a counselor and the patience of a teacher.

➤ Work with a tax and financial planning professional (preferably a CFP, EA, CPA, or AFC) that understands tax resolution is your #1 priority. Seek out fee-only advisers who clearly define the services offered and how they are compensated. In general, you should not purchase any investment or insurance products as you focus on resolving tax problems and other debt issues.

➤ Determine your life plan and how the journey to financial freedom will help you make your goals and objectives a reality.

➤ Always have an understanding of your actual net worth. Keep in mind that the net worth statement has absolutely no bearing on your worth as a person. Regardless of your actual net worth, be sure to understand that personal wealth has many different meanings to each individual. For some it is a measure of accomplishment and success. For others wealth serves as a tool for accomplishing life goals.

➤ The tax resolution process may require you to tap into an emergency fund if you already have a savings fund. If this occurs be sure to establish a plan to rebuild your emergency fund prior to beginning any other savings or investment plans. Keep in mind that you will need a source to make payments to the IRS if you setup an Installment Agreement to pay your tax debt over time, or if you qualify for an Offer in Compromise. Maintain a "Starter Emergency Fund" of at least $500-$1,000 in the event of emergencies as you progress through the tax resolution action steps.

➤ After you have established and implemented a plan to resolve your tax debt, focus on eliminating high-interest consumer debt. Pay off all forms of debt excluding your mortgage and student loan prior to beginning a savings or investment plan.

➤ Establish an emergency savings account and fully fund it with 3-6 months living expenses. Use your personal spending plan to determine how much you are capable of saving each month.

➤ When seeking life insurance you should only focus on term insurance. Do not purchase cash-value life insurance since there are better investment alternatives.

➤ Set aside at least 15-20% of your income into a long-term investment vehicle. In general, investing should be a long-term goal after you resolve your tax liability. Keep in mind that the expected long-term rate of return of your investments is probably much less than the interest and penalties on any tax liability. Therefore, it usually advisable to resolve any tax liability and pay off your consumer debt before beginning an investing program suited to your risk tolerance.

➤ Make arrangements to have a will prepared immediately if you do not have one in place. Be sure to name a guardian for any minor children. Review your will on a regular basis and have your will updated as significant life events occur (birth of a child, divorce, inheritance, etc.).

➤ Review your beneficiary selections for all of your bank accounts, investment accounts, life insurance policies, and retirement accounts. Make sure that you update your beneficiary selections as needed.

10 Common Tax Resolution Myths

If you are seeking professional guidance with a tax resolution issue you should pay attention to these common myths that some tax representation firms perpetuate through various media outlets.

1. MYTH: The IRS offers a "one time only" opportunity to resolve your tax liabilities.

   FACT: The impression that tax resolution is a one shot deal is completely false. This "act now before you lose your chance" approach implies that the Offer in Compromise (OIC) program is a new service with the IRS. OIC's were initially introduced in the 1990's in order to increase voluntary tax compliance, reduce taxpayer burden, and improve IRS productivity. The Tax Increase Prevention and Reconciliation Act of 2005 made major changes to the program and altered the rules for lump-sum offers and periodic-payment offers.

   These marketing techniques are intended to encourage you to "act now" and sign up for a service. Many tax resolution clients actually become repeat clients and contact the same firm or a different tax resolution company. Is this the client's fault or a problem with the tax professional? Most typically the client is ultimately responsible for changing negative financial behaviors. However, it is up to the tax professional to provide as much education and guidance as possible to keep clients out of future tax problems. Although tax resolution is not a one-time opportunity, delinquent taxpayers should view it as a one-time only event that needs to be dealt with correctly the first time.

2. MYTH: If someone owes taxes to the IRS and has negative cash flow they should easily qualify for an Offer in Compromise.

   FACT: The IRS has the authority to settle or compromise federal tax liabilities by accepting less than full payment under certain circumstances. OIC's are generally accepted if the taxpayers can establish that they have either no means of paying the tax or do not actually owe the tax. The IRS calculates a taxpayer's collection potential by looking at equity in assets and monthly disposable income using a special formula that only includes "allowable" expenses based on national and local standards.

   A taxpayer can be living paycheck to paycheck with significant tax and consumer debt and the IRS may still have a legal right to collect on the entire amount owed. This is a common situation that many clients are faced with as they enter the tax resolution process. Cash flow problems also stress the urgent need to change overall financial behaviors and develop a coordinated plan to achieve financial freedom.

3. MYTH: It is best to work with a large tax representation firm that has ex-IRS agents working for them.

   FACT: Enrolled Agents (EAs), Certified Public Accountants (CPAs), and attorneys are the only professionals who have demonstrated special competence in tax matters and have earned the privilege of practicing or representing clients before the IRS. Enrolled Agents, like attorneys and CPAs, are unrestricted as to which taxpayers they can represent, what types of matters they can handle, and in which IRS offices they can practice. Past service and technical experience with the IRS is one category that can qualify a person to become an Enrolled Agent.

The most important thing to look for when seeking professional help is integrity and expertise in tax resolution planning. Note the word "planning". This is an essential element that tax resolution professionals should be focusing their attention. IRS experience definitely helps professionals understand the tax representation process. It does not always guarantee expertise in the important area of tax resolution planning.

4. MYTH: If someone is drowning in debt he or she should easily be able to qualify for "pennies on the dollar" resolution.

   FACT: First of all, avoid any companies that use "pennies on the dollar" advertising or provide guarantees that you will qualify for an Offer in Compromise. The OIC program is the most widely advertised and promoted tax resolution technique marketed on television and the internet. OIC's are also grossly oversold to people experiencing significant cash flow stress due to broader financial problems related to consumer debt. If you have the assets or future income potential to pay off your tax debt over time you will not qualify for an Offer in Compromise (except in special circumstances). The IRS only uses "allowable expenses" in the tax resolution analysis. Certain expenses such as credit cards, tuition, retirement contributions, and cable television bills are not allowable expenses during the tax resolution process.

5. MYTH: Large tax representation firms can perform their services more efficiently and at a lower cost than local Enrolled Agents, CPAs, or tax attorneys.

   FACT: Costs vary from firm to firm. The level of customer service and professionalism also varies. If you take action and actively participate in the "LifeSpan Process of Tax Resolution and Financial Freedom" you will know where to find the most cost-effective solutions to your tax problems, whether or not you choose to use the services of professional tax representation.

6. MYTH: Tax resolution companies have a regulatory body that provides them with a specific set of guidelines and a professional code of ethics.

   FACT: Currently there is no existing regulatory body to protect consumers doing business with tax representation firms. Most individual practitioners such as CPAs, EAs, and attorneys have professional standards they must uphold, but tax representation firms as a whole do not have anything other than legal precedent and IRS policies and procedures to guide them. The IRS issued a consumer alert to taxpayers in 2004 advising them to "beware of promoters' claims that tax debts can be settled for "pennies on the dollar" through the Offer in Compromise Program".

7. MYTH: Tax resolution firms represent me by appearing directly in front of the IRS on my behalf.

   FACT: The majority of tax representation work occurs over the phone, internet, and through regular mail correspondence. Effective tax representation most often avoids the need for a one on one meeting with the IRS or appearances in Tax Court.

8. MYTH: The IRS may have forgotten about you if they do not contact you after a few years of not filing or paying taxes.

   FACT: One of the biggest problems with the IRS collection process is the fact that it can often take years before the collection process actually begins. The tax system in our country is based on voluntary compliance. If you let months and years pass the IRS will eventually track you down, and you will be hit with enormous penalties and interest. This cycle of procrastination and avoidance only creates a bigger tax and financial problem. Delays and avoidance behaviors only intensify tax problems. Besides, if you owe taxes then you need to get the problem resolved quickly. Not paying taxes is essentially stealing from the federal government and all of the honest Americans who paid their taxes. Ignoring the problem will only make it worse.

9. MYTH: Taxes and finances are too confusing to understand. Besides, individuals are not capable of resolving tax problems by dealing with the IRS on their own.

FACT: Financial ignorance can be overcome through action and some basic education. Tax resolution and financial planning is 75% behavioral and 25% knowledge and technical expertise. Everyone has the ability to deal directly with the IRS themselves with proper guidance and preparation. Professionals play an important role in the tax resolution process. The ultimate responsibility lies with the individual to make smart financial decisions. Knowledge will only get you so far. You have to be able to take action and use financial knowledge to your benefit. Too many people with tax problems are paralyzed by fear because they do not understand basic concepts of money and taxes.

10. MYTH: If someone has a tax problem they do not need a financial plan.

FACT: This common misconception is the entire reason that the "Tax Resolution and Financial Freedom" process was created. Tax problems are most often the result of poor planning, economic hardships or emergencies, financial ignorance, fear, and procrastination. The only way to resolve tax problems and take control of your life as it relates to money is to establish and implement a tax and financial plan. Whether you call it financial planning or counseling the end result should always be an improved sense of direction when it comes to financial matters.

Choosing a Tax Resolution Planner

1. Seek a CPA, Enrolled Agent, or tax attorney who specializes in helping people with tax problems. Avoid working with sales consultants who are not the actual professionals who will be dealing with the IRS or state taxing authority.

2. Ask about the tax professional's general approach to the tax resolution process. Does he or she simply focus on the tax debt or do they provide income tax planning and financial counseling?

3. Do not sign any post-dated checks or high-interest finance agreements. Get the terms of the tax resolution engagement in writing and do not feel pressured to sign anything until you have reviewed the client-practitioner contract or engagement agreement.

4. Find out if individuals other than the person you are speaking with will be working on your case. If so, ask about their qualifications and preferred methods of communication. Do not be alarmed if your tax professional uses a team based approach. Simply be sure that each team player's role is clearly defined.

5. Determine what your responsibilities will be during the course of the tax resolution process.

6. Do not set unrealistic expectations for your tax professional or for the tax resolution process in general. Dealing with tax problems can take time and involves a considerable amount of effort on the part of both taxpayer and tax professional. Take ownership of your tax issues and play an active role while working with your tax resolution professional.

7. Trust your instincts. If the promises of a tax resolution planner sound too good to be true then they usually are. Remember that not everyone will qualify for an Offer in Compromise. The Internal Revenue Service determines whether or not taxpayers qualify for various tax resolution options. This means that tax professionals cannot guarantee a particular outcome for your dealings with the IRS.

8. Inquire about the cost of services. Make sure that the fees for service are based on the estimated amount of time that will be needed to deal with the tax problem rather than the amount of taxes owed.

Seven Rs of Financial Behavior Motivation and Change

<table>
<tr>
<td colspan="3">
<h2 style="text-align:center">REPLICATION</h2>

In order to motivate financial behavior change in a way that achieves financial well-being and has a broad impact, it must be possible to replicate outcomes. As you begin to take action and work on taking control of your money, consider these key factors. Keep in mind that the ultimate goal of the tax resolution process is to reach both tax and financial freedom.

Source: National Endowment for Financial Education
</td>
</tr>
</table>

Core "Rs"	Individuals w/ tax debt	Key Questions
Readiness	A person becomes aware that making change is something to consider. In the earliest stages you may be neutral, positive or negative about the possibility of changing how you handle personal finances.	Are you ready to make a commitment to change past financial behaviors? How prepared are you to change your financial decision making by following a tax and financial plan?
Resources	Without the proper resources, no matter how "ready" you may be, it is easy to become discouraged about taking the steps to tax resolution and financial freedom. For example, a person cannot be expected to change financial behaviors that led to tax problems if they are not aware that tax resolution professionals are available to help them make positive changes.	Do you feel confident that you have the resources available to get out of debt? Have you researched all of your options? What professional resources or social support network do you have available to assist you with this process?
Relevance	Life circumstances often trigger recognition of a need to change. For example, it is relevant to establish a personal spending plan when one realizes the need to solve cash flow problems caused by excessive debt. Individuals generally seek specific solutions that resolve their tax problems in the quickest and least painful way.	Do you feel that the tax and financial planning process is a relevant and useful way to resolve your tax debt? Do you understand the connection between your views about money and how you have handled financial decisions in the past?
Respect	The individual must feel genuine understanding, concern, and empathy for himself, his tax resolution professional, and his life situation.	How does your tax debt and financial situation affect how you feel about yourself?
Responsibility	Individuals need to understand the importance of taking responsibility for their personal financial management.	Are you ready to take control of your financial situation?
Reward	Whether it is real or perceived, the individual needs something positive that will reinforce continuing the new and positive behaviors related to planning.	What are some short and long term rewards for your constant diligence, patience, and hard work?

Bottom Line: The ability to replicate tax and financial planning behaviors is the success test for whether an individual's financial behavior change becomes a habit. If you continue to repeat the same positive financial behaviors over and over again (follow a spending plan, save for emergencies, plan for major purchases, avoid problematic debt, follow a tax and financial plan) you can overcome debt problems and take control of your financial future.

<h2 style="text-align:center">REPLICATION</h2>

Index

use with Installment Agreements, 102
Personal umbrella coverage, 156
Planned Major Purchases
    buying a car, 179
    buying a home, 179
    positive financial behaviors, 26
    purchasing a business, 180
    smart use of debt, 56
Potential traps, 4
Power of Attorney, 82, 111, 156
Pre-contemplation, 29
Preparation, 24, 27, 29
Pre-tax retirement accounts, 165
Pre-tax retirement savings. *See Retirement Accounts*
Problematic debt
    avoidance of, 164, 175, 179
    debt reduction plan, 137
    definition of, 136
    initial focus during path to financial freedom, 134
    tax debt is the most problematic, 135
Prochaska, James, 29
Procrastination
    barriers to change, 28
    causes of tax problems, 18, 33, 193
    common characteristics of people in debt, 23-24
    problem financial behaviors, 26
    replacing it with a plan, 119-120
    unfiled tax returns, 77
Purpose, 37, 43, 46

Q

Quick sale values, 54

R

Readiness, 28, 30, 42, 195
Real estate investment trusts, 55
Reason for not filing, 77, 78
Reducing taxable income, 122-123
Registered Investment Adviser, 50
Relevant, 30, 42, 195
Rental property, 55, 71, 79, 89
Replication, 30
Resources
    assessing during tax resolution process, 40
    external (social support), 47-48

financial, 51-61
    internal, 41-46
    professional guidance, 48-51
Respect, 30, 195
Responsibility
    individual accountability, 14, 17, 20
    primary agent of change, 30, 31, 195
    of financial planners, 9
Retirement Accounts, 6, 165, 166
Retirement Assets
    quick sale value, 87
    tax resolution alternatives, 97
Retirement Planning, 9, 148
Reward,
    financial freedom, 12, 21, 188
    motivation and change, 30, 195
Risk tolerance, 168-171, 190
Rule of 115, 167
Rule of 72, 167
Russell 2000, 167, 171

S

S Corporation, 77, 124, 182
Saving
    creating a spending plan, 64
    discontinue until tax debt is resolved, 130
    emergency funds, 143-147
    importance, 72
    emergency funds, 143-147
    national savings rate, 2
    resolve tax debt before starting a savings plan, 67
    saving for retirement, 122
    transfer spending plan items to savings, 72-73
Saving vs. investing, 162
Securities and Exchange Commission, 50
Self-assessment, 40, 46, 62, 151
Self-efficacy, 21, 25, 26
Self-employment tax, 5, 118, 122, 181
Self-esteem, 21
Separation of Liability, 86
Seven Major Goal Areas of a Life Plan, 150, 151
Seven R's of Motivation and Change, 30, 33, 195
Shifting income, 123
Short Term Periodic Payment Offer, 95, 111-112
Short-term liabilities, 55
Small business owners, 82, 124, 181
SMART goals, 37, 39

www.ingramcontent.com/pod-product-compliance
Lightning Source LLC
Chambersburg PA
CBHW061754210326
41518CB00036B/2351

* 9 7 8 0 5 7 8 0 1 4 7 7 7 *